A LATTERDAY CONFUCIAN

Harvard East Asian Monographs
131

William Hung in 1949

A Latterday Confucian
Reminiscences of William Hung (1893–1980)

SUSAN CHAN EGAN

Published by the Council on East Asian Studies, Harvard University, and distributed by Harvard University Press, Cambridge (Massachusetts) and London
1987

*CT
3990
H86
E35
1987*

The Council on East Asian Studies at Harvard publishes a
monograph series and, through the Fairbank Center for
East Asian Research and the Reischauer Institute of
Japanese Studies, administers research projects designed
to further scholarly understanding of China, Japan,
Korea, Vietnam, Inner Asia, and adjacent areas.

Library of Congress Cataloging-in-Publication Data

Egan, Susan Chan.
    A latterday Confucian.

    (Harvard East Asian monographs ; 131)
    Bibliography: p.
    Includes index.
    1. Hung, William, 1893– . 2. Scholars — China —
Biography. 3. Scholars — United States — Biography.
I. Hung, William, 1893– . II. Title. III. Series.
CT3990.H86E35 1987   951.04'092'4 [B]   87-20193
ISBN 0-674-51297-9

                                    I have said before
That the past experience revived in the meaning
Is not the experience of one life only
But of many generations — not forgetting
Something that is probably quite ineffable:
The backward look behind the assurance
Of recorded history, the backward half-look
Over the shoulder, towards the primitive terror.
Now, we come to discover that the moments of agony
(Whether, or not, due to misunderstanding,
Having hoped for the wrong things or dreaded the wrong things,
Is not in question) are likewise permanent
With such permanence as time has. We appreciate this better
In the agony of others, nearly experienced,
Involving ourselves, than in our own.
For our own past is covered by the currents of action,
But the torment of others remains an experience
Unqualified, unworn by subsequent attrition.

                          (T. S. Eliot, The Dry Salvages, *Four Quartets*)

Contents

Part V

Preface

This biography could not have been written had William Hung not been willing to open his past to me on almost every Sunday afternoon for more than two years between 1978 and 1980, telling me the story of his life. He directed me to his published work and made available to me unpublished papers and manuscripts. The only condition he imposed on me was to make the biography an honest one.

I have relied on many other publications to clarify the circumstances surrounding Hung's life. A list of these appears in Part II of the Bibliography. For readers interested in Hung's scholarship, each mention of one of his publications in the body of the text is followed by a number in parentheses that refers to a numbered entry in Part I.

Despite the documentation in the Bibliography, I have written a book of which William Hung would probably disapprove because it has no footnotes to give references for specific statements and quotations. The various sources of information that I have used are so intertwined in my mind that there are whole sections of the biography for which I would be hard put to identify the precise sources. Roughly speaking, eighty percent of it is based on my taped interviews with Hung himself, ten percent on my impressions of him, his surroundings, his family, friends, and acquaintances over the eight-year period I knew him. The rest is based on research, interviews, and comments solicited from individuals close to him. The tapes will be deposited at the Harvard-Yenching Library with the stipulation that they not be available for twenty years to protect the privacy of individuals about whom Hung expressed strong opinions.

It has been my good fortune at all stages of the project to have the help of a number of persons who have first-hand knowledge of many of the events discussed: his brother Fred Hung of the University of Guelph and his students James Liu of Princeton, Y. T. Wang of the University of Pittsburgh, Wang Chung-han of the Central College of Nationalities in Peking, and Timothy Wixted of Arizona State University. The late Ruth Crawford Mitchell, whom Hung fondly referred to as "my American sister," freely shared with me her reminiscences and correspondence dating as far back as 1912. Not all of their suggestions, however, were adopted; and errors of fact as well as of judgment are mine alone.

My discussions of Hung's works are based on my own readings of them and his comments recorded during our taping sessions. I have also relied heavily on the advice of several scholars, notably Yang Lien-sheng, Teng Ssu-yü, James Liu, and Loh Wai-fong, who were kind enough to share with me their views. Here again, errors of fact as well as of judgment are mine alone.

I am grateful to Chiang Yung-chen, who alerted me to the trove of correspondence relating to Hung held in the United Board for Christian Higher Education in Asia collection at the archives section of Yale University Divinity School Library. By consulting them, I was able to form a clearer picture of Hung's relationship with Yenching University and of Hung's financial conditions at various stages of his life. The letters in Chapters Eleven, Eighteen and Nineteen are quoted directly from this source. I am indebted to Francis Cleaves, the executor of Hung's estate, and to Bonnie Oram, William Hung's granddaughter-in-law, for making available to me some of Hung's papers and family photographs; to Don W. Borg, Alumni Editor at Ohio Wesleyan University and Jane A. Drury, Director of Alumnae Affairs at Wheaton College, for helping me verify many of the names, dates, and events in the lives of William and Rhoda Hung. Acknowledgments are also due to the helpful staff of the Harvard-Yenching Library, the Widener Library, and the Harvard Archives, as well as the Yale University Divinity School Library.

Chou Shan, Grace Muran, and Hilary Horton have generously given me their professional advice as editors; the manuscript benefits from their comments. Paul Griffith the late editor of *Fellowship in Prayer*, which included a portion of the biography in its May 1982 issue devoted to William Hung, has also been helpful. Katherine Keenum, the editor of this biography at the Harvard University Council on East Asian Studies, helped me pull it all together. She tirelessly challenged me on points of accuracy and clarity; the book is much strengthened as a result.

I am grateful to Patrick Hanan, K. C. Chang, Tu Wei-ming, John King Fairbank, the late Joe Fletcher, and especially to Francis Cleaves and James Liu for their encouragement in the completion of this project. Lastly, I must give credit to my husband, Ron, for his support and advice. When writing the biography of a Sinologist, it is a distinct advantage to be married to one.

Part One

Graduating class, Anglo Chinese College, Foochow, 1915
William Hung is standing, second row, sixth from left

CHAPTER ONE

Childhood in Foochow

WILLIAM HUNG'S EARLIEST NAME, Hung Cheng-chi ("Right Continuance"), was given him by his father, to be entered into the clan's genealogical register. When he was ready to enter school, his father gave him his school or official name, Hung Yeh ("Great Enterprise"). In the Foochow dialect, this is pronounced "Hung Ngiek." In his twenty-third year when he left Foochow for Delaware, Ohio, he gave himself the Western name William.

HUNG WAS BORN on October 27, 1893, during the reign of the Kuang-hsü Emperor, in the city of Foochow. At the time of his birth, Foochow was the capital of a province and a well-known seaport in international trade, but it remained a city impassable by wheeled vehicles because of its hilly terrain and narrow streets. Paved with stone slabs, the streets ran up and down in steep, stony steps. A high wall enclosed the city, where stately banyan trees, luxuriant bamboos, and many brilliant flowering plants grew in the subtropical climate. But there was also the melancholy sight of thousands of graves dotting the hillsides. Even as a boy, Hung was saddened by the fact that so much land had been taken by the dead and was lost to the living. The Hungs, being poor, did not have a homestead; his parents, his paternal grandmother, an uncle, two aunts, and several cousins lived together in one rented house after another. The cramped quarters gave rise to an atmosphere in which the surface harmony barely covered the strains underneath.

But Hung spent most of his childhood outside the walled city, at his maternal grandparents' home in a southern suburb, on an island called Nantai in the Min River delta. In the city, William was merely the third grandson to Grandmother Hung; in Nantai, he was the proud first grandchild to Grandparents Lin.

The Lins had their own spacious domicile, a complex of nearly a dozen buildings facing a street that ran along a branch of the Min River. At the front end of the complex was a big wooden structure housing Grandfather Lin Chung-kao's Ever Lucky (Yung-chi) Tea Company. At certain times of the year, twenty to thirty women worked in the big hall sorting leaves, under its great exposed beams and skylights. After the sorting, another team of workers would come to pack the tea into tin-lined wooden chests. On one side of the hall were several rooms, occupied mainly by the company staff. The corner office with its upstairs chamber, was reserved for business guests from out of town. As the eldest grandchild, Hung was occasionally allowed to use this as his bedroom; he remembered with fondness the lichee tree standing just outside the window, whose branches held ripening fruits he could pluck by reaching with his hand. The residential buildings were behind the tea company and were all set at right angles to each other around two paved courtyards. Most of the buildings were two-storeyed, with a suite of three rooms on each floor. The upper-storey rooms were approached by wooden staircases that led to long verandahs running the length of the buildings. The roofs were made of gray tile, and on some of the ridges stood glazed figures of people and animals. Grandmother Lin's bedroom was in the central building adjacent to the main hall, facing south onto the first courtyard. In the same courtyard, Grandfather Lin occupied a suite of rooms in the building on the east and had direct access to the company offices. The structures on the west were sometimes rented out to tenants. The rest of the rooms were divided among Hung's mother, his sister and brothers, an aunt and an uncle. The servants' quarters, a dining room, and the kitchen were found in the back. The boundary of this vast complex was marked by a plank wall. Through its cracks young William could peer into the backyard of another family, also home of a tea merchant, whose residence was laid out on a similar plan, their tea company facing a street at the other end.

Life was rich with the sights, sounds, and smells of a Chinese city. Pedlars of all kinds passed through all day, each with the special chant or yodel of his trade. Earliest in the morning came the man who collected the nightsoil to be returned as fertilizer to fields in the countryside. For this, the men paid a small fee which became part of the servants' income. During the day, there was the tinker who mended household utensils, the knife and scissors sharpener with his whetstone, the quilt puffer who made quilts soft and fluffy again by beating them with a bow-like instrument. Then the water cart rolled around, bells tinkling, to fill earthern jars at every household. Vendors sold hot food from stoves dangling from carrying poles of cakes from the wicker basket balanced on their heads. They clanged their bells to sell malt sugar blown by mouth into molds of horses, men, and dogs – a tempting sweet, but one forbidden to little William, whose parents considered it unsanitary.

When William's milk teeth began to come loose, the itinerant dentist was invited into the house frequently. This august personage wore a string of teeth around his neck, like a Hawaiian lei, and carried a box of medicine on his back. He worked by smearing a painkiller on the afflicted tooth, tying around it one end of a silk string, and tying the other end of the string to a door handle. He would give the patient a sudden slap on the shoulder and simultaneously kick the door closed. Before the patient realized what was happening, the tooth had come off.

Hung remembered catching crabs from the bank of the river that ran in front of Grandfather Lin's house. Down the river, there would be two women singing and treading the waterwheels. As the wheels moved up, buckets were lifted out of the river and tipped over to pour water into a canal that branched off to irrigate vegetable and fruit gardens. The women who worked the wheels belonged to the aboriginal tribes of Foochow who had settled there long before the area became thickly populated with ethnic Han Chinese from the North around the tenth century. These women were distinguished by the huge hairpins they wore, which stuck out menacingly from their hair. They did not bind their feet and walked about freely around town, doing all kinds of men's work.

One day when he was wandering by himself, William walked and walked until he found himself on a long, silent street with blank walls on both sides. He was totally lost. He came to a gate in the wall; but lacking courage to knock, he sat down on one of the stone bases of the gate and cried. The vermilion doors opened behind him and an older boy came out to ask him what was the matter, then offered to take him back to the Ever Lucky Tea Company. "It is practically next to our back door," the boy assured him. He took little William's hand and led him through what seemed an interminable series of gardens with moon gates and what must have been several dozen courtyards before they got out into the street. Sure enough, Ever Lucky Tea Company, with its familiar gate shiny with tung oil, was right down the street. As Hung looked back on the event, he thought this must have been one of those fabled residences in which many generations of a clan lived together.

Grandmother and Grandfather Lin were warm, loving people with eclectic beliefs. One or the other of the children would sleep with Grandmother Lin at night. Grandfather Lin engaged a wet nurse to take care of little William. Once when William fell ill with high fever, Grandfather Lin went around to pray and make solemn vows in all the temples and shrines in the neighborhoods, whether Confucian, Buddhist, or Taoist, as well as at all the Catholic and Protestant churches. He hoped that at least one of the spirits might bring about his grandchild's recovery. Grandmother Lin boasted she had psychic powers. She maintained that whenever any of her grandchildren were born, she would be somehow conscious of the event even though it might have taken place many miles away. William did not know whether to believe his grandmother, but all through his life he maintained an open-minded attitude towards supersensory perception and was fascinated by theories on the workings of the subconscious.

Hung's mother, Lin Fei, was Grandfather Lin's eldest daughter and his favorite. He had nothing but the greatest respect for his son-in-law, Hung Hsi, a literary man of impeccable character. But it soon became apparent to him that a daughter married to a scholar-official was subjected to a life of painful separation and uncertainties. When his younger daughter came of age, therefore, he arranged a marriage with a fellow merchant, a man who owned a string of pawnshops. Since the Lins had no son, they adopted a boy. This turned out to have been a mistake. For this boy was weak-minded and later squandered the family fortune.

WILLIAM did not see a great deal of his father during his early childhood. Hung Hsi, who passed his second-degree examination in 1891, made several long trips north to Peking, the imperial capital of China, in attempts to pass the third-degree examination, which was held every three years. When William was five years old, Hung Hsi left for Shantung to begin his official career. Whenever his father was back in Foochow, William and his mother, his sister and brothers, would travel by sedan chairs into the walled city to join his paternal family. His mother also went there to await the births of her children, in observance of the rules of a patrilineal society.

Before Hung Hsi's family joined him in Shantung in 1901, there were to be six children in all: Hung Yeh (William), a boy Hung Tuan, a girl Hung Chih-p'ing, Hung Shen (David), and Hung Shou (Arnold). Hung Fu (Fred) was born in Shantung, as was another boy, who died in infancy of smallpox. They were all two years apart, coinciding perhaps to their father's various trips home from Peking and Shantung, with a five-year gap between the fifth and sixth child, owing to the Confucian prescription of three years of abstinence after the death of a parent, in this case, of Grandmother Hung.

Hung had vague recollections of being taken to watch his father perform as one of thirty or forty ceremonial dancers at the seasonal sacrifices of the local Confucian temple. Dressed in colorful costumes and carrying sticks, feathers, or pennants, the dancers moved in unison to the music. On that day, sheep and hogs were sacrificed according to rituals handed down from the Han Dynasty (206 B.C.–A.D. 220). It was a treat when his father brought home the piece of pork that was his share; for at Grandmother Hung's the normal fare was rice, vegetables, and sometimes a little salted fish or a fowl.

Once, having spied some white sticks on his mother's dressing table, little William reached up for a few to examine them. They were brittle and made a crisp *pieh* sound when he broke them. He broke several. It turned out that a friend of his father had brought over a fan to have Hung Hsi inscribe a poem on it. These ivory pieces were parts of the frame; they had been taken out of the fabric so that the cloth could be laid flat on the table for the brushwork. As soon as Hung Hsi saw the broken pieces, he guessed who the culprit was. He chased after William with a big stick; but the boy hid behind Grandmother Hung, who told her son, "You'll have to beat me first before you beat him."

Ordinarily, however, Hung Hsi was an even-tempered man who did not raise his voice. It was Lin Fei who administered discipline. When the offense warranted, she did not hesitate to give her children a few whacks on the behind.

William's earliest memory of his mother's discipline went back to a scene that took place when he was about two years old, at Grandmother Hung's house. In front of the house were vendors who sold all kinds of goodies: water chestnuts, cooked snails, hawberries glazed with sugar and arranged in a row on a bamboo stick. Hung was walking on this street with his wet nurse, Mama Ch'en, when he found a copper coin on the ground. Mama Ch'en asked Hung to hand it over to her, but he refused: "It's mine. I found it."

"At least give it me so that I can clean it for you. The thing is filthy," she said. So she did just that, shining it up so that the copper coin with the square hole in the middle was gleaming.

At that time, children had their hair tied up neatly in several braids that stuck out of their heads like budding horns. They wore overall-like clothing with a slit in the seat of the pants that opened up when the child squatted down to do nature's bidding. Little William put the coin in the pocket of such a garment. That night, Mama Ch'en filled the low, oblong wooden tub in the kitchen with kettles of hot water to wash the child thoroughly before she carried him off to bed. As usual, Lin Fei came to supervise the bathing. She discovered the copper coin in William's pocket, took it out, and put it into her stomacher. The child saw and cried out, "Mother, don't take that! It's mine."

"Why is it yours, and where did it come from?"

"I picked it up on the street."

"You shouldn't be picking up things in the dirty streets."

Mama Ch'en hastily explained she had washed it.

"Give it back to me. It's *mine.*" Little William demanded impatiently.

"Well," his mother said, "If you insist on dividing up what is yours and what is mine, I will give the coin back to you and you can leave the house."

She placed the coin in Hung's tiny hand, folded up all his clothes, put it on one side and bid the stark naked two-year-old child goodbye. William started to cry inconsolably and between sobs, told his mother he did not want the copper coin anymore. It was his first lesson on the nature of property ownership in a Chinese household.

WHEN WILLIAM WAS ABOUT FOUR years old, he was considered ready to start formal studies. An arrangement was made for him to receive a traditional Confucian education with the children next door. On the first day, the teacher came over to the Hung house. After Hung Hsi and the teacher had knelt down on red rugs and bowed to each other, the teacher sat down on a red-cushioned armchair and William was told to kneel down and kowtow three times to him. Next, the teacher lifted William up onto his shoulder and carried him with a package of school supplies next door. On a table in the study was a plaque with the inscription, "The Place of the Perfect Great Master Confucius." William was told to kneel down again in front of this plaque and kowtow three times. Then all the pupils stood in a cricle and bowed together once, and the class began.

From that day on, William went to school every day from seven o'clock in the morning until seven o'clock at night, with three hours for lunch and an afternoon nap, and one hour for supper. There were no weekends off. The only vacations were fifteen days around the Chinese New Year and a day off each on the Ch'ing-ming Festival in the spring for visits to ancestral graves, the Dragonboat Festival, the Mid-Autumn Moon Festival, and the birthdays of the Empress Dowager, the Emperor, Confucius, and the students' own parents. Apart from these days away from classes, absences were allowed when the pupil was sick at home or was to accompany his parents on visits to relatives. The best no-school days, however, came when the teacher himself went on leave for some reason; for on these rare occasions, the children could play with each other.

There were generally six other children in the school, three of whom were sons of the neighbor who engaged the teacher; the others were students the teacher recruited on his own with the permission of his employer. The first lessons were to learn to write simple words with the inked brush. This was done by tracing characters that were outlined in red: *shang, ta, jen, k'ung, i, chi* ("up," "big," "man," "Confucius," "second," "self"), and so forth. These characters are simple enough graphically, and combined, they are sometimes explained as a letter from Confucius to his senior; but to a little child, the words make no sense together.

The method of instruction was mainly memorization. Each day, a student was assigned a certain passage in the Confucian texts. The teacher punctuated the passage, read it aloud, and explained its meaning. The student repeated the reading and explanation after him. Then he returned to his own seat to read the assignment aloud again and again until he could recite it easily from memory. Hung, with his near-photographic memory, had no problem with the instruction. But other students ran the constant risk of having the teacher's tobacco pipe land on top of their skull with a resounding *tok* whenever they missed a word. More serious offenses might be given heavier punishments— strikes on the hand or a forced kneeling in front of the Confucian tablet.

For a beginner, the text was a primer called *Three Character Classic* (*San-tzu ching*), attributed to a thirteenth-century Confucian. The text starts with the statement, *Jen chih ch'u, hsing pen shan* ("At man's beginning, his nature was good")—an assertion diametrically opposed to the doctrine of original sin that Hung would struggle with later in his life. Hung's second primer was *The Hundred Family Names* (*Po-chia-hsing*), a listing of one hundred family names with no apparent logical connections among them. It began *Chao, Ch'ien, Sun, Li,* because these four represented the four leading families under the Sung Dynasty (960–1278) when it was written. The sequence is thought to represent the comparative social status of the time, but a child could hardly be expected to appreciate such distinctions. It was very hard to memorize. The third book that young William was taught was more interesting. It was *The Thousand Character Text* (*Ch'ien-tzu wen*). One thousand characters, all different, are grouped into two hundred fifty lines of four characters each. They are pithy descriptions of natural phenomena, formulations of moral precepts, allusions to historical events, and statements of literary principles.

In calligraphy, William graduated from tracing red outlines of characters to copying rubbings or reproductions of famous writers' hands. In mathematics, he learned to add, subtract, multiply, divide, and perform square-root calculations on the abacus, using a rhymed manual, which he had to memorize.

AFTER WILLIAM'S AUNT LIN was married off, the building in which she had lived was rented out to a family with a little girl just about William's age. They were allowed to play together. This girl had a Chinese doll house in which were little beds, little tables, little chests, and a family of little people. The little people had sets of clothes, which the girl washed and folded neatly, arranging them in the little drawers. Hung was struck with wonder and admiration for his playmate. He told Grandmother Lin that when he grew up, and when she arranged to get a wife for him, he would like to have this little girl. Grandmother Lin was greatly amused by her grandson who even at this tender age, placed orderliness above all other qualities in his choice of a wife. She told him, however, that he already had a fiancée in the neighboring town of Lien-chiang, and that the girl was just as good as his playmate. When William's mother was carrying him, the wife of a close friend of his father was also expecting. To seal their friendship, the two fathers had betrothed their unborn children to each other should they prove to be a boy and a girl.

The Lin maidservants started to tease William about the Lien-chiang girl. They would taunt him, "Look at him, so young and already has answers for everything. Wait till the Lien Family girl does her job on him. We hear she has a clever mouth too."

"Oh no," William would come right back at them, "You don't know anything about the Lien Family girl. I am sure I can take care of her."

As it happened, the Lien Family girl died while a teenager in an epidemic, thereby sparing Hung a traumatic moral crisis faced by many educated young men and women of his generation, of whether they should break a marriage vow made by their parents in order to marry the person of their own choice.

As WILLIAM HUNG recalled fragments of his childhood to a friendly listener in 1977, more than eighty years later, over a pot of tea in his kitchen in Cambridge, he sometimes roared with laughter over his own antics, sometimes sighed over the utter unpredictability of life. As a child, the world around him had seemed so permanent.

CHAPTER TWO

The Story of the Hung Clan

DURING ONE OF HUNG HSI's brief stays in Foochow, he spent some time coaching a fellow clansman to take the civil service examinations. This clansman, though one generation below William, was already in his twenties, so William called him informally Big Brother I-seng. Once he brought William three sticks of sugarcane over six feet long. William greedily ate all three, and for days his jaws were sore from chewing. From Big Brother I-seng he learned that there was a whole village of Hungs in Hou-p'u ("Behind the Marsh") not far from Foochow. It was a humble farming village with proud ancestral memories. Gradually from his father and his married Aunt Hung, who occasionally came to visit, he pieced together the history of his father's family.

THE HUNGS traced their ancestry to the clan of Kung-kung ("communal work") of the legendary Chinese diluvian age, around 2300 B.C., when a great flood was caused, it was said, by a leak in the sky. The clan of Kung-kung were the hydraulic engineers of the time. Their head directed his clansmen in building dikes. When he failed to contain the flood, he was banished by the Emperor Yao. Around the first century A.D., one of the prominent Kung-kungs offended some mighty political power and the whole clan was annihilated except for one person, who escaped to the western part of China near the border of Chinese Turkestan. He had to change his surname but wanted to do it in such a way that if there were other Kung-kungs alive, they would recognize the clan name. He chose the word Hung, which rhymes with Kung-kung, and is written with two Chinese radicals, the left side being a symbol of water, and the right side Kung, meaning "communal."

There was no man of distinction from the Hung clan until Hung Hao (1088–1155). Hung Hao served as a minister during the turbulent period when the northern half of China was conquered by invaders who established their own empire, the Chin, as a rival to the Sung dynasty. Hung Hao served both Emperor Hui-tsung, the last Sung emperor of a unified China, and Emperor Kao-tsung, the first ruler of the much diminished empire known as the Southern Sung. When Hung Hao was sent north by Kao-tsung as an ambassador, the Chin court tried to persuade him to serve them instead. When Hung refused to switch loyalties, he was placed under house arrest. It was thirteen years before he was released. No sooner had he returned south to the Sung court, however, than he got into political hot water by criticizing the chief councilor Ch'in K'uei, a favorite of the emperor. For this, he was banished to a remote outpost of the empire. He died in exile, leaving behind him one of the first geographies of Manchuria, *Accounts of the Piny Wilderness* (*Sung-mo chi-wen*).

Hung Hao had three famous sons: Hung Kua, a minister in whose collected writings, *P'an-chou wen-chi,* is found the history of the Hung clan; Hung Tsun, the first Chinese numismatist; and Hung Mai, a historian. Because of these three prominent brothers, descendants of this branch of the Hungs came to be known as the "Three Talisman Hungs." At the time of the Mongolian invasion of China in the following century, a descendant of Hung Tsun the numismatist, fled to the vicinity of Foochow and married into a local, landed family. The family grew into a clan and the clan into a village known as Hou P'u. Many generations of illiterate and semiliterate Hungs tilled the land in Hou P'u. They maintained there a family temple and a book of genealogy. Among the first things William's father did after he passed the examinations and became eligible for official appointment was to pay his respects to this family temple. He compiled and published a genealogy of the Hung clan up to his time. In the 1940s, when William Hung's brother Fred was working for the Chinese Nationalist government, he made a visit to the village and was honored by the village elders.

William's great-grandfather inherited a good-sized property and a grocery store. He also owned a boat which plied the Min River transporting rice. This made him a fairly rich man in Hou P'u in the middle of the nineteenth century. This great-grandfather invested the profits from his business in more land, usually that of a relative who found himself short of cash for funeral or wedding expenses. A deed would be made with the understanding that if the seller should in the future be able to raise the amount in so many iron coins, he should be able to redeem the land. In the meanwhile, he became a sharecropper, tilling the same fields but dividing the harvest with the new landlord. The great-grandfather, however, died young, leaving behind his wife and a little boy just as China was entering a period of severe economic dislocation precipitated by the opium trade forced on China by the British. There began the first of many rounds of currency debasement. A decree declaring the invalidation of iron coins was made, and people holding iron coins were permitted to exchange them for copper coins at a much reduced exchange rate. Men who had mortgaged their lands to William's great-grandfather saw a great opportunity to redeem them at a reduced cost; and they now beieged William's great-grandmother, demanding their land back in exchange for the debased iron coins. Panic-stricken, the hapless widow fled with her young son to the walled city of Foochow. For a time, they lived on the jewelry she had brought with her; but that eventually was exhausted, and William's grandfather was sent to work as a cook's apprentice. Upon completion of his apprenticeship, he obtained employment with the family of a Manchu official.

One day, a woman in tattered clothes, whose hair was all clotted with dirt, appeared at the door of William's great-grandmother's house. As soon as she came in, she threw herself down on the ground and knocked her head on the floor. She identified herself as the girl to whom William's grandfather had been betrothed at infancy. Her family had also left their village, she explained; but her parents were killed by bandits, who sold her to a family in Canton. The family was childless and treated her as a daughter; but as she grew older, there were discussions about making her a concubine. She had escaped, travelled several hundred miles, and endured innumerable hardships, until she made her way to the door of her betrothed. She became William's grandmother.

Grandfather Hung's career as a cook took him to different parts of China. He lived to see his eldest son pass the first-degree civil service examination. On his deathbed, he ordered his wife to bring him "the iron box." In it were the land deeds that William's great-grandmother had brought with her when they fled the village. He then asked for a match and burned the papers. As he explained, "Drawing on the merits that our ancestors have accumulated, you, my oldest son, were able to get an education and pass the first-degree exam. As an educated man, you are in a powerful position, so you might be tempted to return to Hou P'u and demand the lands back. It would be difficult for the illiterate farmers to resist you. Now I am burning the deeds because I, too, want to accumulate some merits for you and your children."

WHEN GRANDFATHER HUNG DIED, in the year 1876, William's father was only ten years old. Soon, bad times fell upon the family. First Uncle Hung had to hire himself out to be a tutor while he prepared for the second-degree examination. Second Uncle Hung passed the military service examination (consisting of tests in horsemanship, archery, and strength), but he was rapidly sinking into the never-never land of opium smokers. Aunt Hung, married to a farmer, was unable to provide much financial assistance. There simply was not enough money, and William's father was apprenticed to a stationer in a small store in the city.

The life of an apprentice was not easy. In return for free labor, the shopkeeper provided clothing, food, and shelter to the boy and taught him the trade for a set number of years, upon which the boy would graduate to being an employee. Not until then would he receive any money. The store was his home. His bed space was found behind a curtain at the end of the store. Hung Hsi rose with the sun, drew water from the river to prepare breakfast for himself and his master. After washing the dishes, he took down the wooden plank that constituted the door of the store, and got ready for customers. He learned to fold the sheets of paper properly, binding them into notebooks and ledgers; to mend those with defects; and to keep track of the writing brushes, inkstones, inkslabs, and other merchandise that met the simple needs of the merchants of the neighborhood and the "market school" next door.

In China at that time, as had been true for nearly two millennia, just about the only respectable thing an educated person could do was to serve the government. And in order to be eligible for a public appointment, one had to pass the civil service examinations. An unsuccessful candidate could try again, and many tried every year until they grew old and died. One such unsuccessful candidate ran the "market school" next door to eke out a living. His students consisted of neighboring merchants' sons, who simply wanted to learn the rudiments of writing and arithmetic. As was the custom, however, no attempt was made to modify the method of instruction to fit the purposes of the students. All students were given the same Confucian classics and told to recite them aloud until they had memorized them. Hung Hsi had learned a few simple characters from his eldest brother, so as he went about quietly performing his various tasks, his ears would prick up at the chanting next door, while he listened for familiar words and passages. One day, the school teacher and a literary friend strolled over to pick up some supplies. As they waited to be served, they argued about some passages in the Confucian classics. The apprentice pointed out to one of the gentlemen that they had quoted Confucius erroneously. They were dumbfounded. The teacher made some inquiries into the boy's background and offered to teach him in exchange for cooking and the performance of other household chores—if the shopkeeper was willing to release him from his apprenticeship. The shopkeeper got in touch with the family and negotiated a settlement for a sum which Aunt Hung was eventually able to pay.

Hung Hsi made rapid progress in his studies. He mastered the Confucian texts known as the Four Books and familiarized himself thoroughly with the orthodox interpretation of them written by Chu Hsi in the twelfth century A.D. This was essential for an official career because the civil service examinations were based entirely on these texts and Chu Hsi's interpretation. The examiner would give part of a sentence from the Four Books on which the candidates were to write "eight-legged essays." In the eight-section essay, the candidate had to demonstrate that he could identify the fragment, its context, what Chu Hsi said about it, and how Chu Hsi differed from other commentators. The essays had to be orthodox in outlook, yet show some originality. Literary skills were also very important. William's father failed in his first attempts to pass the examination. After several years, the teacher suggested that he continue his studies with a man named Ch'en, who also taught him gratis. Mr. Ch'en recommended him for various teaching, writing, and copying jobs. With the money, he was able to support himself and send some to his mother. He also joined a literary society made up of people who wanted to help each other master the "eight-legged essays." Some twenty unsuccessful examination candidates would meet several times a month in a local temple to write essays, criticize each other's writings, and compare their works to the best models. They would have a monk prepare simple and inexpensive meals and spend the whole day there. In time, Hung Hsi passed the first-degree examination.

With the acquisition of this first degree, living conditions for him improved markedly. He was able to earn a comfortable livelihood as a kind of free-lance writer. Illiterates came to have their letters written. Merchants asked him to paint their store signs. Actually, owing to a broken bone caused by a fall while he was fetching water from the river as an apprentice, Hung Hsi did not have the steady hand necessary to execute the bold graceful strokes of big characters. But he was able to compensate for this partly by the use of a painstaking and ingenious process. William remembered seeing his father spread the writing paper on the floor, sprinkle several handfuls of rice onto the paper, and shape the rice into the desired forms of the characters. Then he traced the outline carefully with a charcoal stick. Finally, he swept the rice away and filled in the outline with ink. For such work, he would receive one or two taels, enough for a few days' food. From time to time, he would receive the lucrative commission of fifty to one hundred taels to write a tomb description recounting the life of a deceased man.

IN 1891, Hung Hsi passed the second-degree examination, held every three years at the provincial capitals. The following year, a national examination was to be held at Peking; candidates who passed would be *chin-shih,* assured of an official career. But the trip to Peking from Foochow took over a month. A servant was needed to help carry luggage and provisions. On the way and once the candidate arrived in Peking, he would need board and lodging. What was a poor scholar to do? Present in every neighborhood at that time were professional matchmakers who made it their business to look after promising young men. Among the various wealthy young ladies brought to the attention of William's grandmother was the daughter of a prosperous Foochow tea merchant. She was nineteen, stately-looking, the first woman among the genteel families of Foochow to have "natural feet." The tea merchant Lin Chung-kao had two daughters and an adopted son. He wanted his oldest daughter to marry a literary man. So a "chance meeting" was arranged on a festival day for Hung Hsi and Lin Fei to catch a glimpse of each other. The parties concerned were pleased with what they saw, and Hung Hsi asked the matchmaker to convey an inquiry to the Lin daughter: "I am a disciple of Confucius and I intend to live according to his teaching. If I succeed in passing the examination, I will be a public official. I want to be a clean and honest official. Therefore at home we will have to live without luxuries. All my life I have never worn any silk, and we never had servants at home. It would be too much to expect you to live the way I have lived, but what I can offer still means a standard of living very much below what you are accustomed to. If you are willing to agree to this, then let me propose marriage and

I believe you will be a great help to me. But if you find it difficult to accept a life of austerity, we need not go any further."

Miss Lin's reply was quite straightforward: "I am satisfied with the man. I will be happy to marry him. If he can live that way, there is no reason why I can't."

William's father and mother were married in the year 1892. It was understood that the Lin family would help their new son-in-law with his trip to Peking. Hung Hsi took the third-degree examination three times, at intervals of three years each; but he never passed it. Fortunately, under a system called Grand Selection, candidates who passed the second-degree examination could qualify for official appointments. They had to register with the Board of Appointments and were interviewed by the Vice Minister. Mediocre candidates would be assigned to posts as commissioner of education in the counties. But Hung Hsi, along with other more impressive candidates, was appointed a "magistrate-in-reserve," ranking seventh on a nine-grade official system, in which grade one was the top. Since, to avoid conflicts of interest, officials were never appointed to posts in their native province, Hung Hsi was sent to Tsinan, in the Province of Shantung, more than five hundred miles north of Foochow.

A magistrate-in-reserve was expected to take up his residence at the provincial capital. He was expected to ingratiate himself with the provincial governor and prove his abilities in the governor's offices, the yamen. Ideally, he should have his wife with him; for a young man without his wife was held to be too prone to sexual adventures, and no governor would appoint such a man to a position of responsibility for fear of bringing disgrace on himself. As long as his wife was unable to join him, Hung Hsi received only temporary appointments from time to time; and he continued to support himself by writing.

Second Uncle Hung had a great deal to do with why William's father could not have his family with him in Shantung. By now, Second Uncle Hung was married and had several children of his own; but because of his opium habits, he was never able to make ends meet. William's grandmother, in the perverse ways of motherhood, was especially fond of this son and reasoned that as long as she remained in Foochow, her younger son the official would have to send her money, which she could then share with her favorite. In a Confucian society, the primary duty of a married woman is to her in-laws; her husband comes second. Thus it was out of the question for William's mother to join her husband and leave her mother-in-law behind in Foochow. A warm, level-headed woman with a mind of her own, Lin Fei did not hide the fact that she resented this. She and the children spent much more time in the comfort of her father's house than with her mother-in-law.

ANOTHER FAMILY TENSION caused the Hung home in the city to be not a very pleasant place. By this time, First Uncle Hung was long dead. He had made his living as a private tutor. At one of the families where he was employed, the beautiful daughter of the house had come home young and childless to live after her husband died. Soon First Uncle Hung fell in love with her. When she became pregnant, he took the only honorable course available—he married her, even though, according to the prevailing custom, respectable women were not to remarry. This was considered a taint on his character. He died not too long afterwards, leaving his young wife and a son, whom William called Big Brother Yen. William's grandmother, herself a widow of uncompromising propriety, despised her pretty daughter-in-law.

"Even now," Hung said, as he recalled this unfortunate woman in 1978, some eighty years later, "I can close my eyes and see her in the thin black blouse and black trousers which she wore every season of the year, her flesh showing where the fabric was worn through. She did all the heavy chores in the household. My grandmother did not like Big Brother Yen either, even though he was the eldest of her grandchildren. She probably associated him with too many bad events. Later on, my father took him to Shantung and tried to bring him up in the world."

CHAPTER THREE

Early Years in Shantung

IN 1901, when Hung was about eight years old, his strong-willed paternal grandmother died. His father hurried home from Shantung to observe the customary three years of mourning. Then, still a magistrate-in-reserve, he returned to Shantung, taking with him his wife, four sons and a daughter, his nephew Yen, a cook, and a tutor for his children. They went partly by land and partly by water (William remembered the cook, Nung-nung, teaching him how to angle for fish on the Grand Canal). It was another three years before Hung Hsi actually landed a position as a magistrate. Until then he was given various temporary assignments, including that of special investigator sent to examine the facts of a murder case.

One of the choice jobs involved overseeing the transport of taxes to Peking. The trip, involving some danger, paid well. The silver ingots were placed in a tree trunk that had been split lengthwise and hollowed out like a canoe and then rejoined, tied with wires, and sealed with paper. Bodyguards from private security firms escorted the convoy. They were armed with heavy iron nails called *piao,* which could be hurled at antagonists. Preceded by a red banner on which the name of the security firm was displayed prominently, the party stopped in towns and cities, where they were entertained by local officials and sent on their way with some customary gifts.

DURING THEIR FIRST FEW YEARS in Shantung, Hung and his brothers continued their education under their Foochownese tutor, Master Hsieh. Sometimes, they were joined by their sister. They recited their lessons in one room; and Mr. Hsieh, in an adjoining room, would call them in one by one to give them the lesson of the day. Everyone was responsible for a lesson a day and a composition a day. At this point in his life, Hung had a great passion for vernacular novels, which he surreptitiously rented from stores by the day. They were not considered healthy reading material for youngsters, and Hung had to read them under his blanket in bed when he was supposed to be taking a nap or during recitation period while his mouth continued to make the proper sounds. Every time his recitation went haywire, a threatening, rumbling noise could be heard issuing from Mr. Hsieh's room, bringing Hung back from the imaginary world to the reality at hand.

"My taste ran chiefly to novels with a lot of fighting. There's *Journey to the West* (also known as *Monkey*), *Battle of the Gods, The Seven Knights-Errant and the Five Righteous, The Seven Swordsmen and the Thirteen Knights-Errant, Water Margin.* I did not at that time understand those episodes in *Water Margin* dealing with sex, and it was not until many years later that I could appreciate *Dream of the Red Chamber.* Later I also read *Strange Stories from a Studio,* which, of course, is not in the vernacular. In fact, I found the elegant classical language of this book a great help in developing my literary style. The allusions are always apt.

"My favorite stories were those concerning Monkey in the *Journey to the West.* I cried when I came to the part where Monkey was captured by the goblins and he sobbed over how he had been unfaithful to the master."

The happiest time of the day came when the children gathered around the father after dinner to hear him tell stories. Many of these ended in doggerel verses that stuck in Hung's memory.

One story was about a civil examination in which the candidates were asked to write poems about a soup dumpling. A candidate ended his poem with these two lines:

> It takes the sweet or plain with equanimity.
> Rising or falling, it floats with calm sublimity.

The examiner took one look at the poem and decided the man should be a big official, because he could take the adversity as well as the success of life.

Two comic stories told about how the eunuchs surrounding the first emperor of the Ming dynasty (1368–1644) vied with each other in the composition of four-line poems. It was said that one day, snow began to fall and the emperor remarked casually,

> A flake here, a flake there, yet another flake!

Thereupon, a eunuch was prompted to rhapsodize,

> Two flakes here, three flakes there, yet four or five flakes.

Another eunuch continued idiotically,

> Six flakes here, seven flakes there, yet eight or nine flakes.

The brilliant minister, Liu Po-wen, who could hardly stand it any longer, cried,

> The snow vanished among the white plum blossoms.

Another time that it snowed, the emperor saw a white dog lying on the ground with the snow falling on it. He remarked,

> The white dog has suddenly grown in size.

A eunuch, eager to score a point, intoned enthusiastically,

> A black dog would have turned white.

The emperor then turned to Liu Po-wen and challenged him, "What do you say to that?"

And Liu Po-wen responded,

> The good mountains and rivers of the Ming Dynasty,
> Stretching ten thousand miles, all in one hue.

Hung Hsi also liked to tell them stories about his first teacher, Mr. Ch'en, who even during his lifetime, was legendary for his scholarship and his sense of justice. It was said that when the Min River overflowed into the city of Foochow one year, the governor-general's groom rushed home to rescue his wife and children, as a result of which the horses in the stable were left unattended and drowned. The groom was put in jail and sentenced to be executed. His wife came to see Mr. Ch'en, who wrote a poem for her and taught her what to do. The following morning, when the governor-general came out of the yamen and the runners were clearing the way for him, the woman threw herself in the middle of the road, crying, "Grievance! Grievance!" According to accepted custom, the governor-general stopped his sedan chair and let her speak.

"My husband was your groom. He was negligent in taking care of your horses because he was trying to save me and the children," the woman said. "Now he is in jail and it is rumored you might execute him."

"That's right," said the governor-general.

"I have asked a learned man to write you an appeal. I beg you to read it."

The poem read:

In former years when the stable of Tung-lu was burned,
The Great Sage was concerned only that people were hurt.
Now the flood overflowed the Southern Gate,
Great Man, what heart have you to ask about horses?

The first two lines of the poem refer to an incident in the *Analects* of Confucius in which he asked whether people were hurt in the conflagration of a stable. Upon reading this, the governor-general told the woman to go home and he released the groom.

HUNG'S FATHER smoked a water pipe and drank only on social occasions. His sole indulgence was playing an elegant, complicated game called *shih chung* ("poetic bell"). His friends liked to play this game at the Hung residence because they liked the Foochownese cook, whose specialty was golden fried oysters, and because they were fond of the Hung boy, William. William was entrusted with the responsibility of preparing for the game and of keeping time. After lunch on game days, he would arrange inkslabs, writing brushes, and paper on the table and paste on one wall seven sheets of paper, each inscribed with a word having an even tone, and on the opposite wall, seven sheets of paper each with a word having an oblique tone. The papers were carefully folded and the tips glued together so that the words were not visible. Around three or four o'clock in the afternoon, the guests began to arrive, each bringing with him a small bag of copper coins. There were usually a dozen players, fewer on rainy days. At the start of the game, William asked one of the players to point to one of the sheets of paper on the wall; he peeled open the one indicated to reveal the word. Then another player pointed to a sheet of paper on the opposite wall and a word with the opposite tone would be disclosed. The players would then write couplets using the two words revealed. In the first round, the two words revealed had to be used as the first words of either line; in the second round, the two words revealed had to be used as the second words of either line, and so forth.

A fast player might be able to complete several couplets using the two words revealed within the alloted time of twenty minutes. Everybody stopped when William rang the bell. William then went around the table, collecting the couplets into a little wicker basket and redistributing them to the players. Each player glanced through the anonymous couplets in his hand, put aside those he thought below par, and copied down those he felt were good. He might award one copper coin to one couplet, three copper coins to another—the best couplets were awarded seven coins. Then he handed the pile of poems to the person sitting next to him so that these could also be judged by his neighbor. Couplets written by the player himself would naturally be passed on discreetly. After William, the timekeeper, rang his bell signalling the end of the judging session, the fun began. Each player in turn would read aloud the couplets he had copied down and place the coins due to the writer in front of him as he did. The honored writer would stand up, bow with a big grin on his face, and run over to collect the money. Sometimes as soon as a player read the first line, several other persons who had also liked the couplet would join in to read the second line with him; and the happy writer would bow quickly and run around the table to pick up his rewards. There would be a moment of general merriment as smiles and words of congratulations rained on the writer. With seven rounds of this game and all the papers on the wall peeled open, the game would be over. The table would be cleared for dinner amid animated discussion of some of the more clever lines or more ludicrous couplets of the afternoon.

One time, the even-tone word disclosed was *yen* ("dazzling"), and the oblique-tone word was *chien* ("diminish"). While the adults were writing their couplets, a mischievous idea crept into William's mind; and he too, composed a couplet:

> The flowers are still in bloom, the fragrance has not diminished;
> Though it's late in the spring, the colors are dazzling.

When the players read aloud the couplets they picked, it turned out that this was among the ones that almost all of them had favored. "Aïyo!" cried William gleefully, as he ran around the table to collect his money. The players were astounded. William's father scolded him, but his friends were all pleased. Not only was it a reasonably good couplet, but in it was artfully hidden the compliment of a young boy to an older generation of men.

AMONG HUNG HSI's friends was one Yao Nan-ch'üan, who was not a frequenter of the poetry meetings. He was richer, higher up in the official hierarchy, and busier than the others. He rode a sedan chair covered with blue felt and carried by a team of four coolies. He was a "prefect-in-reserve" and a noted medical practitioner. A native of Cheking province, he had taken the second-degree examination with William's father and had become a good friend. William was a sturdy little boy, but the health of his brother Tuan was fragile. Usually, when Tuan fell ill, their mother would consult the standard *Pharmacopoeia,* a list of some four hundred kinds of herbal medicine first compiled during the third century A.D. Since she could not write, she would ask William to write the prescription down on a piece of paper and have it filled at the local medicinal herb store. Once, however, when Tuan ran a very high fever and none of their mother's remedies worked, they sent for Uncle Yao. Uncle Yao took the pulse of the patient; looked at his eyes, nose, and tongue; and wrote down a prescription. He said he would come back the second day. The medicine failed to alleviate Tuan's ailment, so Uncle Yao added a few items to the prescription the second day; but it still would not work. The third day, Uncle Yao issued a completely new prescription, telling William's father that he had come across an exact description of the disease in an old book the previous evening. The prescription called for the herbs to be boiled in water, the patient to drink the liquid, the herbs to be boiled again in fresh water, and the patient to be given the liquid a second time. The family followed the instructions; but upon drinking the medicine, Tuan lost consciousness and began to froth at the mouth. The parents argued with each other about whether to force-feed the child the second dose. William's mother was certain the prescription was wrong, but the father insisted that his friend Yao Nan-ch'üan could not have made a mistake. They forced open the poor boy's mouth with a pair of chopsticks and poured the medicine down, whereupon Tuan went into convulsions. The mother cried, and the rest of the family crowded helplessly around the stricken child. It was past midnight when they heard a banging at the gate. William took a lantern and went out to look. A sedan chair entered, carried by four porters and led by two others carrying lanterns. As soon as Uncle Yao stepped into the door, he asked, "How is the boy?" Upon being told what had happened, Uncle Yao exclaimed, "Thank heavens he is still alive!" Lamps were lit and William was told to fetch the prescription written the day before, now all crumpled up. Uncle Yao took a look at it and shook his head, "Your ancestors must have accumulated many good deeds. I thought I'd killed the child."

He ordered William to make some ink on the inkslab. Calmly he smoothed out the paper and wrote at the end of the prescription, "Add one jujube date."

William got into the sedan chair and, prescription in hand, rode to the herb store in magnificent style, two orbs of soft light swinging before him in the still night. He roused the store clerk from his sleep and had him fill the prescription. It was dawn before Uncle Yao departed, saying as he left, "If this doesn't work, I might as well give up practicing medicine."

But the boy recovered rapidly and the family thenceforth revered Uncle Yao Nan-ch'üan as a living Buddha.

William had shown Uncle Yao some of his writings, and Uncle Yao came to like him a good deal. Quite a while afterwards, William mustered enough courage to put the question to him, "How could one jujube date make such a difference?"

Uncle Yao told William that since he did not know medicine, it would be difficult to explain the reason to him. "But I can give you an analogy. When a person is attacked by a disease, it is like a country invaded by enemies. The enemies throw the whole country into chaos. But if the army is stronger than the enemies, it will be able to vanquish them. In my haste, I forgot to put down the jujube date in the prescription. But I could not fall asleep that night. As I reviewed all the things I did during the daytime, my mind turned to your brother; and it occurred to me that I might have omitted something in the prescription. I sat up with a start and hurried to your house. The jujube date is what is known as *chung-chün* ("headquarters") in medical terminology. It is the regulating element. Without it, the stronger the army, the more havoc it wreaks."

One would never think of paying a family friend such as Uncle Yao for his services. Instead, gratitude was shown by sending him presents on the New Year. Towards the end of each year, the Hungs received boxes and baskets of goodies from Grandfather Lin from Foochow: dried lichee nuts, dried longan, dried plum, a great variety of candies, and, of course, crates of tea leaves. Lin Fei would divide them into big portions for friends. But William's father, to whom material things had always come hard, always felt that his wife was overly generous and took a little bit out of each portion, saving treats for the children. William's mother would insist on putting them back. So it went for days, one taking out and the other putting back. Friends like Uncle Yao who knew that the Hungs were poor would send back some "return presents"—gold ingots for instance, sometimes enough for the Hung family to live on for several months.

BY THE TIME WILLIAM was ten or eleven, he had come to realize that his life when he grew up would be very different from his father's.

Changes and rumors of change were coming to China. The Hungs had no newspaper except for the *Peking Gazette,* which consisted mainly of court news and official documents. Missionaries in Shanghai published a newspaper called *The Globe Magazine (Wan-kuo kung-pao,* later translated as *Reviews of the Times),* but it never reached people like the Hungs. Current events could only be discussed behind closed doors. After the family moved to Shantung, William's mother could at times obtain copies of the contraband *Journal for Renovation of the People (Hsin-min ts'ung pao),* published in Japan by the great reformer Liang Ch'i-ch'ao, who had a price on his head. (Lin Fei was such an outspoken and ardent admirer of Liang Ch'i-ch'ao that she said if she were a man, she would go work for him.) From this paper, the Hungs found out about the unjust treaties the Western powers had imposed on China and how dangerously close was China to being divided up by the Western powers and Japan. They also found out about the One Hundred Days of Reform in 1898 in which the young Kuang-hsu Emperor was persuaded by Liang Ch'i-ch'ao and another reformer, K'ang Yu-wei, to proclaim a broad program of modernization. For this, the Emperor was placed under house arrest by his aunt, the Empress Dowager, who revoked all his well-meaning decrees.

Even the Empress Dowager, however, could not stop the wheels of history. It soon became obvious to all that the old bureaucracy of Imperial China could adequately cope with neither foreign armies nor foreign ideas. In 1905, when Hung was twelve, the Court finally decided to abolish the venerable civil service examination system that had shaped, screened, and selected officials for Chinese governments for the past one-and-a-half millennia. It was an unthinkable act, yet there it was. New schools were established to teach new subjects, to provide new orientation for a new generation of Chinese who would serve their country in new ways. This generation was Hung's.

CHAPTER FOUR

Adolescence

HUNG'S FATHER received his first official appointment as magistrate around 1906. As far as appointments went, the district of Yü-t'ai in the province of Shantung was no plum. It was marshy and bandit-infested. The previous magistrate had left in a hurry for some reason, and Hung Hsi was instructed on short notice to fill the vacancy. Hung Hsi, Big Brother Yen, and William set off for the district immediately. Several weeks later, Lin Fei and the rest of the family arrived in resplendent sedan chairs, band music and blasts of cannons welcoming with great fanfare the lady of the new magistrate.

As magistrate, Hung Hsi was a king in his district; and the yamen was his palace. In later years, when William Hung came across yamen in other parts of China, he found them all built on the same plan. Outside the yamen proper was a freestanding wall on which proclamations were pasted. On top of the wall were generally inscribed eight characters to remind the magistrate, "Your emolument comes from the fat of the people." At the gate of the yamen were a flagpole, a drum, and a stone device on which firecrackers were ignited to alert the populace when the magistrate was about to come out. Inside the gate were the offices of assistants and secretaries. Past them were steps leading to the main hall where the magistrate held court in his function as the district judge. He sat behind a tall, imposing, solid-fronted table, which was placed squarely in the center of the hall. A door on one side of the hall led to a sitting room where the magistrate received his guests on a brick platform called a *k'ang,* heated in the winter by coal or firewood underneath. Etiquette dictated that as soon as the magistrate lifted his teacup and invited the guest to drink, the guest had to leave. A door on the other side of the main hall led to the magistrate's study. Behind the main hall, separated by a courtyard, was the building that contained a dining room and bedrooms for out-of-town guests. Behind this building were the residence of the magistrate's family and the servants' quarters.

The magistrate's top-level staff consisted of a legal assistant, a tax assistant, and a secretary. The legal and tax assistants learned their profession by apprenticeship; and these two professions were almost monopolized by men from Chekiang province, particularly from the Shao-hsing area. The secretary was an educated man, often someone waiting to take his examinations. He took care of all documents. Beneath these three persons were scores of local clerks attached to the yamen. In reality they collectively held more power than the magistrate. Magistrates came and went; but the clerks were always there, often passing positions from father to son. Moreover, they were knowledgeable about local customs and had useful local connections. Their salaries were miniscule; but they made their living by imposing charges for their services, some legitimate (e.g., for preparation of documents or explanation of procedures), others of a dubious sort. They also received favorable treatment from local merchants when they made purchases. In addition to the bureaucracy, a small military force was under the command of the magistrate. At Yü-t'ai, this consisted of a standing army of more than a hundred. Weapons—knives, swords, spears, and a few old guns—were kept in an arsenal and not issued in normal times. Since there was never enough money in the magistrate's budget to cover expenses, many positions were left unfilled. Servants were employed to perform some of the more menial chores at the yamen; but it was customary for the magistrate to bring his own cook, his own barber, and a hairdresser for his family. It was also customary for the magistrate to bring with him his own printer to print his proclamations, his personal writings, and perhaps an updated local gazetteer.

"The magistrate's duty, first and foremost, was to collect taxes," William Hung remarked. "The size of the population was estimated, the taxes computed; and the magistrate was responsible for exacting the money out of the population. There were poor people who sold their children and rented their wives out so that they could pay their taxes. The taxes were sent to the provincial capital, and ultimately to Peking. The second duty was to maintain peace and order. Other functions—educational, cultural—were just 'frosting on the cake.'"

Theoretically, the magistrate was the teacher of all the scholars in his district. Long after their father had died, when William's brother David was travelling around China as an engineer under the Nationalist government, strangers would come to see him saying they were "students" of his father and insist on inviting him to dinner. In his cultural role, the magistrate was responsible for keeping the local Confucian temple in good repair and erecting stone arches in praise of the virtues of women who stayed unmarried after their husbands died, or other instances of exemplary behavior.

The court sessions, which were held every third, eighth, thirteenth, eighteenth, twenty-third, and twenty-eighth of the month, were known as the thirds and the eighths. Hung Hsi would sit behind that imposing table in the main hall, six of his guards standing at attention on each side of him, some holding swords, others holding bamboo sticks. On the table were kept ready two inkslabs and a container of bamboo tallies on which official summonses and subpoenas could be inscribed. The bulk of the cases were family quarrels and property disputes. One case might concern an old woman who claimed that her daughter-in-law had mistreated her; another might involve contention over the division of an inheritance. The magistrate made the judgments in his wisdom and the bamboo stick was used rather liberally. Ordinarily offenders were flogged on the bare buttocks; but serious criminals were flogged on the back, often resulting in death. In some cases, the legal assistant was ordered to conduct an investigation and to make recommendations for a verdict while the defendant was held in jail. Only rarely did murder cases come up. On these occasions, Hung Hsi relied heavily on a twelfth-century book of forensic medicine called *The Magic Mirror for Deciding Lawsuits* (*Che-yü kuei-chien*). To help determine the cause of death, a long pliant stick of almost pure silver was used to insert into the anus of the corpse to probe for telling residues in the intestines.

HUNG HSI liked to wander through his district incognito. Since he was more than six feet tall and strikingly handsome, it was not easy for him to wander around unnoticed. Yet he did find out a great many things about his district this way. It reached his ear, for instance, that his "fast horsemen," responsible for fighting banditry, were in fact in league with the bandits, sharing their loot. One night, Hung Hsi told William and two trusty servants to stand guard in the water closet with guns while he asked the officer in charge of the fast horsemen into his office. He told the man quietly that he had found out about the illicit liaison.

"What would you do if you were in my place?" he asked.

The officer immediately got on his knees and knocked his head on the floor. He said, "A bandit, if captured, has his head cut off. It follows, therefore, that I who associate with the bandits should have my head cut off. But killing me will not stop the banditry. I beg the Great One to spare my dog's life. I shall guarantee that as long as you are magistrate here, there will be no banditry in the district."

Hung Hsi let the man go, and the latter kept his word.

ANOTHER INCIDENT from the Yü-t'ai era was etched in William Hung's memory. He came to spend a great deal of his time with the legal assistant, who was a bachelor and had his own residence and servants outside the yamen. He frequently invited William to drink with him, always having at hand a roasted chicken or other such delicacy to go with the liquor. Hung Hsi had warned him against liquor; but William would invoke Confucius's statement that there are no set limits to what a man should drink, as long as it did not cause him trouble. One day, he received a note from the legal assistant saying he had just received from Shao-hsing a small jar of old wine from the reign of the Chia-ching Emperor (1522–1567), that was fit for a poet. Would he come? William, who at that age rather fancied himself a budding Li Po, hurried over. The wine was almost gelatinous (a small depression appeared in the center of its surface), but it was very pungent. They nibbled on the food as they drank, but the next thing Hung remembered, he was lying in bed at home with his boots and coat on. He sat up and ordered the servants in; they told him laughing that he had been found in the gutter, dead drunk.

"Where's Father?" William asked as he pulled himself up from bed and rushed to his father's study.

Kneeling on the floor and kowtowing, he said apologetically, "I am sure Father is very hurt."

"There's no limit to what a man should drink, as long as it doesn't cause him trouble," Hung's father responded ironically.

"I am still young. Confucius has said, 'A man stands on his own at thirty.' From now on, I shall not touch a drop of liquor until I am thirty."

Much chastened, Hung kept his promise. He did not drink again until he was thirty-three.

Li Po (701–762), the Taoist celebrator of wine, women, and song, was the poet whom William admired most in his youth; but his father saw to it that he also encountered another T'ang poet, Tu Fu (712–770),

whose poetry showed a deeper knowledge of the sufferings of mankind.
When Hung Hsi began teaching his son the art of versifying, he gave
him a copy of Tu Fu's poetry, telling the boy that not only were Tu's
poems worthy of emulation but so was Tu's life. Li Po's poems, he said,
appealed immediately to the palate, like bananas or lichee nuts; but like
olives or betel nuts, Tu Fu's poems tasted better the longer one chewed.
By the time William took that next drink at thirty-three, he had tasted
more of life's complexity and become a collector of books on Tu Fu.

HUNG HSI's tenure at Yü-t'ai was cut short in about a year by a serious
illness. When he was about to leave the district, he confessed to his son
that although he was able to stop banditry in his own district, the inci-
dents increased dramatically in the neighboring districts. The bandits
had to eat somehow.

With the father ill and unable to earn money, the family came near
destitution. They moved back to Tsinan, the provincial capital of Shantung, to live on a quiet street. Nung-nung, the cook whom they had
brought with them from Foochow, had to be discharged. Only one
woman servant was retained to help the mother take care of the younger
children. Hung, who wanted to go to a modern high school, had to stay
at home to take care of his father. There were frequent trips to the
pawnshop; one sad day, even the magistrate's long silver stick used to
probe corpses had to be pawned off.

Two good things issued from this gloomy period, however. One was
that since William, as eldest son, had to stay home to take care of their
father, Tuan could be sent off to school in his place. Tuan had always resented having to play second fiddle to his older brother. When he was
only a toddler, he composed a little song in Foochownese, which he
sang to himself: "*T'ien nea, t'ien nea, mo yao te nea* (Alas, alas, never
be a number two)!" For once, he got some advantage out of being second
in line.

The other good thing was that during this period, Hung really came
to know his father well. As he nursed Hung Hsi, the father would discuss with the son his philosophy of life.

"He taught me that a man should have public morals, the touchstone
of which is money, as well as private morals, the touchstone of which
is women. He himself had not known any women other than my
mother. Some of his attitudes were similar to the Christian doctrine of

stewardship: that money and talents were given us not to keep but to use for the benefit of others."

Under his tutelage, Hung began an earnest study of the Chinese classics. No longer just memorizing the words to show off as he had done when he was younger, nor to pass examinations, he was studying to distill from the books the principles of how to live and how to integrate knowledge.

One day, when Hung Hsi thought he was dying, he called all his sons to his bedside and told them, "Poverty is the natural and proper state of a scholar. My sons, I have two bits of advice to give you. Never be a government official, and never marry a woman from a wealthy family."

He must have felt himself compromised by both.

As HIS FATHER gradually got better, Hung prepared to take the examinations for the high school affiliated with the Shantung Teachers College. He was then about thirteen. Applicants were tested on Chinese, English, and mathematics. Since his brother Tuan was in the first year, Hung decided he should try for admission to the third year. He taught himself algebra from a Chinese textbook written by the missionary-educator Calvin Mateer. The clear, rigorous discipline of mathematics appealed to his mind, and he retained a love for it all his life. For English, his father engaged a tutor who came in two hours every afternoon to teach him, starting from a, b, c, d. They used a textbook called *The English Language with Chinese Commentary* (*Ying-wen han-ku*), which did an excellent job of explaining the intricacies of English grammar; but just how badly he was taught pronunciation Hung did not find out until much later. His tutor had learned his English from a Japanese, who learned it from a German teacher.

At the time Hung was preparing for his entrance examinations, the first public library opened in Tsinan. It was located in a park, just as private libraries were usually in gardens. An entrance fee of two copper coins was charged the users. No notetaking was allowed. Hung would get two copper coins from his father, take some steamed buns with him, and stay in the library the entire day. He found a copy of *Master Lü's Spring and Autumn Annals* (*Lü-shih ch'un-ch'iu,* a third-century-B.C. encyclopedic work) and liked it so much that he committed the whole book to memory.

The day they were posted, Hung went with a neighbor to see the results of the examination. His education thus far had been haphazard; this was the first time he had been pitted against his peers. Anxiously, his eyes scanned the rows and columns of names on the bulletin board. He half expected to have failed. Suddenly his friend shouted, "You are number one!" Hung followed his finger to the top of the list; and there it was, in two incredible characters, Hung Yeh. He was so stunned that for a moment his immediate surroundings lost the solidity of reality and he thought he would faint.

STUDENTS ADMITTED TO THE SCHOOL were furnished with books, uniforms, pencils, and other supplies in addition to a free meal every day of soup, two steamed buns, and tea. As the head of his class, Hung was also awarded a monthly stipend of two taels of silver, not a negligible sum to his needy family. Hung needed all his pride to sustain him in school, however, for he found himself unhappily the butt of his classmates' jokes. He was ridiculed for his blue cotton gown, sewn with many years of wear in mind by his mother: The hem was let down every year as he grew taller. The gown's resulting horizontal stripes of different hues, growing deeper toward the bottom of the skirt, earned Hung the sobriquet of "Pagoda Boy." A second target of derision was Hung's southern accent, which his classmates claimed made him sound like a sparrow. When Hung came home flustered, his father would try to cheer him up: "Just pretend that it's a dog howling at you. If you really want to reason with the dog, you argue that he is wrong and you are right, that you have not stolen anything and he has no right to bark at you. But what can you do? Get down on all four and bark back at the dog? It's a waste of time. The smart thing to do is to walk away and forget all about it."

Nevertheless, Hung felt intense pressures to excel in school. Chinese literature was the most important subject; and the book selected as the text was *The Tso Commentary on the Spring and Autumn Annals,* from the fifth century B.C., known as the *Tso-chuan.* The class had to write a composition on the book every month. At home, Hung would pick by himself a topic from *Tso-chuan* every day and write a composition on the topic. The topic the teacher happened to choose was frequently one of the topics Hung had already practiced on at home. The class was allowed an hour to finish the composition; William would finish in twenty minutes and stride proudly out of the room.

He was at the head of the class again the following year, but the pressure was unabated. Having found a poem somewhere called "The

Monkey Show," ("Hou-tzu-hsi") which he felt described his situation, he copied it and pasted on the wall at home:

> At the sound of beating drums you climb up the pole.
> The second time is going to be harder than the first.
> Monkey, watch carefully where you step,
> For those are cold, hard eyes that stare up at you!

His was not the only class in which a non-Shantungnese had placed first. In all the other classes, the top honors were won by non-Shantungnese like Hung, for the boys who did best were boys whose fathers were scholar-officials, boys who were practically nursed on poetry and history. Since under the Ch'ing bureaucratic system officials were not allowed to serve in their native province, none of these specially successful pupils were local children. The resentment among the local families grew so great that the authorities had to establish a separate school for the non-Shantungnese boys. The new school was to be run entirely on student tuition and was called the Resident Guest School (K'e-chi hsueh-hsiao). During his second year of schooling, Hung was transferred to it. Shortly thereafter, his father received an appointment to be magistrate of the district of Ch'ü-fu, Shantung, and Hung moved into the dormitory.

Hung was much happier at the Resident Guest School, where he shared a sense of comradeship with his schoolmates. He remembered playing games like kicking the shuttlecock with them as well as studying. Almost all the teachers who taught the modern subjects had received training outside China. Most had studied in Japan, the mathematics teacher in France. There was one who had cut his pigtail abroad and not grown it back. He usually wore a hat to which he had attached a fake pigtail; but once a while, he would remove his hat—a daring act because the Chinese were required to wear pigtails to show their loyalty to the Manchu conquerors. What struck the boys, however, was not any political symbolism but the extreme ugliness of short hair.

The school was converted from an old examination compound. Each student occupied an examination cell big enough to hold a bed, a desk, and a small bookcase. There were janitors assigned to clean the place, to pour tea, to distribute mail, and so forth. Meals were supposed to be included in the tuition; but the food was terrible, consisting mainly of a steamed bun and some dried preserved vegetables or dried preserved fish. Most students gave the cook a few coins to add an egg or a dish of beansprouts to supplement the paltry fare. Richer students ate all their meals outside.

Hung's own food problem was solved in a deal with a fellow student named Shih Chia-chü, who had flunked algebra repeatedly: Hung agreed to give him remedial lessons in exchange for his cooking the meals. Hung had fond memories of lying comfortably in bed inside a mosquito net while Shih worked on the small brick stove outside, reciting aloud the quadratic equations. With the two of them splitting the food costs, they were able to have meat at least once a week. As the arrangement worked out exceedingly well, Hung went on to teach Shih geometry the subsequent year.

"From this first teaching experience, I discovered the basic principle of teaching mathematics. In mathematics, every layer is built on the foundation of the previous layer. The trick is refusing to let the student go on to the next lesson until he has completely mastered the one at hand."

The reliance of other students on the school cook to purchase supplements for their meals had a tragic ending. Many of them had run up substantial bills with him over the course of several months. When he asked for payments, the students would just hem and haw. The cook became desperate: He had incurred debts all over town to buy the food, yet he dared not offend these sons of officials. One morning when the students went to the dining room for breakfast, they discovered he had hanged himself from the beam. On his pigtail were many little pins, and on each pin was a little paper slip on which was written the name of a person and the amount owed. An indignant student removed the paper slips from the dead man's hair and pasted them all up on the bulletin board. Stricken with shame, the guilty ones quickly paid up and sent the money to the cook's family. It was rumoured that the cook's ghost lingered in the dining room, and for the better part of a year nobody dared go near the place.

At the Resident Guest School, Hung was also confronted with a moral crisis that had less melancholy consequences but concerned him personally. Among his classmates were several who frequented brothels. They laughed when they found out that Hung, at the age of sixteen, was still a virgin. They made a point of describing their adventures graphically in front of him to make him blush. Finally, they were able to convince him one day that he should at least go to one to see what it was like, and offered to pay his expenses for him. "You will see that the girls are not as depraved as you might imagine. In fact, some of them are better people than we are."

They took him to a house with an elegantly painted gate. They knocked on the door and were answered by a pack of dogs barking wildly. Already feeling guilty and apprehensive, Hung, who had been afraid of dogs since a bite in childhood, turned around at the sound and fled. He ran straight back to the dormitory and into his room, panting. As he sat down on his bed to rest, he noticed a letter had come from his father. It read, "My son, you are coming to the age of sexual awakening. This is a time of crisis in a man's life. If a woman loses her chastity, society looks down upon her. A man may not have to suffer the contempt of other people if he loses his chastity, but he has his own standards, and he may look down on himself. You should keep your body free from defilement, like a precious vessel. A scholar should set his goal to be a sage, and there are things he would not do. I have eight characters I use to manage myself in these matters. I have written them down for you on a separate piece of paper."

The eight characters — *shou-shen ju-yü chih-chih ju-chin* — meant, "Guard the body like a piece of jade; hold onto your purpose as if it were gold." When he read them, Hung broke out in a cold sweat.

DURING THE SUMMER between his two years at the Resident Guest School, William visited his family at Ch'ü-fu, where his father was the newly appointed magistrate. That summer, the tax assistant took a leave of absence and went back to Chekiang province. William was given the responsibility of collecting the taxes and recording them for his father. He remembered very distinctly staying up late one night counting the money; after several attempts he was still short of a copper coin, so he slipped one in from his own pocket.

Collecting taxes may have been the primary duty of a magistrate, but at Yu-t'ai, bandits had been Hung Hsi's prickliest problem. At Ch'ü-fu, a descendant of Confucius was. At Ch'ü-fu, as the place where Confucius had been born and was buried, a great temple had been maintained down through the ages. The emperors of China had come frequently to make sacrifice and pay homage to the Great Sage. It was customary for the reigning emperor to confer upon a lineal descendant of Confucius the honorary title of Duke of Perpetuating Sageness (Yen-sheng-kung) and enfeoff him with land for his support. As the magistrate of Ch'ü-fu, Hung Hsi had to reckon with the seventy-sixth-lineal-generation descendant of Confucius, K'ung Ling-i, who owned more than fifteen thousand acres (two thousand *ch'ing*) of his district.

It was an irony that Confucius, who himself led an ascetic life, had enriched his descendants in such a fantastic way. This particular Duke of Perpetuating Sageness was emphatically everything Confucius was not. His appetites scandalized the populace, and it was rumoured that he exacted from his tenant-debtors the right to deflower their brides. The Duke would send little slips of paper to Hung's father directing him how he should decide this or that piece of litigation. Hung Hsi made a rule of ignoring them. One day, the Duke appeared at a court session and stood there to watch the proceedings. As he was of higher rank, Hung Hsi was obliged to conduct the rest of the business standing up with him. Afterwards Hung Hsi made it very clear to the Duke that his presence was not welcome at court. The new magistrate's policy towards the Duke was widely applauded by the people of the district. He became known as "Hung the Clear Sky."

William saw K'ung Ling-i once at Ch'ü-fu in the summer of 1909, when he had come to visit on a very hot day, bringing with him a great piece of ice that had been cut out from the river the winter before and buried deep underground for use in summer. The Duke was tall and very handsome. He maintained a company of Peking opera singers at home and was reputed to be quite a good singer himself. He sent William several invitations to the opera performances, but Hung Hsi forbade him to go.

Later that year, William and his brother Tuan came to an agreement about what to do with their lives. Tuan, who was then thirteen, would go to the Armed Defense School (Wu-pei hsueh-hsiao) in Shantung; and William, then fifteen, would try to get into the new Naval Academy, which was recruiting students in Shanghai. With one brother in the modern army and another in the navy, they would defend China against the foreigners.

CHAPTER FIVE

Transitions

WHEN HUNG LEFT for Shanghai to take the examination for admission to the Naval Academy, his mother went with him. She planned to continue farther south to see her parents. After arriving in Tsinan by mule cart, they took a train to Tsingtao, where they embarked on a boat for Shanghai. A violent storm overtook them at sea, and the boat sought refuge on a small island for several days. When they finally reached Shanghai, the examination date had already passed.

Lin Fei suggested that, as long as they were in Shanghai, Hung should go pay his respects to his father's old friend from Foochow, Kao Meng-tan, general editor of the Shanghai Commercial Press, then already a thriving publishing house innovative in spreading modern knowledge in China. Mr. Kao told Hung that two routes were open to young people who wanted to serve their country: One was the military, the other, diplomacy. He advised Hung to go to Foochow and enroll in the Anglo-Chinese College, an institution run by American missionaries, where Hung could improve his English and absorb Western knowledge.

There was a glad homecoming for the daughter and the grandson in Foochow. Hung was given the guest room with the lichee tree outside his window as an honor. There he lived for the next five years. Having taken Kao's advice, he set out every morning for the hour-long walk from his grandfather's house on the island of Nan-t'ai in the south suburb to the foreign school on the hill across the Min River. To reach it, he had to cross two bridges. The first was the mile-long Longevity Bridge (Wan-shou-ch'iao), constructed with great granite blocks brought down the river by boats in the Ming dynasty (1368–1644). This took him to the Middle Sandbar (Chung-chou), bustling with vendors and wayside teashops. He then crossed another bridge to get to Granary Front Hill (Ts'ang-ch'ien-shan), where the Anglo-Chinese College was situated.

The Anglo-Chinese College was run by the Board of Foreign Missions of the Methodist Church. It had about seven hundred students, most of them children of merchants who had the foresight to provide their children with a Western education. All subjects, except Chinese literature, were taught in English. After eight years of instruction, the students graduated with the equivalent of an American junior college degree. Hung wanted to enter as a fourth-year student; but when an oral examination revealed his English to be unintelligible, he was sent down to the first year.

At the Anglo-Chinese College, Hung's old, worn cotton gown again made him conspicuous among his classmates in silk and satin. They playfully dubbed him "Master Mencius" for his frequent quotation of the Confucian classics. Although, as usual, he did well in his studies—he was promoted every few months as his English improved—he became extremely antagonistic to the religious teaching of the school. He made it his business to learn the Bible very well. He underlined in red ink all the passages with which he disagreed, and tacked up his refutation of those verses on the bulletin board for all to see.

On October 10, 1911, a plot for an uprising against the imperial government was accidentally discovered in Wuchang, thus precipitating the Chinese Revolution. When the news reached Foochow the next day, all the students cut their pigtails to show their solidarity with the revolutionaries. Within a few months, the three-hundred-year-old Ch'ing dynasty was toppled and a republic declared in China. When the initial news of the revolt trickled to Shantung in the north, the whole province was thrown into turmoil. The governor sent down orders for the districts to organize militia units for resistance. Committees of the gentry were formed in each district to elect a general. In Ch'ü-fu, the Duke of Perpetuating Sageness, as the first gentleman of the land, had first claim to the honor; but Hung's father was elected. It was a slap in the face to the Duke. He wrote a letter to the governor claiming that Hung Hsi was unsuitable for the post, as a result of which the latter was recalled to the provincial capital to await further instructions. The gentry at Ch'ü-fu were incensed. A delegation of seven old men, all over seventy years of age, was sent to Tsinan to reason with the governor. They gave notice to Hung Hsi's newly named replacement to stay away until the dispute was resolved.

Meanwhile, William Hung was leading a revolution all his own at the Anglo-Chinese College in Foochow. He continued to excel scholastically. At a schoolwide gathering during his second year, he heard his name called on the stage; and to his great surprise, he was awarded a set of the *English-Chinese Dictionary,* fresh off the press from the Shanghai Commercial Press, for having the highest grades in the whole college. His attacks against Christianity, however, intensified, and he attracted a following among the students. The main thrust of his argument was that Christianity was incompatible with Confucius's teachings and that Confucius's teachings were far superior to Christianity. He loved to point out contradictions in the Bible. One of his favorite themes was that Jesus himself was an unfilial son. He pointed out, for instance, that according to John 2:3–4, when Jesus's mother came to tell him at the marriage feast of Cana that there was no more wine, Jesus responded rudely, "Woman, what have I to do with thee? Mine hour is not yet come." A person who behaved that way toward his mother, Hung contended, was not worthy to be head of a religion. A move was therefore afoot among the faculty members of the Anglo-Chinese College to expel Hung for his disruptive activities. It was, however, successfully deflected by Mrs. John Gowdy, the principal's wife. She maintained that it was not right for a Christian school to expel a student who had been exemplary in all other respects simply because he opposed Christianity.

When Hung's father wrote to him about his situation in Shantung, Hung impulsively wrote back asking Hung Hsi to come help defend Confucianism against the foreigners in Foochow. That his father agreed to come to Foochow to assist him was a remarkable testimony to the confidence he placed in his eighteen-year-old son.

As soon as Hung Hsi arrived in Foochow, he left for the village of Hou P'u to pay his respect to the dead ancestors. It was early spring; the graveyard was chilly; he caught pneumonia and died soon after at the home of his father-in-law. He was forty-six years old.

Hung sent a telegram to Shantung to his mother and wrote a long letter to his brother Tuan. But Lin Fei could not come to Foochow immediately, for Tuan was critically ill. Then Tuan died. Lin Fei sold whatever jewelry she still had, bought a small plot of land not far from Tsinan, where she buried her son; and hurried south with her four younger children to bury her husband. The land near Tsinan she handed over to Big Brother Yen and his northern wife so that they would have some means of subsistence, trusting they would take care of Tuan's grave.

Hung moved his father's coffin from the Lin residence, which was not a proper resting place, to a temple in the city and then set out to organize a memorial service for Hung Hsi. With the invitations to several hundred relatives and friends of his father, he sent the customary "address in mourning" (*ai-ch'i*), which gave a detailed account of Hung Hsi's life—his conduct as an official, as a man, as a scholar. Condolences inscribed on yards of white cloth flowed in from all over. Many of his father's friends came to the memorial service, bringing with them records of loans incurred by the dead man. These they burned reverently in front of the coffin, a gesture for which the family was grateful.

The following year, when Lin Fei arrived in Foochow, she first had to marry off the fifteen-year-old daughter who was betrothed to the heir of a distinguished Ch'en family in the city; for an old rule said that if a daughter was not married immediately after the father's death, she had to observe the customary three years of mourning. The Ch'en family had only this one son, and they were not inclined to wait. Only after the wedding could she get on with the business of burying her husband. Hung Hsi was buried with his pigtail, still a loyal imperial official several months into the Republic. Hung selected a passage from the *Biographies of Dutiful Officials in the History of the Former Han Dynasty* (206 B.C.–A.D. 8) (*Han-shu hsün-li chuan*) for his father's tombstone. It said, "He passed from this world leaving love behind him. His memories lingered among the populace."

THE SUDDEN DEATH of his father was a shattering blow to Hung. It left a great void in his life. A few days after Hung Hsi died, Elizabeth Gowdy came to see William and asked him to describe his father. After listening, she said that a person like Hung Hsi, if he had had the opportunity, would surely have become a Christian. Hung retorted that according to Mrs. Gowdy's religion, those who did not believe in Jesus were sent to hell. Mrs. Gowdy answered that that part of her religion was for the uneducated, that it was really not clear whether there were a heaven and a hell, but that if a heaven did exist, a person like his father belonged there.

Then she said, "I know you have studied the Bible very well, and that you disagree with it a great deal. But the way you read the Bible is not the right way; it is not the right way to read any book. Books are the depositories of the experience of men; they contain both the good and the bad. If you are invited to a feast, you choose foods that are tasty to you, food that you can digest, leaving the plates and bowls on the table. One should not eat the plates and bowls. The Bible has been transmitted in a succession of languages. When you read it, you should pay attention to those parts that you find beneficial to you. It is inevitable that there should be mistakes, contradictions; but even some of the contradictions you may discover at some future date are not really contradictions. You are wasting your time trying to remember only those parts that annoy you."

For some time now, even though Hung had stuck to his guns, his opposition to Christianity had been weakened by several men who had come to speak at the College. The famous evangelist Sherwood Eddy had come. He started out with a demonstration of the qualities of air, which could not be seen or touched, yet was very real. He brought out an empty kerosene can. After screwing the cap tightly onto the can, he placed it on a heating element. As the air expanded in the can, the can expanded with it. With a dramatic flourish, he poured a cup of cold water over the can, whereupon it collapsed immediately. This served as a springboard for a discussion on the nature of God, who is invisible like the air yet is also very real.

In another talk, Eddy declared in a vibrant voice that China also had had its own prophets in the past: Confucius, Mencius, Chuang-tzu, and so forth; that the whole world had much to learn from China. China, however, had always suffered from both internal and external enemies. Now China was a republic and Americans were the first to recognize the Republic. The best among Americans love the Chinese, and some of the best of the Chinese youths had studied in America and were now coming back to be leaders of China. He envisioned millions of new friendships blossoming across the two continents. At the conclusion of his talk, Eddy extended his hand to his Chinese interpreter and their hands clasped. As they pulled their hands apart, the audience saw that there was something between them: It unfolded to become the flag of the new Chinese Republic and an American flag, tied together. The whole audience was electrified. Rising to their feet, they cheered. Hung was very much moved.

Eventually, Mrs. Gowdy's demonstration of Christian love and her liberal interpretation of Christian doctrines won Hung over. He was converted to Christianity.

We have a letter that Hung wrote to Mrs. Gowdy in English, dated

August 25, 1912. Three years later, Mrs. Gowdy sent this letter to Ruth Crawford Mitchell, a person who was to play a big role in Hung's life. It lays bare Hung's earliest struggles with Christianity and Confucianism:

. . . I am sorry that my mother will not be able to come in this year because my younger brother is so sick that he can not rise from the bed. She must wait until he is well. (My cousin has now come back because in Shantung there was revolution against the people who cut off their queues.) I have sent your books to my mother through post. As they helped me very much in the resurrection of our Lord Jesus Christ, I believe that they will help her very much too.

. . . [T]here were men who indeed were good men, who indeed obeyed the commands of God, but they were not what we call Christians and they were Confucians. Whether they could get the grace of our heavenly Father and the saving power of our Lord Jesus Christ, or not we do not know. But I believe that they were not less in goodness than those whom we call Christians.

If we have the question, "Was Jesus Christ sent only for the people of Israel or for the whole world?" We Christians shall answer "He was sent for the whole world." But as I think, this is not true. Why is it that Jesus Christ traveled only where He traveled and why did He not come to China? Why is it that at early times, the Chinese had no chance to know about Jesus Christ until now while some of the Jews knew Him when He was born? God loves His people and likes them to follow His order. But they gradually separate from Him and followed the wish of Satan. So God sent Jesus Christ to the West and sent Confucius to the East to save the people out of sin. We Christians believe that Jesus Christ is the son of God; but we do not know whether Confucius was also His son, or His relative or His servant. No matter what they be before God, they were both the messengers of God, the saviours of people . . .

In her cover letter, Mrs. Gowdy wrote, "Better not let William Hung know that I gave you the letter . . . William must not get too exalted an opinion of himself and I do hope he will be saved from the cancer of personal ambition and self-seeking in his career. We shall pray much about this."

At Hung's request, he was baptized on New Year's Day, 1913, by Bishop James W. Bashford. Hung was then nineteen years old. A few months later, his mother was also converted to Christianity. Eventually the whole family was baptized. Lin Fei ordered David, who had a good calligraphic hand, to write a little slip of paper to put beside each place setting at the dining table, "Do not forget to pray before every meal."

AS HE BECAME MORE RELAXED at school, Hung came to know his twenty classmates better and to enjoy their company. One of the best liked was Yang Hsi-tung, a quiet, affable person who did beautiful calligraphy in the hard, lean style of Cheng Hsiao-hsu. When classmates visited him at home, they found that he had a maidservant and a manservant all to himself. It was at Yang's home that Hung had his first taste of coffee. Another popular person was Jimmy Ch'en, son of a minister. Athletic and handsome, he had a sister who, they all agreed, was the prettiest girl in Foochow. Sometimes, on their way to school, they would see her walking toward the girls' school she attended, and the class clown Lin Li-te would make himself ridiculous over her. There was a Ch'en Yuan-lung who, at Hung's baptism, remarked rather testily that Hung had his heart set on being a bishop. Ironically, not Hung but Ch'en Yuan-lung became a Methodist bishop.

At church, Hung was given the job of translating the Sunday lessons from English to Chinese. As the only student who spoke Mandarin, the official dialect that was widely spoken in northern China, Hung also served as interpreter for preachers who came from the north. Four distinguished foreign guests came to visit in 1913: Mason F. North, General Secretary of the Board of Foreign Missions of the Methodist Church, who brought his son Eric M. North; and William I. Haven, General Secretary of the American Bible Society, who brought his daughter Gladys Haven. Interpreting for American visitors was ordinarily the responsibility of Prof. Wang Kan-ho, a graduate of Cornell College in Iowa; but he could not handle all four at once, so Hung was asked to act as the younger Dr. North's interpreter. Eric North took his talks and speeches very seriously, and Hung was invited to meet him frequently to go over what he planned to say.

The missionary most widely liked by the students was Ralph Ward, who not only spoke tolerably good Chinese, but cooked good Chinese food. After dinner one evening, he spread out a map on the floor and, getting down on all fours, pointed out to the students the countries that had evil designs on China. He told them China had better wake up to the harsh realities of international politics.

In 1914, the students were allowed to organize a Student Council. A man named Ch'i Hsuan was elected president and Hung was elected vice-president and secretary; but when Ch'i Hsuan soon absconded with the funds, Hung became president. Hung organized a school fair with booths selling items made by the students and entertainments for which entrance fees were charged. The coffers of the Student Council were thus replenished; and with some of the money, a ditto machine was bought.

The ditto machine was put to good use that November when the

Student Council received a letter from Japan signed simply by "The Chinese Student Association in Tokyo." The gist of the letter was that the Association had learned through secret reports that Japan had presented twenty-one outrageous demands to China, compliance with which would result in China's becoming a virtual colony of Japan. It urged all students in China to unite and resist. After an emergency meeting of the Student Council, thousands of copies of the letter were distributed in the city. The local authorities took a serious view of the matter and arrested all the "troublemakers." To obtain their release from jail, Hung ran around frantically among his father's friends begging them to offer their personal guaranty that these students would not cause any further disturbance. He explained that they had been deceived by the Chinese students in Tokyo. It was not until February of the following year that the Twenty-One Demands became public knowledge. Under duress, China was compelled to accept most of the demands and the road was paved for subsequent Japanese expansion in China.

AS GRADUATION DREW NEAR, Hung had to make some decisions about what he was going to do with his life. As an adult and now head of the household, he was expected to support his mother and bring up his three brothers. There were several options available to him: He could join the Maritime Customs Service, where his knowledge of English and German would serve him well; he could accept a job offer from a small newspaper newly established in Peking; or he could serve in the Salt Revenue Administration. The Salt Revenue Administration had the highest initial pay, but the agency was known to be rife with politics. Hung's own inclination was to work for the newspaper, yet his future with such an enterprise would be very uncertain.

One day, Edwin C. Jones, who was acting as principal while the Gowdys were on leave, called Hung into his office and took out a telegram from his drawer. It was from a certain Hanford Crawford of St. Louis and asked whether a student named Hung Ngiek was still enrolled at the Anglo-Chinese College. If he was in the graduating class, would he be interested in continuing his education in the United States? Crawford offered to underwrite all expenses. Mr. Jones said that apparently this man, a Methodist layman, was wealthy; for he contributed a thousand dollars a year to the College.

"I did not know who Hanford Crawford was. The only words that could describe what I experienced at that moment was *deja vu.*" Hung felt himself taken back to the day in Shantung when he had just discovered he had passed the entrance examination in first place. Once more, what reality had to offer far exceeded his wildest dream.

Hung hurried home to discuss the matter with his mother. Lin Fei expressed no opinion. Instead, she told Hung to get her a sedan chair to take her to see Grandfather Lin. With a heavy heart, Hung walked behind the sedan chair. This was a grave matter. If Hung should take the offer and go abroad, the financial support of the family would fall once more on the shoulders of Grandfather Lin. But after Lin Fei apprised her father of the situation, Grandfather Lin exclaimed, "We should give thanks to your ancestors for all the merits they have accumulated through the generations. Your father, too, conducted himself impeccably as an official. This is what they call reward for good deeds. It is a great opportunity for you to pursue your education abroad. As to the support of your mother and brothers, you may leave it to me."

Hung got on his knees immediately and kowtowed gratefully to his grandfather.

"However," Grandfather Lin continued, "You should first go back and ask this Mr. Jones to send a telegram at my expense, asking whether there are any conditions attached to this generous offer."

The reply to the telegram came, stating that there was no condition, "so long as he remains a good boy." Subsequently, money arrived by cable in care of Mr. Jones to prepare Hung for the trip. Tailors were summoned to make suits for him; luggage was bought. As he did not know which American college he should apply to, he consulted James Bashford on one of the bishop's trips to Foochow. Bishop Bashford recommended two places, the University of Wisconsin and Ohio Wesleyan. The reason he was so enthusiastic about these two college, he conceded, was that he had graduated from one and served as president of the other. He suggested that Hung complete his last two years of undergraduate work at Ohio Wesleyan and go on to graduate school at the University of Wisconsin. After Hung told him he would follow his advice, Bishop Bashford disclosed that Hanford Crawford was a trustee of Ohio Wesleyan.

"I am sure he will be very pleased with your choice."

The news of Hung's going abroad was greeted with disbelief at the school. Everybody knew he was a bright student, but everybody also knew he was poor. How did this fellow get so lucky? Many of his classmates badgered their families to send them abroad, too. Land, houses, jewelry were sold. Out of the twenty classmates, seven eventually came to the United States. Four came with Hung the year they graduated. Three of them enrolled at Ohio Wesleyan, while Yang Hsi-tung, the rich calligrapher, attended Cornell College in Iowa, the alma mater of their professor, Wang Kan-ho.

HUNG GRADUATED from the Anglo-Chinese College in February, 1915. As the school year at Ohio Wesleyan was not to start until September, he spent the months in between teaching Bible at the College. On Sundays, he joined gospel teams that took him up the Min River to the inland towns and villages. It was during this period of his life that he first became close to his brothers David and Fred. Fred, then a small nine-year-old, loved to climb on his lap. David, six years Hung's junior, was holding his own in school. At a gathering where Hung was present one day, David was asked by his schoolmates to tell a story. He made one up about a scholar who went about making pompous remarks; it sent the audience into fits of laughter. Hung had not thought his normally taciturn younger brother had that in him. He began to discuss literature and history with David, correcting his papers, giving to David what he himself had received from their father. The other brother, Arnold, was more inclined to live his life on a sensory level. He was always rather distant to his big brother.

Bubonic plague raged in Foochow the spring of 1915. Hung's mother, amid bustling plans to select a suitable wife for Hung to preclude his bringing home from abroad a foreign wife, was suddenly stricken. She died in a high fever at the age of forty-one. She was buried next to her husband on the Granary Front Hill (Ts'ang-ch'ien-shan).

That summer, when he was all set to leave, Hung received a letter from the district of Ch'ü-fu in Shantung. The gentry had learned from Big Brother Yen that he had graduated from school. They now wanted the son of Hung the Clear Sky to come back to their district and run for the post of district magistrate in the coming election. Hung was moved by the invitation. He wrote back saying he hoped that his ability to serve his country would improve with a few years spent abroad.

Part Two

William Hung as a young man

CHAPTER SIX

Ohio Wesleyan

WILLIAM HUNG crossed the Pacific Ocean in the fall of 1915 aboard a Canadian steamer called the *Empress of Manchuria.* While the vessel was at anchor for two days at Yokohama, Hung took a train to Tokyo to check out the Tokyo Chinese Students Association. Inquiries led him to a Chinese YMCA where he found a roomful of smashed furniture, which had resulted, he was told, from a big fight among different revolutionary factions. He was also informed that the person responsible for the letter sent to the Foochow Anglo-Chinese College on the Twenty-One Demands was named Li Ta-chao, but that he had already left Tokyo for China. That was the first time Hung heard of Li Ta-chao, who was to become one of the foremost leaders of the Chinese Communist Party and whose protégés included Mao Tse-tung.

AT SAN FRANCISCO, an anxious and slightly dazed Hung was met by an agent of Hanford Crawford, who put him on a train to St. Louis. After speeding across a largely unsettled continent for several days, he arrived in St. Louis, where he was met by Mr. Crawford himself. Hung recalled in a flash that he had seen this man with big beard before in Foochow. Yes, indeed, Mr. Crawford confirmed, it was in Hung's history class at the Anglo-Chinese College.

Hanford Crawford, president of the Scruggs, Vandervoort, and Barney Dry Goods Company of St. Louis, a prominent community leader, and distinguished layman of the Methodist Episcopal Church, had taken his wife and daughter on a world trip upon the latter's graduation from Vassar in 1912. When they reached China, they visited the Anglo-Chinese College to which he had been sending money. Invited to see classes in session, they dropped in on Lacy Sites's history class, where the subject under discussion was the Napoleonic War. Dr. Sites called on Hung to analyze the cause of Napoleon's downfall, and his answer impressed Crawford greatly. In his conversation with the principal, John Gowdy, he was told that Hung was the brightest student the school had ever had and that all the teachers thought Hung should go on to higher education abroad, but that they knew Hung's family could not afford it. The same generous impulses that led Mr. Crawford to donate a thousand dollars a year to the College prompted him to offer to pay for Hung's education in the United States.

Hung's first ride in an automobile was followed by his first ride in an elevator. When they entered the Crawford apartment, Hung was startled to find that all the furniture was draped with white sheets.

"Has there been a death in the family?" he asked.

Mr. Crawford was taken aback by this question until he realized that in China white sheets were used in mourning. He explained to Hung that Mrs. Crawford and their daughter Ruth were both spending the summer in the East at a place called Marblehead Neck in Massachusetts. The furniture, being largely unused, was covered with linen to protect it from dust. Since no dinner was served at home, he took Hung to his club and to a Charlie Chaplin movie afterwards.

HUNG ENTERED OHIO WESLEYAN as a junior with a double major of chemistry and mathematics. Ohio Wesleyan in the 1910s was no isolated, parochial college. It bore the marks of men like Bishop Bashford, its president from 1889 to 1904, whose belief it was that "the universe is fireproof and it is safe to strike a match anywhere in search of truth." Most of the faculty members were similarly large-minded. Discipline, however, remained strict. Chapel service was mandatory. There was to be no smoking, drinking, or dancing; and the rules were enforced by a stern Dean of Men, William Hormell.

Hung threw himself with fervor into his schoolwork. There was an exuberance in everything he did those two years at Ohio Wesleyan. He behaved like a man liberated from all suppressive influences. He found much that amused him and much to admire in the American system. Life itself seemed to be intoxicating, with unlimited possibilities. A fellow Chinese student from Singapore named K. A. Wee even taught him to play tennis. His classmates called him "Happy Hung."

The professor whom he held in highest esteem was an old bachelor who taught Bible, Rollin H. Walker. Professor Walker had inherited wealth and studied in Germany. The students nicknamed him "Saint John." When Saint John prayed during the chapel services, he gave the impression that he was talking face to face with God. He donated more money to the university than he received in salary. When he knew of a student in need, he would surreptitiously slip money into his pocket. If he was thanked, Saint John took the money back.

Russell B. Miller (the object of much conniving because he owned the only automobile in town) taught Greek. The text he used in Hung's class was the Four Gospels. Miller would call on individual students to read the text and translate the passage into English, but for a long time, he did not call on the lone Chinese student in the class. When he finally did, Hung stood up and gleefully recited the whole chapter, from memory, in Greek! He never called on Hung to translate again. But when they got to the feast of Cana in John 2:3–4, the question arose of why Jesus addressed his mother as if she were a servant, and Miller asked Hung if he had any good explanation. Hung, bitten by the irony of having now to explain a verse that only a few years earlier he had used as a weapon to attack Christianity, closed his eyes humbly to pray. An answer did present itself to him. He said, "The Bible does not indicate in what manner Jesus responded to his mother. I think Jesus said it in jest, to tease his mother. He said it with a wink in his eye, meaning there was still wine left but as soon as it was all gone, he would make sure there was a fresh supply."

At this, his classmates broke out in cheering applause.

Hung remembered Trumbull G. Duvall's psychology class as the place where he first learned about the concept of the subconscious. Throughout his life, Hung was interested in the mysteries of the mind, having been exposed in childhood to his maternal grandmother's claims of second sight and the popular Chinese folk practice of interpreting dreams, which flourished despite Confucian strictures against all things supernatural and irrational. Hung always maintained the attitude that there was a substratum of human experience that we did not completely understand.

ALTHOUGH HANFORD CRAWFORD maintained a balance of a thousand dollars for Hung in his bank account at all times, Hung found he needed to draw at most several hundred dollars from the funds. Upon his arrival at Ohio Wesleyan, he learned that he was the recipient of a tuition scholarship, which he suspected had something to do with Bishop Bashford. He also worked at several jobs to earn money; for when he discovered that almost all the students worked to pay for their education and that even the son of the registrar picked apples alongside common laborers, he thought he should have a job, too. He went to see the general secretary of the university YMCA, Charles Laughlin, who had helped him find a place to live within five minutes of the campus at Eight Liberty Street. Through the YMCA's employment office, he was given his first job, to wash the gymnasium floor at seventeen cents an hour. It was hard work; the part he hated most was scraping up old chewing gum. Laughlin suggested that he buy a pair of overalls to wear while doing the work. Hung did not know what overalls were, but later he carefully folded up the pair he bought and took them back to China as a curiosity. The idea of a college student doing hard physical labor was at that time a shocking one in China, where there had long been a sharp division between those above who used their minds and those below who sold their physical exertion.

Later, Hung worked at the Alumni Office for twenty-two cents an hour, folding letters, stuffing envelopes, and sticking stamps on mailings to be sent out to alumni. Several other students were employed at this task, but Hung conceived the idea of performing each step in batches, resulting in much improved efficiency. His supervisor, Raymond Thornburg, of the class of 1915, retained him on his permanent staff. Thus commenced a friendship between Thornburg, whose nickname was "Pinkie" for his red hair, and William Hung, which lasted more than six decades.

Pinkie was a short, stocky man, underneath whose easy manner lay a quick calculating mind that would one day make him a successful industrialist. His parents were divorced, and his mother supported him by sewing and doing laundry. He told Hung that while he was a student, he had supported himself by running a small business. The assets of the business consisted entirely of an iron and an ironing board. College men in those days prided themselves on the crisp crease of their pants. The laundry shop charged twenty-five cents for ironing pants; Pinkie successfully undercut it by charging only twenty cents, with free pick-up and delivery thrown in.

Inspired by Pinkie's example, Hung embarked on an enterprise of his own, tutoring children in mathematics. One evening, he dined at the house of a Presbyterian minister whose son was having trouble with math in school. Hung volunteered to help and discovered that the boy had been memorizing the textbook without comprehending it. After young Johnny began receiving regular drill sessions, he made rapid progress in school and the parents insisted on paying Hung twenty-five cents an hour. Soon the word got around in Johnny's school that there was this "marvelous Chinaman" who could teach math. Hung found himself with almost a dozen students. He bought a blackboard and ran a veritable night school. Some of the money he saved and sent back to Foochow for his brother's education.

Later, his chemistry professor, G. O. Highley, recommended him to do urinalyses for a sanatorium near the university. He was paid twenty-five cents per tube of urine. This he performed in the laboratory early in the morning and would average four or five analyses in an hour. He felt quite rich.

In the summer of 1916, Hung and several friends from Ohio Wesleyan pooled their money to buy an old car in New York City. They spent a month at the YMCA motor school learning about automobiles. Classes were held in the morning on the history of the automobile, its structure, its parts, and so forth. In the afternoon, they learned how to drive. The teacher, a New York taxi driver, flunked Hung in driving and told him he would do well never to take the wheel because he was a resourceful but absent-minded driver. On their subsequent trip to the Adirondacks, therefore, Hung's role was confined to making repairs. William Hung never did learn to drive, but he knew a great deal about how cars functioned.

That summer, Hung also began widening his acquaintanceship among other young Chinese studying in the United States. It was an ambitious generation with high expectations about their place in China's future, and they were curious about each other. At a conference sponsored by the International Committee of the YMCA, Hung met several Chinese Christians who were convinced that it was Christianity that China needed. Two of them, Timothy T'ing-fang Lew and Jimmy Ch'uan, came to visit Hung afterwards in Ohio. All three of them, as well as K. A. Wee, were to be deeply involved with Yenching University.

In the summer of 1916, Hung also went to see the Crawfords in Marblehead Neck. On the way, he stopped over in Cambridge, Massachusetts, where he intended to check out other promising Chinese students. Under a majestic elm tree in front of Weld Hall at Harvard, he saw a Chinese student reciting poetry aloud to himself, totally oblivious to his surroundings. After a while, still rapturous, he stood up and paced under the tree, his shirttail flapping vigorously in the early autumn wind. Hung could not restrain himself from laughing at the comical sight. His friend Ch'en Hung-chen drew him aside and told him that this was the most admired person in Chinese student circles. Coming from one of the leading families of China, he had been abroad for many years and spoke all the major languages of the world; yet he did not want any degree. The man was Ch'en Yin-ch'üeh (also known as Ch'en Yin-k'o), who became an internationally known historian.

Of course, at this time Hung was also deepening friendships with Americans. He came to love the Crawfords as much as his own family. Hanford Crawford's ambition, before he turned a businessman, had been to be a teacher. He spent three years in Europe preparing himself for the teaching profession. It was in Leipzig that he met his wife, née Gertrude Smith, from a Massachusetts family of long-standing religious and social activism. Ruth, their daughter, was a statuesque beauty who was full mistress of every situation. When she attacked a social problem, her mind immediately picked out its international implications. To her, humanity was one, indivisible. She was only three years older than Hung, and Hung referred to her fondly as "my American sister."

During Hung's second year at Ohio Wesleyan, Eric North, for whom he had acted as an interpreter in Foochow, came to teach at the university. Hung took his course on "The History of Christianity." Dr. North was a meticulous lecturer. He was always well prepared, with all his lines of reasoning worked out in advance. Hung came to see an analogy between the study of history and the study of chemistry: While chemistry was concerned with the reactions between or among material substances when they were mixed together, history was concerned with the changes of institutions and peoples when they confronted each other. Hung found himself equally intrigued by both. It occurred to him that perhaps he should choose history as his field of study in graduate school.

Yet the idea of taking Christianity as he knew it back to China was also compelling. While he was at Ohio Wesleyan, he joined a gospel team of students who preached at small towns in the Ohio farmland. To go a step further and walk in the footsteps of men like Bishop Bashford seemed to offer a fulfilling life. Timothy Lew, who was then studying at Union Theological Seminary, pointed out that in New York Hung could eat his cake and have it, too, if he pursued graduate work in history at Columbia and prepared for the ministry at Union Theological Seminary.

In 1917, Hung graduated from Ohio Wesleyan, with Mrs. Crawford present at commencement to see him receive his degree, magna cum laude and Phi Beta Kappa. He was also awarded a fellowship providing him with five hundred dollars a year for graduate study. Taking Lew's advice, he headed for New York.

CHAPTER SEVEN

Friends and Romances

CHINA perhaps will never again produce a group of young men and women — predominantly men — as idealistic, patriotic, and as sure of themselves as the some two thousand Chinese students in the United States in the 1910s. They knew that they were going to be the leaders of a new China. A whole country of crumbling institutions awaited their return. There was no doubt in their minds that the new society that had to emerge would be one patterned after the American democracy. Although China was still ruled by warlords and rife with civil wars, they thought it was just a matter of time. And who would be more equipped to effect the transformation than they, an intellectual elite at home both in China and in the West, where they were acquiring the best tools, the most up-to-date knowledge, and the most impressive credentials? By the 1920s, things would have soured somewhat and there would be the competing claims of Communism to contend with; but in 1917, even with the world at war, the mood among the Chinese students in America was ebullient.

Before the school year started at Columbia and Union Theological Seminary, Hung participated in a conference of the Chinese Students Alliance. Several hundred Chinese came to attend from all over the United States. There were athletic events and dances; but it was above all a political gathering, an occasion for individuals who saw themselves as future generals in the field of Chinese politics to, in Hung's words, "recruit lieutenants and buy horses." The burning topic of the day was the Vernacular Movement in China, led by Hu Shih, who only a few months earlier had been one of them and had expounded his ideas in the newsletter of the Chinese Students Alliance. His campaign to adopt the vernacular language (essentially spoken Mandarin) in serious Chinese literature was running into bitter resistance from the older scholar-officials, who viewed the use of the vernacular as a dangerous departure from fine old traditions.

Not all the challenges to tradition came from men concerned with intellectual issues. In contrast to generation upon generation of Chinese scholar-officials who looked down on business, many of the young men being educated in America were eager to enter banking, trade, or industry. A man Hung ran into at the conference wore what looked like an oversized Phi Beta Kappa key. Upon closer inspection, he found the inscription to be "Kappa Beta Phi." The man slapped Hung's back and laughed, saying, "It stands for everything opposite to Phi Beta Kappa. You are at the top of the class; we are at the bottom. You are dedicated to learning; we are dedicated to making money. We shall provide you scholars with the wherewithal to build the schools and the libraries."

Regardless of their individual ambitions, to the youthful group there assembled, the victory of their generation was all but certain. Little did they know that for much of the rest of their lives, they would be battling not doddering old men, but fiery young ones whose heroes were Marx and Lenin, and by whom men of their liberal persuasion would be ultimately crushed.

IN NEW YORK, Hung fell in with a group of Chinese Christians headed by Timothy T'ing-fang Lew. Timothy Lew was diminutive, less than five feet tall. Moreover, he was afflicted with a sinus problem, which caused him to be constantly sniffling and coughing. But he was charming, witty, and forceful as a speaker. He had a vision of a China transformed by Christianity; and in Hung, he felt he had found someone who shared his vision. Their theology was the kind that was sometimes referred to as the "social gospel." Their Christ was the Christ of Mark 10:21, who said, "Go sell all you have and give to the poor, and follow me." Their hero was Harry F. Ward, professor of Christian ethics at Union Theological Seminary, who, when he was accused of being a Communist, replied, "I am not a Communist. I am worse than a Communist; I am a Christian."

There were at that time several fraternities among the Chinese students in the United States. The most snobbish of these was the Flip-Flap, which boasted of such luminaries as Wellington Koo and T. V. Soong. Lew and Hung agreed they should organize their own fraternity, the members of which were to be restricted to those who had good academic records and were devout Christians. Its motto was to be "We Unite for the Uplift of China." There were seven founding members, among whom were Ch'en Ho-ch'in, who became a well-known educator in Shanghai and T'u Yu-ch'ing, later general-secretary of the Shanghai YMCA. On June 24, 1917, the seven pledged secrecy and named their fraternity C and S, for "Cross and Sword."

"We were so young then. We wanted to emulate the Jesuits, to transform society through education and politics. Cross, for Jesus's 'Take up your cross and follow me'; Sword, to recall the Crusades. We adopted some masonic rites and had vague intentions of recapturing the spirit of the Sworn Brotherhood celebrated in *The Romance of the Three Kingdoms*. We were so secretive I was driven to commit the only thievery in my life."

It happened that, in the fall of 1918, Timothy Lew transferred to Yale to avoid having to take the Hebrew oral examinations at Union Theological Seminary. Hung was left in charge of the business of the fraternity. He received word one day that a founding member, a man named Teng at Princeton, had died of pneumonia. Knowing that Teng kept a meticulous diary, Hung dropped everything and hastened to Princeton, where he represented himself as a seminarian and a close friend of Teng's family, thereby gaining access to the dormitory room of the deceased. He found the diary with detailed accounts of the fraternity's organization, which he tore up and burned on the spot.

It did not take long, however, for discord to creep into the brotherhood. At an election, Timothy Lew was running for the president and won by one vote; his opponent left in a pique. Hung, being the secretary, recognized that one of the votes for Lew was in Lew's own handwriting. To vote for oneself was a violation of the Chinese gentlemen's code of honor, and this incident caused Hung to put some distance between himself and Lew. He regretted having made such a to-do over Teng's diary.

Nevertheless, the fraternity continued to attract new members. These included Chiang T'ing-fu, later to become China's ambassador to the Soviet Union, the United Nations, and the United States; Chang Po-ling, founder of Nankai University and its president for several decades; Chou I-ch'un, who was already the president of Tsinghua University; and Nieh Ch'i-chieh, grandson of Tseng Kuo-fan and founder of the Great China Spinning and Weaving Company in Shanghai.

In 1918, Wang Cheng-t'ing was in the United States seeking American recognition for the government in Canton, in competition with the government in Peking which was run by warlords and closely allied with Japan. Wang was son of a Methodist minister and a YMCA activist. He was one of the signers of the Organizational Law of the Republic in 1911, adopted by the provisional government right after the Ch'ing empire was overthrown. He was Vice-Speaker of the Senate of the various governments formed in 1912, 1913, and 1917. Wang was invited to be a member of the Cross and Sword and accepted. While Wang was in the United States, he was designated by the Canton government to be a member of its delegation to the Paris Peace Conference. After the Conference broke up, several other delegates visited the United States, including Eugene Yu-jen Ch'en, a protégé of Sun Yat-sen, a well-known journalist, and China's Minister of Foreign Affairs from 1926 and 1927; he, too, was initiated as a member.

At a meeting of the Cross and Sword held in a Brooklyn hotel in 1918, Wang Cheng-t'ing disclosed, to everyone's surprise, that there was an older secret fraternity among Chinese Christian students in the United States with exactly the same motto, "We Unite for the Uplift of China." Established in 1907 with the Biblical name of David and Jonathan, its membership included many individuals already in positions of power in China. Timothy Lew called for amalgamation of the two fraternities, not omitting to point out that the members of David and Jonathan would be able to help the members of C and S in their careers. Hung opposed the amalgamation vehemently, on precisely those grounds. He felt that the fraternity should not be used for personal advancement. It was the first time Hung disagreed openly with Lew. In this contest, Lew had the votes; and an amalgamation was effected in due time under the new name of Ch'eng-chih hui (Association for Accomplishing Ideals). This brought Cross and Sword members into the same fraternity as men like Wang Ch'ung-hui, chairman of the Law Codification Committee, later Chief Justice of the Supreme Court, Acting Premier in 1922, Minister of Foreign Affairs from 1937 to 1941, and a judge on the Permanent Court of International Justice at The Hague; Kuo Ping-wen, president of the Nanking Higher Normal School, later the president of Tung-nan University; K'ung Hsiang-hsi (H. H. Kung), reformist, banker, educator, brother-in-law of Sun Yat-sen and later of Chiang Kai-shek, and holder of various top posts of the Republic. The Ch'eng-chih hui subsequently established branches in Peking, Shanghai, and Hong Kong; but by then it had deteriorated into a loose, innocuous association of academics, referred to jokingly as the "Ph.D. Club."

IN ADDITION to seeking out new associates among American-educated Chinese, Hung kept in touch with his classmates from the Foochow Anglo-Chinese College. He had a suite in the dormitory at Union Theological Seminary that nobody else wanted because it was situated on the ground floor where the subway train came roaring out from underground onto street level, and right above the heating furnace, which clanged and chattered all day and night. But the noise never bothered Hung, and he loved the space. The two spacious rooms served as temporary shelter for many of his friends.

Yang Hsi-tung, the calligrapher, had also entered Columbia University, after graduating from Cornell College in Iowa. He told Hung that he was secretly engaged to be married to Jimmy Ch'en's pretty sister. Miss Ch'en was studying somewhere in Canada; but she was very sick with tuberculosis, and he often went to see her. Not long afterwards, he, too, was stricken with tuberculosis and had to withdraw from school. For reasons unclear to Hung, Yang was in financial straits; and he asked Hung for a loan of eighty dollars, pledging as security a fur coat. Hung, not having the money himself, discussed the matter with Mrs. Crawford, who remitted him the amount. Shortly thereafter, Yang Hsi-tung died. Hung took the fur coat solemnly to Mrs. Crawford, saying he thought it should now belong to her. Mrs. Crawford told Hung she did not want it.

"Who knows what kind of germs it is carrying," she said, and proceeded to dump it into the incinerator.

Jimmy Ch'en also made it to the United States. He studied physical education at the YMCA College in Springfield, Massachusetts (which has since closed). When he came to see Hung in New York, he saw Hung's tennis racket and exclaimed, "You know how to play tennis, too? I must say that if someone as decadent as you are can also play tennis, then there surely must be hope for China!"

It was then fashionable to describe anyone who still quoted Confucius in conversation as "decadent." Hung challenged him to a game and beat him.

PINKIE THORNBURG left the Alumni Office about the time Hung graduated from Ohio Wesleyan. He went to work for another alumnus of Ohio Wesleyan, Oliver Wright, who was managing the vast estate of the nineteenth-century capitalist, Potter Palmer, in Chicago. On one of

Pinkie's trips to see Hung in New York, he struck up conversation with the man sitting next to him on the train. The man was headed for Florida to negotiate a difficult financial deal. Having taken a liking to Pinkie, he asked him to come, too, all expenses paid, to act as a sounding board in return for a cut in the profits if the negotiations were successful. Pinkie accepted the offer; and for several days of being holed up in a luxurious hotel in Florida, he was rewarded with twenty-five thousand dollars' worth of stocks. Pinkie could not wait to get to New York to tell Hung of his sudden good fortune. The two friends sat up deep into the night discussing what should be done with the money. Pinkie said he wanted to be his own boss, he did not want to work for other people any more. Hung corrected him, saying that he should remember his boss was always God. Pinkie agreed; he told Hung that whenever as a preacher Hung should be in need of money, he would be there to provide it. But when Hung suggested that he organize his own publishing firm, to publish little-known but worthy authors, Pinkie rejected the idea as being too risky. Besides, he said, he knew nothing about publishing. They decided that Pinkie should consult Oliver Wright. On a subsequent visit, Pinkie told Hung he had bought into a breakfast cereal company facing bankruptcy. He was managing the company and trying to interest some of the hotels and restaurants in New York in the cereal food. He showed Hung samples of the cereals.

IT WAS AT COLUMBIA that Hung had his first real taste of American dating (his only experience at Ohio Wesleyan had been taking the sister of a friend to the senior class picnic). A double-feature movie ticket was ten cents. He was dating two women, both Fukienese. Miss Lin was slender and delicate, elegant in every way. Miss Sung, in contrast, was warm, forthright, and pragmatic. The latter once told Hung that her father was a preacher in China and she knew the life of a preacher would be a hard one. She had, however, saved from her scholarship and part-time jobs a large sum of money that could lay the foundation for their life together. Hung was deeply moved but replied that it was not yet time to talk about that. Later on, Hung found himself being unaccountably snubbed by her. It was long afterwards before he discovered the reason, when he found in an old shirt pocket a letter he had written and forgotten to mail. Miss Sung had written him that she was completing her master's thesis and needed someone to help her type it. Since he had a typewriter and typed beautifully, she asked would he do her the favor. Hung, albeit reluctantly, had written that he would. Naturally, the unmailed answer never reached her.

Newly emerged from a tradition of family-arranged marriages, many Chinese students found themselves launched into uncharted and bewildering seas when it came to Western-style courtship. They were always saying too much or too little, acting too impetuously, or being too inscrutable. The old language associated with love seemed stilted and withered on their lips; the newly-translated Western phrases of endearment sounded alien, if not downright comical. As Hung was working for the Intercollegiate YMCA and was known to be helpful on all sorts of matters, his assistance was also sought on matters of the heart. A Mr. Huang told Hung that he admired a woman named Rhoda Kong very much and asked Hung to say a few words for him. He was going to arrange a dinner for four and perhaps Hung could stay afterwards to convey his love to Miss Kong. Hung knew Rhoda Kong from a Chinese Student Conference he had attended; he had also seen her writings published in the *Chinese Students in America* (*Liu-mei ch'ing-nien*), an English journal of the Chinese Christian Association. She had grown up in Hawaii, attended Wheaton College in Massachusetts, and was doing graduate work at Columbia Teachers College. Attractive, articulate, and outgoing, she was very popular. As it happened, when Hung told Miss Kong that he had a mission to carry out, when they were left alone after dinner, Miss Kong said that she already knew what it was, but it was hopeless. She said that Mr. Huang, brilliant as he was otherwise, had no common sense. He had asked her out to dinner; when she declined, he invited her to lunch; when she declined that, too, he asked her out to breakfast. She said to tell Mr. Huang not to waste his time, for she already had someone else in mind. Hung asked if he might know who. Miss Kong said she would rather not tell just now. Later, when Hung and Miss Kong knew each other better, Hung again asked her who this man was, on whom she had set her heart. She revealed that it was Hung himself.

In recounting the story of his life some sixty years later, Hung was uncharacteristically reticent on the details surrounding his marriage to Rhoda Kong. He said only that she nursed him through a severe bout of Spanish influenza from which he nearly died, that they were married in 1919, and that there was a wedding in New York. From Hung's papers found after his death, we learned that there were not one, but two weddings. There was a marriage certificate signed by Hal R. Boswell, pastor of the Second Presbyterian Church in Newport News, Virginia, on March 5, 1919; and there was an elegant announcement of their marriage on January 22, 1921, in New York. The birth certificates of their first two daughters were dated July 12, 1919, and July 5, 1921. It thus appears that their first child, Ruth, named for Hung's "American sister," was born about four months after they were married in Virginia; and that their second child, Gertrude, named for Mrs. Crawford, was born a little more than five months after the formal announcement.

By today's standards, this is nothing unusual, especially when the principals involved then proceed to build a family. But in those times, it must have been a source of guilt, shame, and anxiety. It is not clear how the situation was handled by William and Rhoda. In correspondence with the Wheaton College Alumnae Association, Rhoda had referred to their first child as an adopted orphan.

CHAPTER EIGHT

Turning Point

THE SEQUENCE OF EVENTS surrounding Hung's marriage might have had some bearing on his decision to withdraw from preparation for the ministry. Years later, he was to write a novel, which was not published, in which the central figure was a man who had to leave the priesthood because of a woman, but who then went on to do great things for China. In 1978, however, in his reminiscences about this period of his life, he stressed the intellectual awakenings he was experiencing and his disillusionments with the church.

In 1918, Hung published a long article entitled "Failure" in *Liu-mei ch'ing-nien,* the journal of the Chinese Christian Association (1). In the article, he drew parallels in the lives of three historical figures who were viewed as total failures by their contemporaries but who left indelible imprints on the world by the values they held. They were the Chinese Confucius, who was born a bastard, led a very unhappy life, and was mocked by some as "a dog wandering around looking for his lost master"; the Greek Socrates, who was charged by the authorities with corruption of Athenian youths and condemned to die by poison; and the Jew Jesus, who died crucified between two criminals. The first had shaped the China into which Hung was born, the second two the Western world into which he had moved. "Failure" may be said to be one of Hung's early attempts to integrate the different worlds in which he lived. In subsequent years, he was to be moved again and again to justify the ways of the East to the West, to justify the ways of the West to the East, and to justify a role for Christianity in the modern world.*

---

*Among his publications in English under this category are a 1921 booklet written for American readers on some of the erroneous notions they held about China and the

It may not be too farfetched, furthermore, to speculate that the article represented to Hung's mind a resolution to renounce personal ambition. Hung had a deep-rooted ambivalence towards ambition. His idealism, his patriotism, and the crying needs of China all demanded that he should exert himself for the public good. Yet where did exertion for the public good end and the drive of personal ambition begin? Since he was a little boy, time and again he had been picked out as the "winner," the "leader," among his peers. Yet he was also conditioned by his Confucian upbringing to believe that personal ambition was incompatible with personal integrity, that manipulating for power and thrusting oneself forward was unseemly, mischievous, and even dangerous. Later in his life, when Hung had the opportunity to do things in a bigger way, his response was always to withdraw. In his unpublished novel, the ex-priest who remade China stayed behind the scenes politically and was unknown to the public.

IF HIS ASPIRATION was to spread Christianity in China—at that time he sincerely believed that this was what China needed—then it would be of paramount importance for him to understand fully the nature of the Christian Church. Was it possible to have a Christian Church free of Western trappings? What could the Church be if the encrustation of rituals and dogmas accumulated through the ages were chipped away? Hung sought for the answers to these questions in church history.

In graduate school, he came under the influence of three professors, all trained in Germany: William Rockwell and James Harvey Robinson of Columbia University and Arthur Cushman McGiffert of Union Theological Seminary. Hung credited Rockwell with having given him a methodology for historical research that he could build on later in his career. Professor Rockwell's lectures were "dry as sawdust." His head was full of names and dates, organized like a telephone directory. He

---

Chinese (2); a 1927 article evaluating the contributions of Christian churches to China (3); an interpretative report of the Conference of the Institute of Pacific Relations that met in Hawaii in 1927 (4); an address on Nationalist China at a 1929 luncheon meeting of the Foreign Policy Association in New York (6); a 1931 article portraying the mental outlook of the Chinese masses and how it was gradually changing (14); a 1932 discussion of the student movement in China (19); and an address given at the University of Hawaii in 1947 on education in old and new China (40). To his Chinese students at Yenching University, he gave a lecture in 1945 on the long history of Sino-American relations which culminated at that point in the victory against Japan (39).

insisted that his students divide all their research materials into primary and secondary sources, and to ascertain the date and provenance of these sources before they decided what to do with them. Every piece of information had to be documented. He made a sharp distinction between facts and values. Facts had to do with who, when, where, what, and how. Values had to do with what was bad, what was good, how good, how useful, how bad, and why. Although values differed from person to person, it was a historian's responsibility to sift out the facts and assign values to them. A historian had to admit that one could not but be subjective, yet he should try at all times to be objective. It was only through a punctilious observation of correct methodology that pieces of proper learning could be added to mankind's store. Recalling his youthful ferment, Hung said in 1978:

"He set me thinking on how arbitrary values are but how, nonetheless, it is values which distinguish human beings from other forms of life. My mind wandered back to China where there were no flush toilets, and vats were used as receptacles for human excrement. Underneath the vats were usually found squirming masses of white worms. That's also life. How is such life different from that of mine, of my mother and my father? The basic difference, I think is that we human beings hold values. We cannot tell whether a worm can think; but only if it should turn out that a worm can ask questions and place facts in a scale of values, assigning to itself a value among all other values — only then might we consider a worm on the same level as human beings. And how does a human being arrive at his values? It is by first reflecting on his place in the scheme of things — on what he needs, what he is capable of, what is his mission, what are his relations to other persons. Then he extends what he knows of himself to his fellow men, trying to understand their motives and values, and by this act of sympathy, make possible communal life. Then he reaches out to comprehend God, whom he sometimes visualizes as a being very much like his father, and sometimes visualizes as a suffering servant, who carries the burden of all humanity. As Voltaire, the Great Agnostic, has said, if there is no God, for the good of humanity it would be necessary to invent one."

James Harvey Robinson changed Hung's views of history. A prolific writer of textbooks, especially known for his studies on the intellectual history of Western Europe, he was a proponent of a "New History." He contended that when people thought of history, they thought mainly of governments and wars; it was now time to break out of this concept and think of history in terms of economic and social trends in institutions and policies. In other words, history should be about how people live and think and how patterns of life have changed over the centuries; history should properly be studied against the background of the whole length of man's existence on earth, and across geographical and political boundaries.

Robinson supervised Hung's work on his master's thesis, "The *Spring and Autumn Annals* and Its Influence on Historical Thoughts of China." The *Spring and Autumn Annals* (*Ch'un-chiu*) was supposed to have been written by Confucius and, as one of the classics, was one of the books Hung had memorized as a child. But in the Columbia University Chinese Library, he found two books which he had never seen before that totally shattered his view of himself as a man learned in things Chinese. The first was *The Catalogue of the Complete Library of the Four Treasuries* (*Ssu-k'u ch'uan-shu tsung-mu*), an annotated and critical bibliography of 3,448 Chinese books from antiquity to the latter part of the eighteenth century A.D., compiled for the Imperial Library under the Ch'ien-lung Emperor. Not all books cited, of course, were at Columbia; but the bibliography itself ran to two hundred volumes. Hung came to realize that he was completely ignorant of much that had been written about the *Spring and Autumn Annals* and that, moreover, the opinions contained in these works were startlingly divergent.

The second book was *The Mirror of History for Aid in Government* (*Tzu-chih t'ung-chien*), a comprehensive history of China from Confucius to the tenth century A.D. Hitherto, Hung had seen only the widely used *Outline of the Mirror of History for Aid in Government* (*Tzu-chih t'ung-chien kang-mu*) published at the direction of the opinionated Sung philosopher and scholar, Chu Hsi (1130–1200), who had imposed on it his own political and moral views. Hung came to the rude realization that the Chinese history he had been exposed to so far in his life represented a narrow, biased view.

"Why, in the field of learning, not only was I unqualified to be considered an expert, I had not even gained entry to the realm. I felt like a little frog who had lived in a little well, who was then taken out of the little well that was his world and brought to an ocean!"

Ironically, it was not Professor Robinson, an iconoclast delighting in poking holes in Christian doctrines, who turned Hung away from the church. It was the influence of a professor at Union, Arthur Cushman McGiffert, who to the end of his life remained a Presbyterian minister. A prize pupil of the German historian Adolf von Harnack, McGiffert placed Christian beliefs on the autopsy table, and with cool detachment applied to it the incisive scalpel of reason. Hung remembered him as starting with the premise that it was futile to seek consistency in the philosophy of any individual. To study a person's thought, one had to ask what his main idea was, what did he advocate, and what was he opposed to. However, if one cut beneath the words, one would find that a person always built into his own system something of what he opposed. One would also find that the strongest point in a person's thought was also his weakest, because that was where he overreached himself. Then, Hung said, McGiffert proceeded to demonstrate how this was true in the history of Christian thought, how the ecclesiastic was influenced by the secular, and how the two became intertwined. He taught that the creeds of Christianity—which Hung had always thought of as statements of faith by Christian thinkers who agreed among themselves, written for transmission to their children and to posterity—were really negative in intent. They were written to exclude people who were not willing to subscribe to particular beliefs. With relentless reasoning, he traced specific items in a creed to specific attempts by the church to suppress specific heresies. Persuaded by this interpretation of church history, Hung was compelled to salvage his Christianity by detaching it from churches; and the thought of becoming a minister became daily more distasteful to him.

WHILE HE WAS GRAPPLING with problems of scholarship and of religion in New York, events were taking place on the other side of the earth that in due course impinged on Hung's private life. After he left for the United States in 1915, China continued to suffer one political convulsion after another. There was a monarchy that lasted six months, followed by a period in which the country was splintered into many regional entities governed by warlords with their private armies. The so-called government in Peking, itself controlled by one or the other of the warlords, had in fact only tenuous control. But it represented China to the outside world and in 1917 entered World War I on the side of the Allies. When Germany was defeated in 1918, Chinese people everywhere were jubilant, convinced that the area in Shantung which the Germans had seized by force in 1898 would now be returned to China. At the Paris Peace Conference of 1919, however, it was divulged that Britain, France, and Italy had signed secret treaties with Japan supporting Japan's claim to German interests in China. Furthermore, it was learned that certain Chinese warlords had accepted secret loans from

Japan in exchange for which they mortgaged railroads in Shantung to Japan. President Woodrow Wilson, in his eagerness to conclude the Treaty of Versailles and get on with his plan for a League of Nations, agreed to legitimize all these claims and secret treaties. The news was greeted with disbelief in China. On May 4, 1919, students, with the support of the new intellectuals and the merchants, took to the streets in an unprecedented demonstration of unity against foreign imperialism and domestic traitors. From this May Fourth Incident grew the May Fourth Movement, which resulted in far-reaching cultural, social, political, and economic changes. In New York, the Chinese students were naturally also dismayed at the outcome of the Paris Peace Conference. When some of the Chinese delegates to the Conference stopped over in New York on their way back to China, there was an emotional outburst over the United States' betrayal of China. The consensus among themselves was that the students should do everything they could to convince their American friends that Congress should not ratify the treaty and the United States should have nothing further to do with the League of Nations. Hung was pursuaded to make public speeches on the subject.

"Between 1919 and Woodrow Wilson's defeat in November of 1920, I must have made at least one hundred speeches: Rotary Clubs, Kiwanis Clubs, ladies' sewing circles, wherever anybody would listen, I'd go. I had one speech that seemed to be very effective. First of all, I'd tell them that I admired Woodrow Wilson. He was an academic man, one of the very few scholarly statesmen who had occupied the White House. But, I said, he should stick to his principles. One of his principles in the Fourteen Points was self-determination, that the people of an area should decide on their government. According to that principle, the Chinese people in Shantung should now be allowed to decide on their own government, and not have their fate handed over to Japan. Another principle in the Fourteen Points was open diplomacy — so I narrated the history of the Shantung decision to the audience. I told them first of all, Japan and England, Japan and France, Japan and Italy, had all entered into secret negotiation, and then they got together and bamboozled Woodrow Wilson. They bargained with him when he was tired, and he betrayed his own principle. I said once you started out wrong, you can't be right. Now the main question before Congress is whether it should acknowledge and ratify the Treaty, whether it should join the League of Nations. You know what my opinions are on the subject. As I am a guest in America, I should not be outspoken on these matters. But if I were an American—which I have not the privilege of being—I would have felt the same way, I said.

"To wind up my speech, I told them a story. There was a very bright young woman teaching a Sunday school class. She wanted every child in the class to live a good, righteous Christian life so that when they died, they'd go to heaven. To let the children know what heaven is like, she described it for them. She said that up there, there are no fights, no snakes, only the good things. When she finished, the children were enthralled. She said, 'Now children, all you who'd like to go to heaven, please raise your hand.' The whole class raised their hands. But at the back, there was a little Johnny who just sat there and remained quiet. The teacher thought perhaps she had not done her job well enough. She tried again, saying, 'I want to tell you some more.' She painted an even more attractive picture, more flowers, nice things to eat, and so forth. 'Now,' she said, 'I'll ask you again, all those who would like to go to heaven, please raise your hands.' But Johnny still sat there unmoved. 'Well,' the teacher said, 'class is dismissed. Johnny, please stay behind. I would like to talk to you.'

"'Johhny, do you understand when I tell you about heaven?'

"'Yes, ma'am.'

"'Don't you see heaven is a nice place?'

"'Yes, ma'am.'

"'Johnny, wouldn't you like to go to heaven?'

"'Yes, ma'am.'

"'But, Johnny, when I asked everybody, why didn't you raise your hand?'

"'Oh, ma'am, I'd like to go to heaven, but not with that bunch!'

"As I finished the story, everybody laughed and clapped their hands, and I'd tell them that the League of Nations might be very nice, but not with that bunch!"

TOWARDS THE END of the school year in 1920, Hung's ambivalence towards the church and his nationalistic sentiments combined to propel him into performing a series of bold actions that led to some of the most important decisions of his life. Hung recalled the events vividly in 1978. As he spoke, his voice grew hoarse with emotions:

"The Methodist Church has a general conference every four years to which Methodist churches from all over the world send delegates. The Conference serves as a lawmaking body, and the bishops are elected there through a ballot system similar to the one used to nominate American presidential candidates in a national party convention. In 1920, the conference was held in Des Moines, Iowa. Mr. Crawford left before it was over to join his family in Marblehead Neck and stopped over in New York to see me. He described some of the highlights to me.

"'You may be interested,' he said, 'that one of the candidates for bishop is your friend Ralph Ward. But I don't think he will get it. At the first ballot, he was just a few votes short; but then it came down. As I am talking here, he is probably already out of the race.'

"I went out to dinner with Mr. Crawford. After I came back to the dormitory, the question of Ralph Ward's candidacy still bothered me. Why did he lack the necessary votes, and why had the votes come down? There must be some reasons. I prayed. I thought back on how in Foochow, Ralph Ward would have students over for dinner and warn us of the grave dangers China was facing. Yes, I thought to myself, Ralph Ward deserved to be a bishop someday, because he was always trying to promote Chinese indigenous leadership. But that must be it, some people must be opposing him on that account. I thought of some of the missionaries who professed to want Chinese leadership—they were always qualifying that remark by saying it had to be gradual.

"The more I prayed, the more I felt God was saying to me, 'Take up the cross and follow me.' So I said, I must go out there even though I am not a delegate. The people from Foochow would know me, some personally and others from my speeches and writings. Early the next day, I told the dean the problem. He was very much interested. He said, 'What do you want to do?' I said, 'I have an exam tomorrow but I would like to go now.' So the dean arranged to have the examination written on a piece of paper so that I could take it on the train and mail it back.

"It was already late at night when I arrived in Des Moines. It was wet and cold, so I took a taxi to the Hotel Des Moines, where the conference was headquartered. The lobby was deserted as most of the people had already gone to bed. The hotel clerk told me that there was no vacancy. I asked him to suggest another place I could go, but the clerk said all the hotels were full at Des Moines. 'You'll have to find somebody who is willing to double up with you.' I said since it was already late and I did not know where to find someone to share a room with, could the hotel put out a cot for me somewhere? The clerk said that was against the rules. However, at that moment, the other clerk at the reception counter started to chuckle and pulled at the fellow's sleeve.

He whispered something into his ear. The fellow smiled, saying, 'Yes, I forgot. We do have a room, but I don't think you want it. It is the bridal suite. Nobody wants it because it costs twenty dollars a night.'

"It was four times the cost of the other rooms, but I took it. Before I left New York, I had gone to the bank and taken out all the money in my account.

"That was the only time in my life that I spent a night in a bridal suite. There were two rooms, an outer and an inner room. As soon as I was alone, I got on my knees and prayed. Now, Lord, I am spending a lot of money, what should I do? I made up my mind and telephoned downstairs. 'Is it possible for breakfast to be served in my room?'

"'Oh yes, sir.'

"'Is it possible to have breakfast served for more than one person?'

"'*Yes,* sir.'

"'Could I have a table?'

"I was assured that it could be set up. Then I went downstairs, got the list of delegates, found the people from China—there must have been more than twenty—and immediately called up the Chinese delegates. None of them were actually staying at the hotel. It was too expensive. They stayed at two places, the YMCA and the YWCA.

"In the Methodist Church, the highest ranking officers are bishops; below them are the pastors. But when pastors have been around for a long time, they are called superintendents, because they take on the additional responsibility of supervising other pastors. I called up the elderly Superintendent Pastor Reverend Yü. He was surprised to find me in Des Moines and at the expensive hotel at that. I asked him whether it was true that Ralph Ward was nominated for bishop but had been receiving fewer votes every day. 'And how does it look now?'

"The Reverend Pastor Yü said Ward would probably withdraw his name in a day or two.

"'What's the matter?' I asked him 'We are good friends. You are for him as bishop. Aren't you?'

"He said he was but he could not go against the current. I asked him to pass the word around to some of the people who were staying with him that all the Chinese delegates were invited to breakfast with me at the hotel the following morning.

"'Are you mad? That's a very expensive hotel!' he exclaimed.

"I told him not to worry and went ahead to call the YWCA.

"So all the Chinese delegates came the next morning. They were from North China as well as South China, and they were all for Ralph

Ward. But they said that the missionaries, who were teachers to most of them, told them not to vote for Ralph Ward. The most vociferous opponent of Ralph Ward, they told me, was a lady who had been in China for more than fifty years. All the missionaries, including my own teacher, Mr. Gowdy, thought Ralph Ward was too liberal, going too fast on the issue of raising Chinese leadership.

"I said, 'You all know that there is nothing against Ralph Ward's character or his piety or his ability. The only thing is his policy to promote Chinese leadership as the number one priority. The opponents also agree on the principle of Chinese leadership, but feel that it should be gradual. By "gradual," they mean no Chinese bishops nor even a bishop who is for the Chinese.'

"At this, I heard someone in the group snicker, saying, 'William Hung is preparing the path for himself. I can see that.'

"It was precisely at that moment, when I heard the snickering, that I made up my mind never to take ordination. There had been some changes in my life already that year, and I decided some very important things at that moment. Inwardly I said, 'God, I am glad you showed it to me. But I said nothing about my personal decision to the others. Instead, I said out loud,

"'That's plain politics; but in church you act the way God wants you to act. What's really important is that we all say Ralph Ward ought to be a bishop sooner or later. We all agree, not because we want to be leaders ourselves but because the Chinese church can never be a real church if it has to be dependent on missionaries. We've got to do something. We are not asking immediately for a Chinese bishop. That is gradual, right?' They conceded that it was right. Then I said, 'I know that in China, we revere our teachers. These missionaries are our teachers. Reverend Dr. Gowdy is my teacher. But we Chinese also say something else. Confucius said, *Tang-jen pu-jang yü-shih*—that when *jen* ('virtue') is at issue, then you should not yield to your teacher.'

"That cinched the argument, and I could see I had them with me. Now I said, 'No matter what happens with Ralph Ward's election, for the sake of Chinese Christians, we cannot let it be said that in this important conference, the Chinese Christian delegates abandoned their friends!'

"And they all thanked Brother Hung for that. They did not realize Brother Hung did it at great sacrifice.

"I urged them to see other delegates to persuade them to vote for Ralph Ward, and if the missionaries questioned them, to tell the truth.

Reverend Yü said the parting prayer and the delegates left to carry out the plan.

"Not being a delegate, I sat in the gallery. When I looked down onto the solemn assembly seated below, I was struck by the fact that most of the delegates were bald. I saw a sea of moons, and I said to myself that unless this church gets a lot more younger people, it has no future.

"Ralph Ward's votes spurted up with every ballot, but someone else received a majority and was elected. Four years later, however, Ralph Ward was elected; and a couple of general conferences after that, the Methodist Church had its first Chinese bishop, Ch'en Yuan-lung, also known as Ch'en Wen-yuan. He was once my rival at the Foochow Anglo-Chinese College."

LOOKING BACK on the decisions he had to make in 1919, Hung summed up the personal insights and philosophical beliefs that crystallized for him then.

"I formulated certain things for my future life. I call it the three negatives and the three positives: *san-yu, san-pu.* I realized that there are three main interests in my life. First, I am very much interested in politics, with the governing of people and the welfare of the nation. But politics is very cruel, and you have to compromise your principles. You sometime have to hurt the persons you love. Therefore I resolved to continue to be interested in statesmanship but never to become an official. Secondly, I am very much interested in religion and in the church. The church is like the face, but religion is the smile. You have to have the face, and the face has to be washed clean for the smile to show. But if the face is dirty, the smile can't be appealing. I resolved that I would never be an ordained minister. In other words, I wouldn't take religion as my profession. Then what could I do? I could be a teacher and a writer; but I would never be a principal or a college president, because in education there are politics too, and you have to hobnob with people who have money, catering to their desires, and mix with the politicians and financiers. So in 1920, I made the decision never to become any of the above.

"Now the positives. The first is *yu-wei,* to work towards concrete achievements. The second is *yu-shou,* to live a morally defensible life. The third is *yu-ch'ü,* to retain a childlike delight in living. Here is why the three *yu's* have to be interconnected: A person who is ambitious to accomplish concrete goals often sacrifices his principles in his eagerness to get where he wants to go. Therefore he has to set himself limits on what he will do, which is *yu-shou*. But a person who is *yu-shou* tends to be long-faced hypocrite; it is important to remember the natural pleasures of life. The most *yu-ch'ü* individuals are poets and artists; but they are not interested in duties, not interested in common welfare. Therefore one has to maintain an equilibrium among all three of these *yu*'s."

Thus in 1920, at the age of twenty-six, Hung drew a line around himself, limiting his ambitions and activities the rest of his life within this self-imposed boundary.

CHAPTER NINE

On The Lecture Circuit

AT THE METHODIST CONFERENCE in 1920, Hung had inwardly re-nounced the ministry but publicly confirmed his ability as a speaker. His power to inform, entertain, and persuade from the podium was to shape both his immediate future in the United States and his long-term career as an academic.

Hung completed his master's degree in history at Columbia in 1919 and his bachelor's degree in theology at Union in 1920. He never fin-ished the Ph.D. in history that he had begun. After one of his talks against Woodrow Wilson and the League of Nations, someone from the audience came up to him and told him he should try to get paid for speaking. Hung wrote to a lecture bureau called the Lyceum. The pres-ident of the firm turned up at Harrisburg, Pennsylvania, to hear him and sign him up.

The Lyceum, and later the American Platform Service, booked Hung on speaking engagements at Rotary clubs, Masonic lodges, syna-gogues, and colleges, from coast to coast. Tall, elegant, speaking flaw-less English, and sparkling with wit, he struck quite a figure wherever he went. The following newspaper excerpts were found in a publicity brochure among his papers after his death:

> The ovation that was paid him at the conclusion of his talk, when the Rotarians rose as one man and applauded until Mr. Hung had acknowledged the compliment several times, assures him of hearty recognition in the future. It was a scene rarely witnessed in Newburgh. . . (*Daily News,* Newburgh, New York)

> He speaks English not only with the utmost fluency, but with the richest vocabulary, and a rare sense of discrimination. A man of great practical sagacity, of keen analytical mind, he has also that deep sense of humor which is often the counterpart of unusual

insight and sane judgment in the appraisal of men and events. (*The Congregationalist,* Boston, Massachusetts)

Professor Hung gave the last of his series of Horizon Lectures this morning at chapel. . . . The lecture was masterful, and following the speech, the student body gave to the speaker an ovation. Orators, teachers, and entertainers have appeared before the student body of De Paw University, but never in the history of the institution has a speaker so well won the applause which was accorded to this great teacher from China today. (Greencastle *Banner,* Greencastle, Indiana)

In the summer, Hung worked for the Community Chautauqua, which organized week-long entertainment and education programs for communities across the country.

"The Chautauqua movement made great contributions to what was later known as adult education in America," Hung observed. "Remember, now, that in those days there was no radio, no television. The Chautauqua would send an agent to call on the minister or the Chamber of Commerce of a town and say, 'We are planning to come on such and such a day. We figure our expense would run to $5,000 for the week. Can you guarantee us revenues of $5,500? We will be selling the tickets. If we do not sell enough tickets, you will make it up. If we make more money than that, you can use it for your church or for the community.' It was a very attractive proposition. So they had the church leaders and town fathers promoting the program for them. The Chautauqua would arrive in several trucks. College men and women employed by the Chautauqua would set up the tents and sell tickets. Chairs were borrowed from the local church. There would be concerts, dramas, and programs for little children. But the core of the program was the lectures, mainly on international affairs, scientific topics, ethics, and religion. So the Chautauqua made money, the lecturers made money, the musicians made money, vendors of cold drinks and peanuts made money, college kids were employed, and the people were educated and entertained."

"I would be given a schedule, today this town, the next day another town. Every day I was scheduled to be somewhere. Sometimes, however, plans were cancelled and I got to watch the rest of the program. I remember watching a Gilbert and Sullivan show which I loved. I generally lectured for an hour on the Chinese language, Chinese customs, China's place in world history. When I began, I made $85 a week. Later on when I became very popular, I made about $185 a week."

Between 1921 and 1922, Hung also held a part-time job as student secretary at the Methodist Church's Board of Foreign Missions. His job entailed keeping in touch with Chinese Christian students throughout the United States, but the main project was organizing a Chinese Exhibit at the American Methodist Church Centenary World Exposition in Columbus, Ohio, in 1921. Hung was given a travel expense account and told to fill up the biggest building on the exposition ground. He combed the country for talented Chinese students. He enlisted the help of the artist Richard Yen to paint dragons over all the columns and make a tremendous Buddha of concrete; he convinced the playwright Hung Shen to organize the entertainment. There were stalls for Peking raviolis, Chinese baked and steamed food, handicrafts, fabrics, and so forth. Hung involved almost a hundred Chinese students, male and female, Christian and non-Christian, in the three months of programs. Hundreds of thousands of Americans caught rare glimpses of Chinese culture, some their only glimpse, that summer in Columbus, Ohio.

WITH HIS WIFE and daughters installed in Groveport on Long Island and his brother David studying engineering on a scholarship at Rensselaer Polytechnic Institute, Hung would return to New York from time to time to visit his family; but he travelled the length and breadth of America for weeks and months at a time. And all the time he was travelling, he tried hard to understand this country. It was an America before radio, television, and supermarkets, an America in which churchmen held an esteemed place in society, in which prohibition was in full force. It was also a booming America, an America experimenting with automobiles and mastering the techniques of mass advertising. People were getting rich in the stock market. Hung's friend Pinkie Thornburg made one fortune in the breakfast cereal business, sold it, and made another fortune in electric clocks. But it was also an America with broad streaks of racism and bigotry, an America in which lynching still occurred, in which race riots and labor strikes were routinely suppressed with brute force. Hung was often amused, sometimes provoked, by the views most Americans held of China and the Chinese. To many, China was one vast land of laundrymen. In an attempt to correct some of these erroneous notions, he wrote a booklet entitled *Get Acquainted,* which was published by the China Society of New York in 1921 (2).

Hung also read avidly. Among his favorite authors in the early 1920s were H. L. Mencken and Upton Sinclair. Whenever he was in a town for a few days, he made a point of visiting the local libraries. He was fascinated with the range of reference tools available to the general public in America and the way information was classified so that it could be profitably used. Dictionaries of all kinds, encyclopedias, indices, maps, charts, chronological tables, genealogical registries – hardly any of these were available in China. Yet how could intelligent decisions be made, and how could scholarship advance, without them? He made a special trip to visit H.W. Wilson, founder of the *Reader's Guide to Periodical Literature* to see how such an enterprise might be organized. He also visited the Library of Congress to find out how they organized their Chinese collection.

When the Washington Naval Disarmament Conference began in 1921, the China Society of New York arranged for some of the leading Chinese in America to meet with Warren Harding; and Hung had the opportunity of shaking the President's hand. Hung thought it was ironic that he had helped to defeat an American president whom he admired and helped to elect a man of whom he disapproved. Hung's ambivalence toward Wilson and Harding was perhaps typical of his political sympathies for decades to come. He often found himself aligned with the conservatives because he wanted to preserve whatever was good and decent of traditional values. Yet he never subscribed to the conservative idea that private property was sacrosanct. The fact that, everywhere, the wealthy had so much and the poor so little was highly disturbing to him. In American politics, moreover, his feelings were often complicated by the fact that China generally seemed to have more staunch supporters in the Republican Party than among Democrats.

IN 1922, an enthusiastic letter came from his friend Timothy Lew, who was now teaching at a recently founded Christian university in Peking. He told Hung that the president of the university and Lew's mentor for many years, John Leighton Stuart, was on his way to the United States, where he would pay Hung a visit to offer him a teaching position. Lew urged Hung to return to China and help them build up this new university in Peking. Not long thereafter, Stuart came to see Hung. He and Hung immediately took a liking to each other. They held common views on Christianity, on education, and on China. Hung was appointed Assistant Professor of Church History at Yenching University but was to stay another year in America helping the vice president, Henry Winter Luce, to raise money for the University.

Yenching University grew out of a dream of Bishop Bashford. There were several small missionary-run schools and colleges in the Peking area, but he saw the need for a full-scale university at the capital city that could develop a new breed of sophisticated Chinese Christians to serve both China and Christianity. In 1911, he held a meeting of representatives from various British and American missions in Peking to adopt a resolution in favor of consolidating all the sundry denominational schools into a Christian University. He wrote in his notebook that day:

We have the witness of history and the testimony of experience as to the wastefulness and the evils of the denominational system in our Christian lands. After prayer and thought I decided to venture out on faith. Hence to-day, March 25th, we held a meeting with representatives of the Anglican Mission, the American Board, the Presbyterian, and the London Missions; and the resolution which I presented in favor of a Christian union university was unanimously adopted. We have either made or marred history to-day . . .

The negotiation process was long and arduous; interdenominational rivalries ran strong; and the form and substance of the merger were not resolved until January of 1919, a few months before Bishop Bashford's death. The new university was to be governed by a board of trustees in New York, consisting of mission board executives, philanthropists, and businessmen, which would approve appointments and the university budget; with a board of managers in Peking to oversee day-to-day operations.

When Stuart took the presidency of the new university, he found woefully inadequate facilities, a faculty and a student body way below the standards of what might be expected of an institution of higher learning, hardly any budget to speak of, and trustees concerned only in defending their sectarian interest. He undertook to find a new location outside Peking ("To move it out of a predominating Methodist influence" was Hung's explanation), and to have a fellow missionary with fund-raising experience, Henry Winter Luce, appointed as vice president.

Luce initially secured pledges of financial support from a Protestant organization called the Interchurch World Movement, but its collapse soon after removed a promising source of funds. Hung, reminiscing in 1978, said, "Last night I tried to think why the Movement failed. Whether you like it or not, the great churches of America really depend on the contribution of the capitalists. The capitalists may have good Christian motives, but that does not alter the fact that churches owe their prosperity very much to capitalism." Referring to a six-week strike by 350,000 iron and steel workers in 1919, during which eighteen people died, Hung went on, "One of the great economic crises of that time was the protracted and bitter steel strike. My feeling is that the steel strike was the cause. The strike pitched labor against capitalists. When the capitalists saw that the leading churchmen of the Interchurch World Movement were sympathizing with labor, they withdrew their support and the Movement collapsed."

It was at this juncture that Hung was brought in to help raise funds. Hung, as the star attraction, was to travel with Luce and speak on Chinese culture, the Chinese language, and the place of China in world history. After his talk, Luce would make an appeal for financial support for this new Christian university in Peking. "In other words, I was the monkey and he was the organ-grinder," he said, laughing.

"What was Henry Luce like? In the Bible, there's a story about a man called Nathaniel. One time, Nathaniel came to call on Jesus and Jesus said, 'Here comes a true Israelite in whom there is no guile.' Every time I come upon that passage, I think of Henry Luce. He was tall, just a bit taller than I am, with a square face and a warm smile. He was so serious, so devout, so innocent, that he sometimes gave the impression of being an old little boy. He would get up and say, 'I am representing a university under very good international leadership, located at the capital city of the newest republic in the world, with the largest number of people. We want you to contribute to this university so that you have a share in it.' And people believed in him, because he was so obviously honest.

"When we were travelling, he wanted to save money for Yenching University; so instead of two rooms, we would share a room with two beds. I travelled with lots of books and generally had to read half an hour before I could doze off. But he liked to get in bed early. Since I had the light on, he would take all the books and build a wall between us to keep the light from shining on him. Then he would wake up very early, while I would not wake up until almost breakfast time. As he did not want to get out of bed for fear he would disturb my sleep, he would have several boxes of three-by-five cards ready at his bedside to sort out quietly in the morning until I woke up. The cards were his files of what he called his DOLS—'my dear old ladies'—the prospective contributors. He would divide them, a bundle for Pittsburgh, another for Philadelphia; these he had to see today, those tomorrow; and so forth. For about an hour and a half, he would work on them and would not make any noise.

"When I said I was like a monkey, I was really like one in my younger days. I was very mischievous and enjoyed teasing him. I would suggest that we invite each other to see a motion picture, and he would oblige. First, we would have dinner. He would look at the menu and always choose the cheapest item, usually, an omelette. Then he would say, 'William, what will you have?' I would feel embarrassed to order anything more expensive. 'All right, I'll have the same thing.' He would be watching the time and say, 'William, we'd better get on.' I'd say, 'Dr. Luce, wait a minute, we haven't had our coffee yet, and you have a pie coming.' I purposely delayed so that when we got in to see the motion picture, the film would have already been running for five minutes or so. And he would be totally baffled. 'Now what is the relationship of this man to that?' he would ask. And I would show off: 'Well, that girl is probably the sister of that man, and the other one is her father.' And my guess generally turned out to be right. 'Oh you are smart!' he'd say. I loved that. He was very slow but very methodical, just like a clock. And I was young and took advantage of him.

"But he loved me very much and enjoyed reading to me the letters of his son. At that time, his son, Henry R. Luce, had this plan to start a weekly newsmagazine with two college friends of his from Yale. Their idea was that since they did not have much capital and could not afford to have their own correspondents, they would just pick up items from the daily newspaper and rewrite them in such a way that they could not be sued for plagiarism. They would inject student smart-aleck humour into the news to make people enjoy reading it. I said, 'Your son Henry has found a gold mine.' So he often wrote to his son, my young friend William Hung said this and that. Later when Henry became a big publisher and I called him at the Time-Life Building at Rockefeller Center, he would say, 'William, you come right over. You gave me a great deal of moral support in those days.'"

Luce and Hung asked their audiences to give "a vital, living gift—a Christian university" to China and raised about $2,000,000 for Yenching buildings in the course of a year and a half. A businessman from the First Methodist Church of Detroit, Arthur Start, was so moved by the fact that a man like Hung was going back to teach in China that he donated $7,000 for a house to be built on campus for the Hung family. Luce told Hung afterwards, "The only problem with tainted money is there t'ain't enough!"

IN AUGUST OF 1923, exactly eight years and one day after he first arrived in America, Hung and family boarded a steamer to go back to China. It was with some trepidation in their hearts that they started this trip. Rhoda had left China when she was a young child. She grew up in Hawaii and spoke no Mandarin, only a few words of Hakka, a southern dialect. Hung, having passed most of his adult life in the United States, felt he did not really know China any longer. He had, moreover, lived only in the remote provinces of that big country. Furthermore, the political and social climate had altered greatly since he left—in many ways, for the worse. The country was overrun by capricious warlords and roving bandits. And Hung himself had also changed, having acquired American tastes, American ways of thinking, and American mannerisms. In moments of candor, he admitted to himself that he felt more at ease in American company than in a Chinese setting.

When their steamer sailed into Kobe, Japan, they were confronted with a fearful picture. The great earthquake of 1923 had hit only a few days earlier. Gasoline tanks along the harbor were still roaring with flames, and the sea was filled with desperate and stunned people drifting about small crafts, pleading for help. The steamer took some fourteen hundred persons aboard. The scene added to Hung's sense of unease in returning to turbulent Asia. The situation seemed to him emblematic of the vast sea of floundering Asian humanity, in dire need of help; but he and others like him in their small Western vessel were severely limited in what aid they could offer.

Part Three

William, Ruth, Gertrude, and Rhoda Hung, ca. 1927

CHAPTER TEN

The Repatriate

WHEN THE HUNGS arrived in Peking, the new Yenching campus that was to be built in a suburb of Peking had not yet been constructed. Classes were held in various buildings in the city. There were 52 Westerners and 28 Chinese on the faculty, instructing 336 young men and 94 young women.

The Hungs moved in with the Stuarts for the first month. Then for three years, they lived at Number Five Mao-chia-wan in an old-style Chinese compound they shared with Donald Tewksbury, an administrator at Yenching, and Bliss Wiant, whom Hung had known at Ohio Wesleyan and recruited to teach music at Yenching. There was a piece of vacant land in the compound, and this Hung quickly converted into a tennis court.

Hung found himself in a China that was undergoing social and political upheaval. Floating freely around him were values, ideas, sentiments, customs and theories of all kinds. He needed to sort them out and let them somehow crystallize around a core that he could safely call his own identity. He could perhaps have made the decision to let that core be the Hung Yeh of 1915 and shed all the ideas and habits he had acquired in his eight years abroad like an unstylish jacket. Some returned students did just that; and to do so would have helped him get along better in an intellectual climate that had become strongly nationalistic and anti-foreign. But instead, he made a choice *not* to negate his American-acquired values, habits, and ideas; and he emphasized that choice by continuing to live a style of life that was decidedly American, exemplified, in part, by the tennis court. He insisted that the university pay him a salary equal to that received by the Western faculty members, which was by no means large but was much higher than the pay scale for Chinese. He became a Mason and joined the Peking Rotary Club. He came to be elected president of the American College Club. His closest friends were Westerners and other returned students.

In many ways, the transition was more difficult for Rhoda, who had lived in the United States all but the first few years of her life. She was greatly depressed by the uncertainty of the political situation. She was appalled by the grinding poverty in which most people lived, the pomp and punctiliousness prevailing in the upper class, and the privileged position occupied by Westerners in China. While still learning to speak Mandarin, she had to cope with ignorant servants, shrewd merchants, and other problems of day-to-day living. She tried hard to do whatever was sensible. In a letter dated December 1, 1923, to the Crawfords, she wrote:

Life in China is ever so much more complicated than in America. The other day William and I with two friends took a walk on the city wall, the best place for walking in Peking. We reached the Hatamen gate and the friends had to turn back because they had Chinese clothing on—the space between Hataman gate and Chienmen [was] closed to Chinese; but all foreigners whether bad or good and Chinese in foreign clothes could enter this forbidden section. A French drunkard could do very ugly things and not be punished except by representatives of his nation. We saw a foreigner strike a coolie that sent that coolie reeling, but the poor creature merely put his hand to his injured face and slinked away. Foreigners demand homage from the Chinese such as unheard of in America.

We were invited out to dinner last week where they served the most elaborate dinner, such as only very wealthy people could serve in America and served five different kinds of wines with it. I tell you this to show that foreigners and upper class Chinese do not live simply. We were surprised to find people we expect to be simple served such elaborate tea, lunches, etc.

You will be interested to know that we are going to be more simple than we ever have been. It is very hard for people to breakaway from the ways they have been accustomed. So I have tried several times and I think it's going to work out nicely: It is this, when I have foreign guests I serve simple but good Chinese food in Western style (Instead of having food in the center of table as all Chinese do and each helping themselves, I pass things around or if only a few people, William and I serve it on to the plate as eating a foreign meal.) and I have a nice Chinese dessert. When I have Chinese guests I serve foreign meals, five courses with the coffee. The Chinese seem to like this very much and they forget that they have had only a few courses and not sixteen or twenty-seven. T. T. Lew does not understand how I dare invite big people and give them such simple food.

HUNG TAUGHT several courses in history and in religion at Yenching. He was also acting chairman of the history department. Of his first year at Yenching, he recalled:

"One of the beautiful things about Yenching was that most of the missionaries and quite a few of the Chinese cared more about the cause than their position in it. Before my arrival, the head of the history department and its only professor was a Swiss Ph.D. from the University of Lausanne, named Philippe de Vargas. Even before my arrival, de Vargas had suggested that I be promoted to associate professor and chairman of the history department. So there were two of us. Naturally, I was expected to teach Chinese history, but I felt I was not qualified. So I got the support of Stuart and the Executive Committee to appropriate some money to employ a real professor of Chinese history. I looked up the head of the department of history at the Peking Normal University, Wang T'ung-ling, who was a greatly admired teacher. He declined the invitation to come to Yenching but recommended one of his graduates, a man from Shansi by the name of Ch'ang Nai-te. Ch'ang came but did not make a great impression on me. He appeared to be a shrivelled-up young man, tousle-haired, and unshaven, wearing always a ragged, blue, Chinese gown. Since he was a recent graduate, we gave him the rank of instructor and assigned him a room in the dormitory. He hardly emerged from that room, so busy was he always, preparing his lecture notes. I did not pay much attention to him. My wife and I would often have other professors over for dinner at our house, but I don't remember ever having invited Ch'ang Nai-te. After a year of teaching, he probably felt neglected and came to see me, saying he did not want to continue. I did not make an effort to keep him. I thought good riddance. It was one of the biggest regrets of my life. For this fellow later became a pillar of the Ch'ing-nien-tang [Youth Party] and figured importantly in the Constitution Movement. He also founded a new school of historical thought. He was a great man and I missed him!

"I had a general history course for which students needed practically no prerequisites. It was mainly a fun course. I told them, 'You are free to sleep in my class, but I don't think you will be able to. First, my lectures are going to be very interesting. Secondly, I always talk very loud, so you can't sleep anyway. When examination comes around, I will not ask you the whos, the wheres, the whats, and the whens; but I will be asking you the hows and the whys. In history, it is the general tendencies, the institutions that are important; the hows and the whys are the juices, whereas the other matters are the pulp.' Then out of the whole class of more than a hundred students, I would pick out a few and encourage them to study historical methods.

"In my historical methods class, I would first try to instill in them a sense of history. I gave them a series of assignments. The first assignment was to have them, in one week's time, hand in a paper on 'Who I am': What is your name? Do you have other names? Where are you from? Are both your parents alive? What do they do? Are there any prominent persons among your ancestors? Where did the clan name come from? Are there any clan records? Any genealogy kept? Where are they kept? The second assignment was to write a history of the city or town they came from and the house they had been living in: Does the house belong to your family? Have you seen the deed? What is the history behind the house, and how did it pass to your family? It was a wonderful way to train them in the use of documents. Very often, their parents became very interested in their paper because the students dug up facts that the parents did not know about."

In the School of Religion, Hung taught a course on the history of Christianity; and one of his lectures produced an unexpected encounter with occultism. To a somewhat sceptical class one day, he argued that conflicts arose between the followers of Peter, who saw Christianity as an extension of Judaism, and those of Paul, who claimed that the New Covenant between God and man as preached by Jesus was a break with the Old Covenant as handed down in the Old Testament. The next day, the students were noticeably restless and ill-behaved. When Hung asked them about their behavior, they claimed that they had gotten in touch with Peter and Paul in a seance the night before and been told that his lectures were wrong, that there had never been any conflict between the two apostles. A stunned Hung invited the class to his house for tea that afternoon and an attempt to duplicate this spiritual communication. After a giggling Rhoda left the room, in the time-honored fashion of seances, a table vibrated and raps gave the correct answer to numerical questions with answers known to a member of the audience. But when questions about how many coins were heads up in a box that had just been shaken or on what day of the week April 1 would fall the following year, the "spirit" could not answer. Hung dismissed them with the cheerful concession that there might be something to the idea of mental telepathy within the group of sitters but a refusal to hear any more about communication with dead saints.

IN ADDITION TO TEACHING, Hung in 1923 took on the responsibility of building a library for Yenching. A glance at what existed dismayed him. There were very few Chinese books, and what English books there were consisted mainly of Biblical commentaries. To acquaint himself with what other books were available to Yenching students, he visited Peking's only public library, which was housed in a musty, dilapidated building and presided over by a couple of tottery, old men. There was no system by which books could be located. Often Hung found himself the only person there. But at least it was free and allowed copying, unlike the public library Hung had frequented as a boy in Shantung.

The best place for books in Peking were the old bookstores in the Liu-li-ch'ang area. There the proprietors were unfailingly courteous, and browsers might linger as long as they pleased. But the university needed so many basic books, and there was no money to buy them with! Hung remembered his rich friend Pinkie and wrote him, proposing a "Mother Thornburg Library Fund." Pinkie sent a check for $1,000. As soon as Hung received the money, he rushed off gleefully to Liu-li-ch'ang and came back at the end of the day in a cab packed solid with books. With that encouragement, he successfully solicited other friends in America; and later, he managed to convince Alice Frame, the Dean of the Women's College that was now a part of the university, to ask her separate board of trustees to divert $25,000 to buy Chinese books for the Yenching Library. Later still, when funds from the estate of Charles Martin Hall became available to Yenching, financial constraints on the library were greatly eased; and it came to be known as one of the best in China.

HUNG'S FAVORITE PASTIME on Saturdays was to get a rickshaw and visit the site of the new campus for Yenching. The site, chosen by Stuart, was something over two hundred acres near Tsinghua University five miles outside the West City Gate of Peking, about midway between the city wall and the Western Hills. It appeared to be a vast ruined garden, and was, in fact, made up of abandoned gardens. Yenching purchased its first sixty acres in 1920 and, through purchase or lease, gained access to the rest of the site in subsequent years. The whole area was full of gardens and palaces, some still standing but most left in a state of disrepair by their impoverished Manchu owners. Tsinghua University was built in a princely garden outside the Yuan-ming-yuan, an imperial summer palace laid waste by the Anglo-French army half a century earlier. Hung would take long walks among the lakes, the artificial hills, the pine groves, of what was to become the Yenching campus, tracing the sources of waterways and making maps of the grounds before they were altered irreversibly by the new construction.

He began to collect books, manuscripts, paintings, and poems that related to the history of the site. His first piece of historical scholarship in Chinese, written in 1928, concerned two funerary tablets unearthed on the campus site, which gave rather detailed accounts of the lives of two obscure, sixteenth-century, Ming officials who were buried there. Hung was able not only to give the information contained in the inscriptions, but to note citations to the two men in other documents (5).

It turned out that one part of the grounds was the site of the famous Ladle Garden (Shao-yuan) built by the Ming painter Mi Wan-chung. Hung was able to secure Mi's own painting of the garden as it existed in 1617 and publish the ten-foot scroll in eight magnificent plates, along with a collection of writings on the garden (23). A part of the campus, which was used as the site for a residence to house bachelor officers of the university, was found to be the former country villa of Prince I-huan (1840–1891). Hung wrote an article on the villa entitled "A Brief History of the Garden of Elegant Refinement" (17).

The principal area of the campus, however, was discovered to have belonged to Ho Shen (1750–1799), a one-time guard of the Ch'ien-lung Emperor's sedan chair, who within a few years became the chief minister of state and father-in-law to the emperor's favorite daughter. It was said that his meteoric rise was aided by the fact that he resembled a concubine of the emperor's father, whom the young Ch'ien-lung had inadvertently caused to be put to death. After the death of Ch'ien-lung in 1799, however, the succeeding emperor exposed Ho Shen's incompetence and corruption, confiscated his properties, and ordered him to commit suicide. The garden was dug up repeatedly by eager treasure hunters lured by persistent rumors of buried wealth. Hung pieced together this poignant story and published first a booklet in English, "Ho Shen and Shu-ch'un-yuan" (25), and then excerpts from source materials with commentary in Chinese (27). He also published a colophon to and identified the author of an incomplete manuscript of poems that he admitted to be mediocre, but that interested him because they contained references to the geography around the campus (10). This piece of earth was becoming very dear to him.

On the ruins of the villas of Mi Wan-chung, Prince I-huan, and Ho

Shen, were to arise what appeared to be new Chinese palaces with traditional green-tiled roofs, red pillars, and intricately latticed windows; yet these were buildings equipped with the latest plumbing and heating facilities. Much of the original landscaping of hills and lakes were eventually restored, complete with a pagoda that concealed the water tower. The buildings came to bear such names as Bishop Bashford Hall and Luce Pavillion, names of fond associations to Hung. And in the southern nook of the campus would be a brick building with a fireplace, built specifically for Hung and his family with the funds provided by Arthur Start of Detroit.

IN HIS ROVINGS among curio shops and old bookstores, Hung often ran into Ch'iu Shan-yuan, an official at the Ministry of Education in charge of relics. Under his charge in Peking was a historical museum, full of interesting objects. These included a full-sized bronze human statue used to examine candidates for medical degrees; it was equipped with tiny holes; its cavity could be filled with water and its surface covered with wax so that liquid would spurt out only if pierced by an acupuncture needle at the appropriate spots. Education, however, was the poorest among all the ministries; and there was no budget to open the historical museum to the public. Hung took up the matter with Stuart, and they were able to obtain $6,000 from the estate of Charles Martin Hall to pay for the initial costs of opening the Peking Historical Museum in 1926. Glass cases were bought, and a new coat of paint was applied to the building. Hung wrote Eric North that during the first four weeks of the public opening, about 185,000 visitors—or roughly one-fifth the population of Peking—went through the museum. Subsequent receipts from admission charges were adequate to pay for maintenance, and Stuart and Hung were both made honorary members. Hung learned a great deal about antiquarian subjects from Ch'iu. Ch'iu later recommended to Hung a recent graduate from Peking University, Jung Keng, to teach at Yenching. Jung Keng became a well-known authority on ancient inscriptions and on Chinese bronzes. When Hung founded the *Yenching Journal of Chinese Studies* in 1927, he asked Jung Keng to be its editor-in-chief.

IN THE SUMMER OF 1924, Hung went back to visit Foochow for nine days. It had been less than ten years since he had left, but he could hardly believe the changes that had taken place there. The city wall had been completely torn down, and the steep streets with steps running up and down were all levelled. When he left, there had not been a single wheeled vehicle within the walled city; now everywhere he looked, he saw rickshaws and bicycles, while sedan chairs had become rare. Hung was invited to many places to give commencement speeches, and another surprise awaited him: When he was a student in Foochow, he was the only person in the whole school who spoke Mandarin; now all the students did.

There were changes in his family, too. Grandfather Lin had died while Hung was in the United States. Grandmother Lin was still alive; and he took her a hundred shiny British coins; but the grand old residence was much deteriorated in the hands of his adopted uncle. He also visited his good-natured Aunt Lin and fifty years later could remember the bowl of rice noodles she cooked for him. Yet even food pointed to how much his ties to his old life were slipping. Because he was on a diet of toast and milk for intestinal trouble that summer, he stayed with a Westerner, Bliss Wiant's brother Paul. And with David in America, Arnold studying at Yenching, and Fred living in the dormitory at the Fukien Christian University, Foochow was no longer really home.

HUNG spent the rest of the summer with his family—the last leisurely one he would have for a long time—living in the very pleasant summer home of a missionary friend on a mountaintop near Peking. He grappled with the problem of how the great store of knowledge the Chinese had accumulated over the millennia might fit into a framework consistent with a college curriculum. The prevailing practice of lumping everything Chinese into a "Chinese Studies Department" seemed to him very unsatisfactory. He came up with a classification of four divisions: languages, mathematics, sciences, and the humanities. Under the humanities, he felt that Chinese literature should be a separate department, but that Chinese aspects of archeology, art, history, language, philosophy and religion should be integrated into their respective academic disciplines. He was to have ample opportunities to put these concepts into practice when he became Dean of Yenching University that fall and was given a free hand to shape its academic future.

Another problem he set himself to tackle that summer was how the incredible wealth of information available in Chinese might be made

accessible to future scientists, historians, and other seekers of knowledge. Basic reference tools needed to be developed, as did a system by
which indexes and concordances could be prepared for Chinese texts.
The latter problem, of course, arises because the thousands of Chinese
characters are non-alphabetic and follow no self-evidently logical sequence. It would be impractical to arrange them in an index by sound
because too many are homophones or have variant readings, and the
pronounciation of some of the more archaic ones is now unknown. Traditionally, characters were classified either by orthography or sound.
That is, they were first sorted into large groups by the 214 calligraphic
radicals or by rhymes and then into smaller sub-groups according to
their number of strokes. But all of these systems are too arbitrary and
cumbersome for practical use in indexing. When Hung had visited the
U. S. Library of Congress a few years earlier, he had been shown a
book by Lin Yü-t'ang that classified the strokes in Chinese characters
into nineteen types (horizontal, vertical, left to right, right to left, etc.);
he was also shown another system, used among librarians, for classify-
ing strokes into the eight types found in the character *yung* ("everlast-
ing"). So Hung played around with the different systems; and working
with thousands of three by five cards, he perfected a system of his own,
which he called the Kuei-hsieh system. (*Kuei* and *hsieh* are two rarely
used characters which mean "put in" and "pull out.") This system
assigns a six-digit number to each Chinese character. The first digit
indicates to which of five generic types the character belongs. The next
four digits identify the kinds of strokes found at the four corners of the
character, and the last digit signifies the numer of squares found in the
character. The advantages of the system are that it is relatively easy to
learn; in it characters are easy to find; and once one is given the six
digits, one can almost visualize a character in one's mind.

In the same year, the Shanghai Commercial Press was to publish the
new "Four Corner Number Dictionary," using a four-digit number system. The four digits identifying the types of strokes at the four corners
of a character were similar to those of the four middle digits found in
Hung's six-digit system, for both systems trace their lineage to the
librarians' *yung* system. The "Four Corner System" instantly became
immensely popular and was widely accepted as a new way of arranging
characters in dictionaries and other reference works. Although the
"Four Corner System" has the disadvantage of frequently having too
many characters falling under the same four-digit number, it is contro-
versial whether Hung should have persisted in using his own Kuei-hsieh

system in all subsequent Yenching University publications, many of which were major reference works. Since the Kuei-hsieh system appears only in Yenching University publications, few people learn to master it. In using these publications, therefore, they are forced to look up the characters under the old radical-stroke count system or the Wade-Giles romanized character system to find the six-digit number before they can locate the character. Hung could have made the minor concession of modifying his system so that the middle four digits would correspond to those of the widely accepted "Four Corner System." This would have made the Kuei-hsieh system much easier to use. But no such concession was made. His insistence on his own system reveals the strong streak of stubbornness in Hung.

It seems, furthermore, an act of pedantic snobbery for Hung to name a new system of arranging Chinese characters "Kuei-hsieh," using two archaic words only the very learned know how to pronounce. It was unworthy of an American-trained repatriate who prided himself on simple solutions for complex problems. The decision to use these two archaic words to label a new system could have risen only from a mind torn with conflicts between attraction to innovations and allegiance to the old—even though for the present, to his colleagues Hung appeared to be simply the stereotypical American-educated, brash, young man on the move.

CHAPTER ELEVEN

Dean at Yenching

THE SITE of the former Yenching University campus, with its lakes, pine groves, pagoda, and palatial buildings, inspires bemused reflections on the brief, brilliant, and tragic history of that institution. The founders of Yenching endeavored to forge a bilingual and bicultural Christian elite in China. And to a surprising extent, they succeeded. Even though the life of the university was cut short in 1952, Yenching alumni have exerted an influence on politics, education, and scholarship in China far beyond what their small number might suggest. For much of the thirty-five years following the Communist accession to power on the mainland, foreign ministers on both sides of the Taiwan Strait were Yenching alumni; and some of the most respected Chinese scholars in academia around the world received their training at Yenching.

In 1924, when at the age of thirty Hung became Dean of the College of Arts and Sciences, neither the nature of Yenching's success nor the sadness of its ultimate fate could have been forseen. It was then only an obscure, disorganized, very highly promising university. At that time, it consisted of three entities: the College of Arts and Sciences, sometimes known as the Men's College; the Women's College, under Alice Frame; and the School of Religion under Timothy Lew, which offered the only graduate-level courses. Over them all was the president, John Leighton Stuart.

Since the Women's College was at that time not yet fully incorporated into the rest of the University, and was physically two miles away from the main campus in K'uei-chia-ch'ang, Stuart, Lew and Hung made up a kind of triumvirate that ran Yenching between 1923 and 1926. Stuart had known Lew when Lew was a boy in Chekiang and had helped pay for his education in the United States. Lew and Hung, of course, had been close associates since their Cross and Sword days. It was Lew who convinced Hung to do his graduate work in New York. It was Lew who persuaded Stuart to invite Hung to join Yenching. And it was Lew who spearheaded the move to get Hung elected Dean by the faculty. Both Hung and Lew were devoted to Stuart, a man whom many regarded as a saint. But between Lew and Hung, there was always some uneasiness. Hung, at least, felt he could not freely give Lew the unquestioning loyalty that the nature of their friendship seemed to demand.

Lew was an impassioned, rather volatile person, who had sweeping visions of a new China, whereas Hung, although he had his histrionic and daring moments, was not inclined to strike out into unfamiliar territory unless he could see clearly ahead of him. The fact that Rhoda disliked Lew did not help their friendship. Rhoda disliked everything about Lew: his short stature, his long hair, his constant coughing, his sinus problem, and what she felt was his incessant effort to better his position.

"One time when we were talking in private, Rhoda said, 'Let's give Timothy a nickname. He is really like a mouse, always looking for holes. Whenever he finds a hole, he bores into it. Let's call him Chit.' So we started to refer to him as Chit in our conversation. One day, Timothy came to see us. My eldest daughter Ruth, then only four years old, yelled out, 'Mother, Chit is here!' We were terribly embarrassed."

There was a consistency in the kind of issues that pulled Lew and Hung apart. They had first disagreed openly when Lew advocated amalgamation of Cross and Sword with the more established fraternity David and Jonathan, while Hung opposed it for fear that the fraternity would be used for personal advancement by the younger members. Lew won that round. Now at Yenching, Lew proposed at a faculty meeting that Yenching start granting honorary degrees. Hung vehemently opposed the idea. When the votes were in, Hung prevailed; and Lew stomped out of the room, slamming the door behind him. In 1925, when Sun Yat-sen died, Lew waged a vigorous and successful campaign to have him buried with a Christian funeral. Hung viewed the whole business as the exploitation of a famous name. Hung felt that even though Sun Yat-sen was a Christian in his youth, his taking a second wife while his first was still alive proved that he had repudiated Christian beliefs. Lew's strategy of forging an alliance between Christianity and the emerging political forces was abhorrent to Hung, and the two friends drifted apart. In the 1930s, Lew left Yenching entirely and became a member of the Legislative Yuan in the Nanking government.

Nevertheless, there was a whole range of matters on which Hung and Lew were in basic accord. Together, they persuaded the faculty to abolish compulsory chapel service at Yenching by arguing that religion was a form of life and that there could be no growth in life without freedom. With Lew's support, Hung took some rather drastic actions to raise the academic standard of the university. He phased out the preparatory school and initiated graduate-level courses in arts and sciences. Keenly aware that good Chinese literature and history departments were essential for Yenching to be respected in China, he fired almost the entire Chinese department faculty and rebuilt the departments from scratch. He established the rule that a student who did not maintain an equivalent of a B average would have to leave Yenching. During the first year, ninety-three students, out of a student body of a little more than four hundred, had to drop out. The student body was later maintained at about eight hundred, and admissions became extremely competitive.

"With respect to my rule that any student whose grade fell below B had to go elsewhere," Hung reminisced, "many people came to remonstrate with me on behalf of their son or daughter. But I always said that without a university education, a person might pick up a trade or go into business; yet with an education, he might not be willing to demean himself to go into trade. As a result, if a poor student stayed in school, he could become a bad scholar and be totally useless to himself and to society."

It is interesting to note that Hung's vision of a modern China did not have a place for an educated and sophisticated business class. Among his generation of Western-style liberals, there remained the Confucian taboo against educated people being engaged in commercial activities. This deep-seated taboo may have contributed to the theoretical bias of the educational system which they advocated and for which they were frequently criticized.

In an article, "The Lean and Fat Years," published in the *Yenching University Alumni Bulletin* in 1973, C. Y. Hsu described what it was like to be a student applying for admission to Yenching and interviewed personally by Hung:

. . . [T]he most terrible 'pass' to go through was that of Dr. Hung. When you were admitted into his office, you stood in front of his desk and presented your registration card reverently. He examined your card, sized you up critically and asked you some tough questions. He spoke English to every student in a loud voice, never a word of Chinese. Many a student who did not speak English well shuddered, perspired and stammered during the interview. If he was lucky enough to get Dr. Hung's signature on his card, he would heave a sigh of relief when he stepped out of his office.

Hung was not a popular dean among the students. There was a great deal of resentment against him.

"They considered me a fake Chinese. Behind my back, they twisted the tones for *tǎ-fēn chǔ-ì* ("grade-ism") and said that mine was *tà-fèn chǔ-ì* ("big shit-ism"). Fortunately, I was able to rely heavily on Ch'en Tsai-hsin to help me with administrative work. Ch'en was an early graduate of [the Methodist college] Huei-wen ta-hsueh [i.e., "College of Convergent Learning," one of the predecessors of Yenching University]; he later got a Ph.D. from Columbia in mathematics. He was a very quiet man, older than most of us, and very fair. He had the title of Associate Dean. When I started out as Dean, Yenching still had a preparatory school. The students in the preparatory school were just entering into adolescence, full of childish pranks, very difficult to deal with. So I asked if he might look after those. He would really have preferred to do his own scholarly work and play chess, using his beautiful ivory set. But out of the kindness of his heart, he dealt with them; and they respected him.

"There was one incident in which even now I do not know whether I acted rightly or wrongly. We had a student named Fu Chin-po, who spelled his English name as Philip Fugh. He was a very bright, handsome, and clever man; and there was no question about his patriotism. His ancestors were in charge of the Manchu palace household. These people were so smooth socially that they could put you immediately into a pleasant mood. Even as a freshman, Philip won the confidence of Leighton Stuart. Later on the names Stuart and Philip Fugh became so entertwined you could hardly separate them. When Stuart became the U.S. Ambassador to China, Philip Fugh was the only non-American who was a confidental secretary at the American Embassy. And when Stuart was incapacitated, he and the Fugh family lived together in Washington. The way he took care of Stuart was beautiful. Philip had a peculiar ability: It did not matter what kind of political setup, no matter who the key persons were, he could always find a way to approach them, sometimes through the sons and daughters or concubines. He was Stuart's right-hand man, particularly in dealing with the Chinese government officials.

"Now Philip always respected me, but as a student he neglected his studies. I think it was in his sophomore year that his grades went way down. Stuart came to plead with me, 'He's got the brains, you realize, why don't you just let him stay?' I said, 'All right, Leighton, I'll make an exception, but he'd better understand that he has to buckle down and study. Next year, if he doesn't measure up, you will have to support me in dropping him.' Stuart agreed. The second year, he failed again, so I had to ask him to leave. Stuart did not make any request, but I don't think he ever forgave me for that."

There were other students whom Hung had to expel for non-academic reasons. He remembered one in particular, a senior surnamed Chang, from a prominent family in Peking. Chang had ordered a servant in the dormitory to get him some water to make tea. The servant had been slow; and when he finally brought in the water, Chang was so annoyed that he took the whole kettle of boiling water and threw it at him. The servant was badly burned, and the whole university was shocked. Hung called on the servant in the hospital to assure him that all his expenses would be taken care of by the Chang family and to apologize, saying "The incident shows that there is deficiency in our education at Yenching." The servant replied that it was all very nice for the Dean to come apologize, but that the proper person to make the apology was the young man himself. Chang refused to apologize to the servant and was promptly expelled.

As DEAN AT YENCHING, Hung found himself spending as much time defending the institution as running it. Sometimes, "defending" took a very physical form. Just a decade earlier, when the Chinese Republic was newly born, Christianity was one of the major forces of social change; now it was being denounced by many intellectuals as an opiate of the people, a tool of imperialism. By the mid-1920s, feelings against Western imperialism and religion were running at an all-time high. Several times, rumors floated about that some of the radicals were coming to burn down the university. Hung, along with Lucius Porter, Randolph Sailor, and other faculty members, would patrol the campus through the night, carrying big sticks in hand.

When the May Thirtieth Incident took place, Yenching found itself politically vulnerable. On this occasion, Hung overcame his usual reluctance to dabble in the uncertainties of Chinese politics and entered into the fray.

In 1925, Shanghai was still ruled by a Shanghai Municipal Council made up of Western representatives, with the British dominating. On

May 30, there was a demonstration of laborers, students, and merchants on behalf of mistreated Chinese workers in Japanese-owned cotton mills in Shanghai. As they marched, the British police force opened fire into the crowd and killed eleven Chinese. In subsequent demonstrations elsewhere in the country, fourteen Chinese were killed by the British and Japanese militia in Hankow, and fifty-two Chinese were killed by Anglo-French troops in Canton. Protest strikes spread across the country. An anti-Christian movement emerged alongside them. The students at Yenching joined the strike, and the faculty felt compelled to draw up a "Statement of Yenching University Faculty" condemning the British from the standpoint of the Christian scriptures.

Two American members of the Yenching faculty community, George and Dorothy Barbour, described the campus in June in diaries and letters, which they later published in their book, *In China When*. . . . Dorothy commented on "the bitter resentment among the students"; and George described an address by Shanghai delegates to a student mass meeting:

They spoke in intensely emotional terms, giving vivid pictures of the 'massacre,' . . . and had the entire student body in tears. Dean William Hung said that till now he had never believed the description of the 'revivals' of the 18th century. Students got up sobbing and hysterical, but Dean Hung, by a strategic move, headed off suggestions for burning of buildings by suggesting that they first ask those in Shanghai to write out a precise statement of just what had happened and put their name to it. This he would then have translated into all languages for transmission to other countries. But even at 2:30 the students were still so much aroused that they voted to remain all summer in Peking . . . Dean Hung pointed out that their home villages knew nothing of the facts and that it was incumbent on them to spend the first part of the summer among the unintelligent country people. It calmed things down.

The Barbours also alluded to another Incident that called for Hung's skill in containing student anger and defending the university in the first, tense days after the May Thirtieth Incident. This time he had to take on an opportunistic Peking newspaper, the *Far Eastern Times,* which had been pro-British in its English edition and anti-British on its Chinese pages. When, in its English editorials, it attacked the Yenching faculty for the "Statement" condemning the British action as un-Christian, Hung was forced to act. As the Barbours wrote at the time, "The *Far Eastern Times* was nearly wrecked by an article by our Dean William Hung, comparing editorials appearing on the same page—the English virulently anti-Chinese and the Chinese anti-foreign. The paper has simply grovelled."

In 1978 Hung recalled, "In Peking at that time, there were four main newspapers. There were the *Ch'en Pao* and the *Ching Pao* in Chinese; the long-established *Peking Leader* in English, edited by an American named Grover Clarke; and a bilingual *Far Eastern Times,* a new paper which had only just opened up under the editorship of an Englishman named Lenox Simpson, who wrote under the name of Putname Weale. Simpson was a foreign advisor to various warlords. It was said that his newspaper was financed with money from Chang Tso-lin, a mustached ex-bandit in the northeast, who was poised to take over Peking. Simpson had the clever idea of boosting his circulation by importing a shiny new automobile to Peking and displaying it in his front office's show window as a prize for the person who signed up the most subscriptions to the *Far Eastern Times.* In 1925, with only a few automobiles in Peking, people would buy subscriptions by the thousands to help a cousin or nephew win the car. Consequently, in just a few months, the paper was able to surpass the old *Peking Leader* in sales.

"The *Far Eastern Times* consisted of a single page daily, one side in English, the other in Chinese. The 'Statement of the Yenching Faculty' was sent to all the newspapers in China; and the *Far Eastern Times,* like all the others, ran it both in the Chinese and English versions. It did not comment on the 'Statement' on the Chinese side of the newspaper; but on the English side, it ran an editorial for several consecutive days condemning it and ridiculing Yenching University, saying it was trying to mix Christianity with politics, catering to uneducated Chinese mobs. Not many readers of the *Far Eastern Times* read both Chinese and English, but the Yenching students did. They called a meeting and threatened to smash the *Far Eastern Times* office. I reasoned with the students, 'I agree that your cause is just, but your action is violent. There is always a better way to resolve things than violence.'

"'What do you suggest?'

"'If you are willing to delay actions for a few days, I will have a way to deal with it to your satisfaction. But I am not going to disclose it to you, because if the plan is not a surprise, it might not work. In another week, if *Far Eastern Times* keeps harping on Yenching, I will go march with you.'

"I had a plan in mind, which was really very simple. I had kept a file of *Far Eastern Times.* Now I took out the file and quickly translated all their English comments on the May Thirtieth Incident into Chinese and translated their reportage in Chinese into English. I set the contradictory reportage and editorials side by side and labelled the Chinese version *Yi-tsai tung-fang jih-pao!* ('How Strange, the *Far Eastern Times!*'), the English version, 'A Journalism of Duplicity.' Then I wrote a cover letter to the editor-in-chief requesting that the *Far Eastern Times* print the articles, in both its Chinese and English versions, on the appropriate sides of the newspaper. I wrote, 'I have thought of having the articles published in the other newspapers. But in accordance with correct journalistic practice, I want to give you the first chance of refutation since it is a charge against you. I am perfectly willing that when you publish them, you add to them your comments. In case you do not publish them, I will have to send them to be published elsewhere.'

"A reply came immediately, 'We are sorry we cannot publish your communication. If you will be so kind as to call on our office, it will be worth your while.' I ignored this offer and sent the English text to the *Peking Leader* and the Chinese text to the *Ching Pao*. In both, I enclosed a letter saying that the *Far Eastern Times* had declined to publish it. Later, the editor of the *Peking Leader* told me that it was a godsend for them. They put it on the first page, stipulating that 'Dean Hung of Yenching University has offered this article to our rival. Since they have declined, it is our duty to publish it.' The first time he printed the article, he intentionally left out an unimportant line so that he could run it again the second day with an apology. *Ching Pao* printed the Chinese text with an editorial calling on the Chinese workers of the *Far Eastern Times* to leave their employment. Having lost their Chinese workers as well as their advertisers (mainly British, who felt duped), the *Far Eastern Times* folded up.

"It created great excitement at Yenching. Because of this, the students became more or less reconciled to me, especially since they found out that this fake Chinese could write such good Chinese, in a vigorous classical style, similar to the prose of Liang Ch'i-ch'ao."

The political situation continued to worsen. A student demonstration in Peking in connection with the May Thirtieth Incident led to forty-seven dead, including a woman student from Yenching who died from bayonet wounds. Since its formation in 1921, the Chinese Communist Party had proliferated in all the larger cities. As long as Sun Yat-sen was alive, he was able to effect some cooperation between the two revolutionary forces of the Kuomintang and the Communists; but with him gone, the alliance had fallen apart and a bitter struggle for power and for the control of young minds was taking place. Hung found himself spending an inordinate amount of time getting students out of jails.

EVEN DURING THESE YEARS when he was deeply enmeshed in administrative responsibilities, and notwithstanding his general severity as Dean, Hung found time to indulge in what was to be a passion of his life: the discovery and nurturing of superior individuals. The Chinese term for this peculiar type of passion is *ai ts'ai* ("love of talent"). Like a connoisseur of fine gems who finds joy in spotting stones of unusual qualities, making sure that they are cut just right, and bringing them to the attention of the world, Hung always kept a keen eye out for exceptional students, spared no pains to take care of them physically as well as educationally, and tried to secure for them the recognition he felt they deserved. During his tenure as Dean of the College of Arts and Sciences at Yenching, Hung came across two students worthy of such efforts.

The first one was Li Ch'ung-hui, son of a Presbyterian minister in Peking. In 1925, when a series of petty thefts at the Fourth Dormitory came to Hung's attention, he gave authorization for an ex-policeman to be hired to patrol the premises. Li Ch'ung-hui, as president of the Student Council, came to see Hung. Saying he was convinced that the thefts were committed by one of the students, he suggested that Hung let the policeman go and leave the matter to the Student Council. The thefts stopped. Hung, wondering what the Student Council had done, called Li into his office. Li explained that they had indeed caught the thief; but he refused to divulge to Hung the name of the person, saying that the culprit was contrite, that all stolen goods had been returned to the owners, and that there was no necessity to pursue the matter further. Hung was very impressed.

Later, when Hung learned from other students that Li was sick with tuberculosis, Hung found out where he lived and went across the city to visit him. It was a cold day; a little coal brazier was burning in the middle of the small, cramped house; the windows were all pasted up with paper; the air was suffocating. While Li stayed in his bed coughing, his parents fussed over Hung. Hung, seeing that it was no environment for someone with tuberculosis to recuperate, wrote his friend Pinkie Thornburg in the United States, describing to him the situation. The expected check for a thousand dollars came with his reply. This enabled Hung to lodge Li at a Buddhist temple in the Western Hills, with a reliable servant to cook and take care of him. On good food, rest, and nearly half a year of salutary mountain air, Li recovered. Pinkie, on his own initiative, paid for Li to go to the University of Chicago Graduate School for his doctorate. Li died while a student there.

The second unusually talented student to whom Hung gave special help had a dramatic career. This was Chang Wen-li, also known as Chang Yen-che. During Hung's last year as Dean, Chang applied for transfer in his third year from Fukien Christian University. His transcript was excellent, but no recommendation accompanied it. Hung learned from Dean Roderick Scott of Fukien Christian that no recommendations had been sent because the university hoped to retain Chang. From Chang himself, Hung learned that organizing and then running an effective, democratic student government had so occupied his time that he felt his studies had been neglected. Hung admitted him, but his reputation had preceded him. The new transfer was elected president of the Yenching Student Council as soon as he arrived. To extricate the council from its financial difficulties, Chang got permission for it to run the university mail service and dining room, which were managed with great success. He became such a celebrity on campus that the university police were known to salute him; the only other person they saluted was Stuart.

Hung asked Chang Wen-li about his plans after graduation. He said he intended to go back to his mountain village in Fukien to start a high school.

"My father is a poor country preacher of the Dutch Reformed Church. His whole year's salary amounts to about thirty-five dollars a month. When I graduated from our little primary school, the farmers in the district pooled together some money and sent me off to high school. To tell you frankly, the farmers in China are the most oppressed people. What we need is a revolution. I have a commitment to go back to the village when I finish my study."

When Hung asked him whether he had learned enough for what he planned to do, Chang answered, no. He hoped some day to study with Thomas Carver at Harvard, but for the time being he was too poor. Hung made a decision on the spot. Taking Chang into his confidence, he told him that he was negotiating to teach at Harvard for a year and offered to take care of Chang's expenses if Chang would accompany him. In the fall of 1928, therefore, Chang Wen-li found himself at Harvard, partly at Hung's expense. Hung also solicited donations for him from Leighton Stuart, Lucius Porter, and other Yenching faculty members, enough for him to spend a year in the United States and return to China by way of Europe. When Chang did in fact return to China, he turned up unannounced at Hung's house with an extraordinary tale. But meanwhile, Hung himself had undergone changes.

OF HIS DECISION to resign from the deanship, Hung said, "In 1927, I woke up to the fact that there would be terrible upheavals in the educational institutions in China. Some of the brightest students we had at Yenching were Communists. While many of the students appreciated my service as Dean, there was a strong undercurrent of resentment against me. Moreover, all these years, I did not have time to reflect, to study, to know some of the better faculty members and good students. It had demanded too much of a sacrifice on my part. And I had greater things in mind for myself and for Yenching. So I begged to resign from the deanship but remained on those committees with responsibilities for the library and university standards. Of course, Stuart still wanted to keep me on; but I had a hunch that in some spots of his heart, he was glad that I would no longer have my hand on the central core of the university administration. I suspected that because many times he had said to me, 'William, this is your decision. But I believe this American method of yours won't work.' He felt that in China, I was too Americanized, that in China you have to be more flexible."

This is confirmed by a letter from Leighton Stuart to Eric M. North found in the archives of the United Board for Christian Higher Education in Asia. In this letter, dated March 8, 1926, Stuart wrote:

[Y]ou will be interested to know that for several weeks past there have been determined efforts on the part of these agitators to provoke a strike unless William Hung was dismissed from the Deanship. He has been so strict in enforcing our standards and in general maintaining severe discipline that this has been rather irritating to a large number of students. It has been aggravated by a certain amount of self confidence, and brusqueness of manner has exposed him to the charge of being not really Chinese, but an Americanized, mechanized, efficiency overlord, lacking in human qualities which Chinese stress. He has had the brunt of putting into effect policies made necessary by somewhat lax discipline and easy going office methods of his predecessors, just at the time of this swelling out of nationalistic feeling and the Communist and other hostile agitations. There has been just enough disaffection among the students enflamed by some of the older teachers of Chinese, whose dignity he has somewhat ruffled to give an occasion to outside agitators. The Chinese papers have recently contained a number of malicious paragraphs intimating that there was soon going to be a big blow-up in this University that outwardly had seemed so placid through all the recent disturbed months.

Stuart may not have fully appreciated all that was done by Hung. In his memoir, *Fifty Years in China,* he mentioned Hung only once, in reference to a speech Hung made. There was no acknowledgment that it was under Hung's deanship that Yenching emerged from an obscure college run by Western missionaries to a nationally recognized Chinese university that participated fully in the intellectual life of China. So glaring was the oversight that in a preface written at Stuart's request, Hu Shih, who had taught at Peking University when Hung was Dean at Yenching, and who between 1931 and 1937 was Dean of Arts at Peking University, felt compelled to fill the gap by paying a side tribute to Hung. He wrote:

As a friend and neighbor of Yenching who watched its growth with keen interest, I would like to say that Dr. Stuart's great success as a university builder lay chiefly in two directions. First, he and his colleagues planned and built up, literally *from scratch*, a full-sized university—the greatest of all the thirteen Christian colleges in China—with one of the most beautiful university campuses in the world. And secondly, this university of his dreams became in the course of time more and more a Chinese university, which, with the help of the Harvard-Yenching Institute of Chinese Studies, was the first of all the Protestant missionary colleges to develop an excellent department of Chinese studies.

I would like to pay a tribute to the Chinese scholars of Yenching, notably to Dr. William Hung (Hung Yeh), who deserves special credit for building up a very good Chinese library at Yenching, for editing and publishing the excellent *Yenching Journal of Chinese Studies* and that most useful series—the *Harvard-Yenching Sinological Index Series.*

It should be noted that in the spring of 1930, when Hung was in the United States, on a leave of absence from Yenching University, there was an attempt by the Yenching faculty to reinstate William Hung as Dean. Hung declined the invitation.

CHAPTER TWELVE

Manuscripts, Murals, and High Finance

THE STORY of how Yenching came to be a major beneficiary of the Hall estate and how the Harvard-Yenching Institute came into being is worth telling here. When Charles Martin Hall, who discovered the electrolytic process for separating aluminum from bauxite, died a rich bachelor in 1914, he had stipulated that a third of his estate should go to educational work controlled by Americans or the British in Asia or the Balkans. By 1929, when all the funds had been distributed, something over fourteen million dollars had been given away in this category. Hall had named two executors for his estate: Arthur Vining Davis, President of the Aluminum Company of America, and Homer H. Johnson, one of the company's legal counsels. In 1921, Henry W. Luce was able to obtain fifty thousand dollars for Yenching from the Hall estate. Furthermore, having found out there were millions more to be disposed of before 1929, he arranged for Stuart to meet the executors in the United States. Luce had already won over Johnson; it was up to Stuart to impress Davis, whom he met over lunch in New York.

According to the story Hung remembered Stuart telling (and differing in some amusing details from the one found in Stuart's own memoir), the meeting went as follows: All through their lunch, the conversation never once touched on the subject of money. It was not until after coffee and dessert were served that Davis said, "I have only five minutes left. State your case." Stuart, perspiring profusely, began to talk about Yenching's need for funds; but before too long, Davis cut him short, "Just tell me how much you want." Stuart suggested a million, to which Davis answered, "You shall have it." It left Stuart with the uneasy feeling that he should perhaps have asked for much more.

Meanwhile, Wallace Donham, who knew Homer Johnson and was Dean of the Harvard Graduate School of Business Administration, had his eye on the money for Harvard. In 1924, Davis instructed Stuart to work with Donham to develop a joint program that would satisfy the stipulations of the Hall estate and benefit both Harvard and Yenching. Under consideration was a Harvard Oriental Institute with a field office in Peking. The idea was the brainchild of Langdon Warner, then Harvard's "China's Expert," a Fogg Museum Fellow who taught courses on Japanese and Chinese art at Harvard. Warner had studied art in Japan and had made several trips to China. His love for China, however, was strictly limited to it arts. The Institute he had in mind would be primarily involved in archeological exploration and publications on art and archeology.

LATE ONE EVENING IN 1925, after Rhoda and the two Hung daughters had gone to bed, Hung received a phone call from a student, Wang Chin-jen, "There is something urgent I would like to see you about."

To avoid waking up the gatekeeper, Hung waited for Wang at the compound gate and led him into the living room. As soon as they entered the house, Wang, with tears rushing into his eyes, sank on his knees before Hung, "Dean Hung, you have to save me. I am a traitor to China."

Hung stared at him and managed to venture, "Wang Chin-jen, I don't think you are in a position to be a traitor. Usually, only people in high places can betray the country. You must have misjudged yourself."

Tears streaming down his face, Wang revealed that in his absence from Yenching the previous year, he had worked for a man from Harvard University called Langdon Warner, acting as his interpreter and making his travel arrangements for him on an exploration trip to the western parts of China. At Tun-huang, they stayed at a small temple right outside the caves, for Warner said he wanted to study the Buddhist relics there. One night, Wang woke up, found Warner missing, and discovered him in one of the grottos working with some cloth over one of the murals. Warner was startled to see Wang and tried to take him into his confidence. He explained that the murals on these walls were of great historical and artistic value. Unfortunately, he said, the Chinese were not interested in such matters; but as the universities in America were eager to study them, he was experimenting with a process, using cheesecloth saturated with glycerin, to see whether he could transfer some of the murals back to America. He said that if he was successful, he was going to return to China and hire Wang again. But he told him not to tell anybody, which led Wang to suspect that what he was doing was not authorized. Now this Warner was back with a big delegation of Americans. They had brought with them huge cans of glycerin and several dozen huge rolls of cheesecloth. Wang was certain that they wanted to take all the murals away.

Hung shuddered when he heard this. If Warner's plan was allowed to be carried out, it would complete the despoliation of one of the most important historical sites of China.

Tun-huang is located in the Lob Desert of western Kansu province, along the old Silk Road, travelled by caravans between China and Europe since time immemorial. Between the fourth and the tenth centuries A.D., a community of Buddhists had built monasteries here. In the cliffs above the monasteries, they carved thousands of Buddhist statues and covered the cave walls with miles of monumental murals. In the eleventh century, Tibetan tribes overran the oasis; the Buddhists fled, leaving behind them not only their murals and sculptures, but also embroideries, paintings, and manuscripts wonderfully preserved in a sealed cave. Among these were what became known as the world's oldest extant printed book, a book printed in A.D. 868, liturgical literature of Nestorian Christians in China dating to the seventh century A.D.; T'ang and Sung versions of the Chinese classics, which became important in determining the authenticity of later texts; many literary pieces in the vernacular, whose appearance altered scholars' understanding of the development of Chinese literature and social history; as well as innumerable writings in Sanskrit, Turkish, and other languages long dead.

In 1907, an Austrian in the service of the British colonial government in India named Aurel Stein made one of his many archeological expeditions overland from India to Chinese Turkestan. When he came to Tun-huang, he heard rumours of a fantastic cache of ancient manuscripts and paintings in the area. He traced it to the hills just beyond the oasis where a Taoist priest named Wang had made his home in an abandoned Buddhist temple in the cliffs. Stein posed as an admirer of the Buddhist saint Hsuan-tsang and convinced the priest to show him the hidden cave where the treasure was stored. He was stunned by the quantity, the antiquity, the quality, and the variety of the manuscripts, embroideries, and paintings before his eyes, many of them in perfect condition. After giving a generous donation to the priest, Stein carted away some nine thousand scrolls and returned to India quietly by the way he had come. He gave his finds to the British Museum and was consequently knighted by the British Crown.

Later on, Paul Pelliot, a prize student of the great French Sinologist, Édouard Chavannes, read Stein's report and also came to Tun-huang. Pelliot had been serving with the French Legation in Peking, spoke perfect Mandarin, and had had extensive contacts with the Chinese literati. He carted away about seven thousand scrolls. Before he shipped them to Paris, however, he showed some of the manuscripts to the scholars Lo Chen-yü and Wang Kuo-wei, who were astounded and excitedly invited other scholars to view them. Pelliot promised that he would have them catalogued and photographed so that Chinese would have access to them. He also told the Chinese that there were many more left in Tun-huang and that the government had better get to them before the dealers did.

In 1911, just before the Ch'ing dynasty toppled, the disintegrating Chinese bureaucracy was finally moved to do something about Tun-huang. An official serving in the Department of Education was sent to Tun-huang to collect the remaining eight thousand scrolls. On his way back, however, a merchant offered him a huge sum of money for some of the manuscripts. Since the official had already reported to Peking that eight thousand scrolls were on their way, they came up with the expedient of cutting many of the manuscripts in half, so that the official still had the right number to deliver and the merchant could sell the rest as specimens of ancient calligraphy. Hung himself later came to own a foot of Tun-huang manuscript. His colleague at Yenching, Jung Keng, one day brought to Hung a manuscript of a Buddhist text written in an interesting Han Dynasty script. It was about thirteen feet long. Jung, who had procured it from a second-hand book dealer, wanted to share it with several friends, at a dollar a foot. Hung took a foot.

Now Hung was called upon to save the Tun-huang murals from being carried off to Harvard. He instructed Wang Chin-jen to go ahead with the trip and act as if nothing was happening. The next morning, Hung went to see the Vice Minister of Education Ch'in Fen, who took immediate action. Ch'in sent a telegram to every governor, district magistrate, and police commissioner along the way to Tun-huang, saying that very soon, a delegation from a great institution in America would be coming for archeological study. He instructed the local authorities to provide these friends with ample protection and courteous treatment, but on no account allow them to touch any historical relics.

Two days later, Langdon Warner called on Stuart at Yenching. Stuart had heard from the Yenching trustees in America that Warner was coming and was expecting him. As a joint program between Harvard and Yenching was under negotiation, Stuart was perplexed and angered to learn that Warner had been in close contact with the government-run Peking University without Yenching's knowledge. Warner had evidently decided that if Harvard must affiliate with a Chinese institution in order to partake of the Hall estate, it should be a prestigious national university instead of the missionary-ridden Yenching. Stuart discussed the matter with Hung, and they consoled each other with the thought that this might not turn out to be the kind of venture they would care to associate with in any case. Nevertheless, Stuart invited the Harvard delegation to have dinner at the Western Returned Student Club, with Hung among the faculty members present. There were speeches after dinner, during which Warner spoke warmly of China's great tradition of arts. Hung also spoke and welcomed friends from abroad who had come to help the Chinese study their archeological relics. He admitted that until recently political and economic struggles had prevented his countrymen from studying the treasures of their past. Now, however, Chinese scholars felt strongly that relics should be studied and, moreover, that art objects should stay in China when there were specialists in the country competent to undertake the work. In those cases when it was necessary to take them out, they should be returned. The speech caused hardly a ripple. Everybody behaved politely, and many toasts followed.

Every place the Harvard delegation went, they were met by a big welcoming party. Out at Tun-huang, two soldiers were assigned to every foreigner. The soldiers were very polite, but they had been given strict instructions that the foreigners were not to disturb anything. Originally Warner had planned to hire several dozen camels to carry the loot over the mountains to India. With no loot to be had, that plan was abandoned; and they went back to Peking. A small mission hospital along their way in the oasis city of Lanchow found itself the surprised and grateful recipient of a tremendous quantity of glycerin and cheesecloth. Warner told Wang Chin-jen in private that the representative from Peking University, Ch'en Wan-li, was the fly in the ointment; for everywhere they went, Ch'en always called on the local yamen, and people would come out to "help" them. Later, Warner wrote a book, *The Long Old Road in China,* a well-written book marred by rather blatant racial slurs, describing principally his earlier trip to Tun-huang. Referring to his second trip, he lamented,

I could not guess that in a short seven months the whole Chinese nation was to stir in
its sleep and yawn so portentously that all we foreigners would be scuttling back to our
Legations. On that windswept track, with the spring still lingering two provinces away,
it never occurred to me that when I came that road again it would be in the fierce summer heat only to be turned back from the very gates of the Tun Huang chapels.

Ch'en Wan-li, who did not speak English, published his own book
about the trip, called *Hsi-hsing jih-chi* (*Diary of a Western Trip*) in
which he indicated that he suspected other people had known of the
Americans' intentions.

AFTER THIS DISASTROUS EXPEDITION to Tun-huang, Langdon Warner
was left out of subsequent Harvard-Chinese schemes to get the Hall
money, but the planning by Stuart and Donham continued. On New
Year's Day, 1928, Hung wrote the Crawfords,

More than two years ago an endowment of one million dollars was given to Harvard
University and Yenching University jointly for the promotion of advanced studies on
Chinese culture. It seems now probable that the fund might be increased . . . and the
work organized under what is known as Harvard-Yenching Institute . . . From the Yenching end I have been associated with the working out of the programme from the very
beginning.

The Harvard-Yenching Institute was, indeed, incorporated almost immediately that month in Massachusetts with a board of trustees composed of three Harvard members, three Yenching members, and three
outside members. Its administrative headquarters were to be located at
Harvard, but its principal activities were to be carried out at Yenching.
According to its articles of incorporation, dated January 5, 1928, the
purposes of the Institute were as follows:

To conduct and provide research, instruction and publication in the culture of China,
and/or elsewhere in Continental Asia and Japan, and/or Turkey and the Balkan States
in Europe and, in furtherance and not in limitation of the foregoing: . . . To carry on,
for properly prepared Chinese and Occidental scholars, research and educational work
of the type appropriate to a graduate school of arts and sciences, and, in so far as it may
appear expedient in order to prepare scholars for admission to the work of the Institute,
to develop through other institutions undergraduate work in China; to explore, discover, collect and preserve objects of culture and antiquities, or to aid museums or
others to do so.

The language of the agreement was vague and showed obvious marks
of compromise. On the whole, it was a triumph for Stuart, and for those

like Hung who were deeply engrossed with him in formulating policies to build a first-rate institution. It made Yenching University an instantaneous international center for Chinese studies. The Institute was to provide funds for Yenching to develop graduate-level programs to which other universities, including Harvard, could send the cream of their students in Chinese studies for further training. It also opened the door for Yenching graduate students to be admitted into Harvard. In addition to having access to $4,500,000 granted to the Harvard-Yenching Institute itself by the Hall estate, the Institute at Yenching was to administer the distribution of some $1,800,000 to other American-controlled (Christian) universities in China to strengthen their Chinese studies program, which naturally gave Yenching tremendous power. And it was an opportunity and a power that Yenching put to brilliant use: Over the ensuing decades, the list of scholars who were trained by the Institute, whose research or publications were made possible by the Institute, or who were otherwise associated with it reads startlingly like an international Who's Who in Chinese studies.

At Harvard, several eminent Sinologists, including Paul Pelliot, were invited to Cambridge to advise on the direction of the Institute at its inception in 1928. Stuart proposed that Hung and Lucius Porter be invited as representatives of Yenching. After this flashy beginning, not much happened until Serge Elisséeff assumed the directorship in 1934. Elisséeff, whose family was prominent in pre-revolutionary Russia, was the first Westerner to have graduated from Tokyo Imperial University. He later emigrated to France and studied under Paul Pelliot. A man of great intellectual capacity and great charm, he was director of the Harvard-Yenching Institute until 1956, when he was succeeded by his student, Edwin O. Reischauer. He expanded the scope of the Institute at Harvard to include Japanese studies and built up a Far Eastern Languages Department at Harvard, the first of its kind in the United States.

With the Communist takeover of China and the dissolution of Yenching University in 1952, the activities of the Harvard-Yenching Institute moved to Taiwan, Hong Kong, Japan, and Korea, where it continues to give aid to educational institutions and to inter-institutional research organizations. It awards fellowships to Asian students for graduate study in the humanities and social sciences. Every year, it pays for the travel and living expenses of more than a dozen Asian scholars to spend a year at Harvard to pursue research in their respective fields. It also maintains the Harvard-Yenching Library in Cambridge, which has become one of the best, if not the best East Asian library outside of Asia.

In retrospect, it might perhaps be accurate to say that the uses to which Stuart and Donham put the Hall estate monies departed from the original intent of Charles Martin Hall. It is safe to conjecture that Mr. Hall, in stipulating that a third of his estate be used for "education in foreign lands, to wit, Japan, continental Asia, Turkey, and the Balkan states in Europe," did not envision a joint Harvard-Yenching program focusing on the investigation of Chinese antiquities. Hall very likely had in mind the promotion of modern sciences in these areas of the world. The current activities of the Harvard-Yenching Institute, with its widely diffused objectives, is probably more true to the intention of that good man. Whether the influence of the current activities of the Institute will prove to be as far-reaching as that of its first decades, only time will tell.

CHAPTER THIRTEEN

Harvard 1928–1930

WHEN HANFORD CRAWFORD received the news in 1928 that Hung was coming back to the United States to teach at Harvard, he was so pleased he sent him two thousand dollars so that the Hungs might take a leisurely trip through Europe on their way to Cambridge. They visited Rome, Paris, and London, wandering around places whose history Hung had earlier studied so assiduously.

HUNG was to hold the title of Lecturer at Harvard and to give a few courses in Chinese history. At age thirty-five, he had come late to Sinology as it was practiced in the West. It was a field dominated by American missionaries and European aristocratic eccentrics, like Baron A. von Stael-Holstein, also at Harvard that year, who told Hung he first went to Peking in 1916 "in pursuit of a lost Sanskrit genitive infinitive." Chinese scholars were regarded as useful only as language teachers or as "native informants." They were held to be generally lacking in "critical faculties." True, Hung knew more of the Confucian classics than any Western Sinologist; he had grown up in a Chinese society and knew its living traditions; but he had neither a Ph.D. nor scholarly publications to demonstrate his mastery of the kind of knowledge and reasoning valued in the West. When he tried to make the acquaintance of noted Sinologists in Europe, therefore, he was given the cold shoulder everywhere. At Oxford, Professor W. E. Soothill tested him on various points of recondite scholarship before he accepted Hung as an equal. Hung was therefore relieved to find a congenial atmosphere at Harvard.

As soon as the Hungs arrived in Cambridge, they went to call on President and Mrs. Lowell. The Lowells were not home; but a few days later, they came to the Hung's apartment at 79 Martin Street and climbed three flights of stairs to return the call. It was not until later that the Hungs found out that a new lecturer was not expected to make social calls on the President of Harvard.

Harvard in the late 1920s still retained the social climate of a small college. Even though the salaries of faculty members were not high, everyone could afford to have maids; and there was much entertaining back and forth. In addition, there were what were known as "shop clubs" in which members of different departments met regularly to present informal papers on some of the more perplexing problems of their respective fields. The history department also had a Thursday lunch presided over by the chairman of the department, Arthur M. Schlesinger. Through these lunches, Hung came to know Robert Blake quite well. When Hung proposed in 1930 that the Harvard-Yenching Institute finance a Sinological Index Series to compile systematic indices to all the Chinese classics and make them accessible to modern scholars, Blake, who was a trustee of the Institute, strongly supported the project.

Hung taught a big undergraduate class, "History of the Far East since 1793," a course first conceived and developed by Archibald Cary Coolidge. Seventeen ninety-three was the year of the famous Macartney Mission in which Lord Macartney, representing King George III of England, called on the Ch'ien-lung Emperor to propose direct trade and formal diplomatic relations between the two countries. The Chinese emperor's haughty response was that China possessed all things in abundance and that the two countries had better remain apart. Historians customarily looked back to this episode with regret, blaming Ch'ien-lung for his "ignorant conceit" but for which China might have eased into the world community more smoothly. In teaching the course, Hung was able to introduce Chinese materials made public after the deposed child-emperor, P'u-yi, was ousted from the Forbidden City in 1912; these threw new light on the reason for the mission's failure. It turned out that a letter from King George to the Chinese emperor had been sent to Naples to be translated from Latin into Chinese at a Catholic school operated to prepare Italian and Portuguese priests for missionary work in China. The Catholics naturally disliked the notion of a strong Protestant presence in China. They contrived to send a copy of the translated letter to China before Lord Macartney arrived there. The Catholics, in transmitting the letter, warned the Chinese that the British had ulterior motives and were not to be trusted – that the letter mentioned the British had a vast network of colonies around the world which she governed with beneficence when, in fact, her biggest colony in America had just rebelled and had successfully overthrown British rule. It was little wonder that the mission failed. Hung caused the lecture hall to shake with laughter with tales of how on the day his lordship was to see the emperor, his carefully orchestrated, magnificent procession got inextricably entangled with a great herd of pigs being driven to the market for slaughter.

Hung's office was located on the fourth floor of Widener Library. He was given a key and allowed to roam freely in the library at any time of day or night. In those more gracious times, there were no guards checking books and bags at exits, and library personnel made daily rounds of the offices to pick up books that the professors no longer needed. Hung was exhilirated by all the resources housed in that building. He was made aware, for instance, of materials that shed new light on Chinese diplomatic history: German diplomatic documents published by the victorious Allies after World War I, materials from the Imperial Russian archive made public by the new Communist government, Tokugawa records newly made available, Western accounts of the Taiping rebellion, and so forth. Hung wasted no time in alerting his friends in China, Chiang T'ing-fu and Chien Yu-wen, both in the fields of modern history, of the existence of these valuable documents. He also found an unpublished Chinese manuscript on the Taiping rebellion that he later published himself. The single book that intrigued him the most, however, was one that at first sight had no connection with China. It was a late-nineteenth-century German book, *Canon der Finsternisse,* by Theodor Ritter von Oppolzer, which calculated the dates of solar eclipses from 1208 B.C. to A.D. 2161, with maps of where on earth the eclipses could be seen. Hung, like many other scholars in China then, was much interested in the reliability of historical dates given in Chinese documents; he saw at once that he had come upon a priceless historical tool for authenticating Chinese historical records.

The book and his interest in questions of dates gave him an opportunity to impress Paul Pelliot, who was also at Harvard in 1928. One day, he was auditing Pelliot's class when the great Sinologist mentioned that the earliest event with a scientifically ascertainable date in Chinese history was in the year 776 B.C., for an eclipse was cited in a poem in the *Canon of Poetry* as occurring on the Hsin-mao day in the tenth month in the sixth reign year of King Yu. Hung restrained himself from correcting Pelliot in front of the whole class but afterwards went up to him and invited him home for a Chinese dinner cooked by his wife. After dinner, Hung was able to demonstrate to Pelliot that although the poem in question said the eclipse occurred on the Hsin-mao day of the tenth month, nowhere did it asign it to the sixth year of King Yu's reign. That assignment was traceable to the astronomer-monk I-hsing in the T'ang dynasty who, after calculating the day of the probable eclipse, had figured that it must have been in the sixth year of King Yu. In truth, more recent and more precise calculation by the German Oppolzer showed that the eclipse that occurred that day could be seen only from the middle of the Pacific Ocean. Pelliot was impressed, and the two men became good friends. It was through Pelliot's recommendation that Hung in 1937 received the Prix Stanislas Julien awarded by the French Académie des Inscription et Belles Lettres.

In the field of Sinology, Pelliot was as revered for his meticulousness as he was feared for his acerbic pen. He left Harvard after only one semester, and Hung picked up his course on Chinese historical research methods. The subject Hung chose to discuss with the class of four students was the authenticity of the so-called "ancient-script" recension of the *Canon of History.* Pelliot had written an article on the subject, which Hung used in class; but he pointed out that there was a numerical error in Pelliot's table comparing the chapters of the "ancient-script" recension and the "modern-script" recension. One of the students, James Ware, stood up immediately and declared, "Pelliot never makes a mistake."

Hung retorted, "I can make mistakes. You can make mistakes. Pelliot can also make mistakes."

The next year Ware, who was leaving to study in France, came to see Hung to ask whether he might question Pelliot about the alleged error in the table. He wrote from Paris that Hung was right, Pelliot had indeed made a mistake.

Hung's encounter with the other despoiler of the Tun-huang treasures was not so pleasant. The Harvard-Yenching Institute trustees had authorized $100,000 from the Harvard-Yenching fund to have Sir Aurel Stein organize another expedition to China. Leighton Stuart heard about it and told the trustees he could not support the expedition; in addition, he urged Hung to go see Sir Aurel to try to dissuade him from going. Hung called on him at the Commander Hotel in Cambridge and had a long talk with him. Stein, by then a wizened old man, lectured Hung, "Mr. Hung, you are young; you do not know. I have been in China long before and many times. The Chinese officials—they do not care. I know how to manage them."

When Stein arrived in China, however, he found that in 1929, fiery Western-educated young Chinese much like William Hung were in charge of the government. He had to request a change in authorization from the Institute to do research in Afghanistan instead.

Hung published his first scholarly writing in English in 1929, a review of Kenneth Scott Latourette's *A History of Christian Missions in China* (7). Hung commended the book's objectivity but pointed out that the author did not make sufficient use of Chinese texts and had entirely overlooked some sources in French. He later felt that the tone of the review was too brazen and suspected that it earned him Latourett'e lifelong enmity.

THE HUNGS originally were to stay in Cambridge only one year; but since Rhoda was expecting a child and Hung was enjoying himself immensely, he applied for a year's extension of his appointment. When Agnes was born, Hung arrived at the hospital to find Rhoda crying in her disappointment that their third child was not a boy. Nevertheless, Agnes was to become the parents' favorite.

Many friends from Hung's New York days visited them in Cambridge those two years. Pinkie Thornburg, who was busy keeping afloat the many companies in which he held a major interest, came a few times. Another visitor, who arrived unexpectedly one day in a big car, was a one-time carpenter from Foochow, named Dick Uong. In 1921, by working on a steamer, he had made his way from the Philippines to New York, where he had jumped ship only to be apprehended in Canada. Back in New York, the immigration officer, unable to find anyone else who could understand Uong's southern dialect, had in desperation called Hung, whom he had once heard make a speech. When Hung was able to learn how determined Dick Uong had been to come to America and that he had a marketable skill, the immigration officer was touched and said if he could find a sponsor who would guarantee he did not become a public charge, he could stay. Hung had placed him with a retired teacher in Albany, New York. When they were reunited in Cambridge, Uong told Hung that after practicing his trade as a cabinetmaker for a few years, he had gone to the University of Maine to study pulp and paper chemistry. Now he was employed as chief chemist in charge of research at the Fitchburg Paper Company in Massachusetts. Having seen Hung's name in the newspaper one day, he had come to pay his respects.

Hung's activities in the United States were not limited to his work at Harvard, for he was in high demand as a public speaker. Nor were his interests limited to historical issues, for he was very much the William Hung who had a stake in the fate of modern China. On a panel of the Foreign Policy Association in New York, he appeared with Arthur N. Holcombe and D. Z. T. Yui to discuss Nationalist China (6); and he participated in many debates with Japanese propagandists in which he combatted his opponents with a combination of logic, eloquence, and an uncanny ability to get the audience to laugh with him. After speaking at a national convention of the Rotary Club, he appeared on the cover of the *International Rotarian.*

A speech at the prestigious Hungry Club of Pittsburgh had the personal bonus for him of giving him the chance to get together again with his American sister, Ruth Crawford Mitchell, who was now teaching at the University of Pittsburgh. His meetings with the elder Crawfords, however, were tinged with sadness. In the stockmarket crash of 1929, the Crawfords lost most of their fortune. When Hung visited them that year, Hanford Crawford was very ill and could relieve his distress only by playing the piano. He expressed regret that he could not fulfill a pledge of $250 to the Fukien Christian University. Hung was glad to be able to send the money in Crawford's name. Hanford Crawford died in January, 1930. His wife, who was never the same after his death, died later that year.

THE HUNGS went back to China by way of the Hawaiian Islands, where Rhoda had grown up and where Hung had been offered a visiting professorship at the University of Hawaii the previous year. At the Honolulu immigration office, Hung was annoyed by the questionnaires he had to fill out—one each for himself, his wife, and his three daughters. On each were the questions, "Are you a Communist?" "Are you an anarchist?" On little Agnes's form, Hung put yes to both questions. When queried by the customs official, Hung insisted that the baby was an anarchist because she did not recognize any form of government, and that she was a Communist because she did not respect other people's rights to their property.

Hung was returning to a China to which he was psychologically reconciled. First of all, since the Nationalists had won the Civil War, people with modern education were in charge. Many of his fraternity brothers had moved into prominent positions and were hopeful of building a humane, democratic government. Secondly, he found himself comforted by an image of the stoic, peasant masses, who despite the turmoil of politics and the hardships of life, endure with a faith in the ultimate justice of the universe. In 1930, he wrote an article describing a popular woodblock print that had been pasted on the walls of merchants' and peasants' homes for centuries (14). It shows a man contentedly eating, with a rice bowl in his left hand and chopsticks in his right. He leans on the leg of a huge ideograph that says *t'ien*. *T'ien* may be translated "heaven," "nature," or "God" and vaguely means all of them to the Chinese masses; for it represents the force that levels, balances, and harmonizes the human and physical worlds. In the article, Hung expressed the fear that this picture, which had long been hanging on the walls of humble homes and shops would soon be replaced by garish advertising posters, pictures of movie stars, and political leaflets. But for the time being, it was a useful emblem of a culture in which the simple achievement of being alive and eating was a source of satisfaction.

Part Four

William Hung in his study, ca. 1961

CHAPTER FOURTEEN

Old Ties and New Friends

HUNG RETURNED in 1930 to a Yenching University much changed in his absence of two years. First of all, it had moved from its makeshift, unheated classrooms and offices in the walled city of Peking into its magnificent new campus in the suburb. Furthermore, the university was reorganized to conform to regulations set down by the newly established Nationalist government in Nanking. The College of Arts and Sciences, for instance, was now split into a College of Arts, a College of Natural Sciences, and a College of Public Affairs. As the government required all institutions of higher learning be headed by a Chinese, a pious man of impeccable character was found in the person of Wu Lei-ch'uan to serve as "Chancellor," even though the real authority still flowed from Stuart's office.

Soon after Hung returned to Yenching, he became engaged in the last of the many conflicts with his old friend Timothy Lew. Lew had also been travelling. Between 1926 and 1928, he lectured at various colleges in the United States and Europe. When he returned to Yenching in 1928, he was asked to be the executive secretary of the Harvard-Yenching Institute in China. With funds from the Institute, Lew proceeded to organize a Research School of Chinese Studies (Kuo-hsueh yen-chiu-so) at Yenching, patterned after those of Tsinghua and Peking Universities. To do research, he recruited old-style Chinese scholars. Hung had always been opposed to the idea of such an institution. He felt strongly that Chinese studies should be an integral part of the college and graduate school, not isolated as a separate entity. To have a school of "Chinese Studies" isolated from the rest of the university was as absurd as lumping European sciences, literature, history, and so forth into a school for "European Studies." Moreover, he believed that Chinese studies should be carried out by people with modern training, who knew something of the world outside China. When one of Hung's prize students, Nieh Ch'ung-ch'i, wrote to Hung in Cambridge to ask whether he should apply for admission to the new Research School, Hung encouraged him to go ahead, thinking that it would be an improvement in Nieh's situation from teaching high school. When Nieh was refused admission, over much less qualified candidates, Hung was furious. As soon as he returned to Yenching, he took Nieh under his wing to work as an editor on the Harvard-Yenching Sinological Index Series and set himself to dismantle the Research School. Timothy Lew, replaced by Lucius Porter as executive secretary of the Harvard-Yenching Institute, was no match for Hung on this issue, especially when he had become preoccupied with other matters of larger national concern. He eventually left Yenching in 1936 to become a member of the Legislative Yuan in Nanking.

Hung's friendship with Stuart, by contrast, remained close. Together, they went on day hikes to the Western Hills. On their way back, they liked to stop at Wen-ch'üan (Warm Spring), where for a small fee they could rent a private room with a pool filled with about two feet of sulphur water. The water came in through one hole in the ground and went out another and was thus kept fresh. Sitting face to face soaking in the tepid water, they rubbed their backs against the rough cement wall of the pool. Soon, Hung would take out his pipe, and Stuart his, which he used only occasionally; and they would spend long hours making observations on events and people amid the swirl of sulphur steam and tobacco fumes.

Hung's stay at Yenching University this time lasted from 1930 to 1946, sixteen years in all if we include the years when the campus was occupied by the Japanese. His official titles were Professor of History, Director of the Graduate Institute of Letters, as well as Editor-in-Chief of the Harvard-Yenching Institute Sinological Index Series. Hung was Executive Secretary of the Harvard-Yenching Institute in 1940 before it was closed down in China by the Japanese, and then again in 1945–1946 when it was reopened.

Hung continued to chair the Yenching Library Committee, and was responsible during those years for acquisitions, not only for the Yenching University Library but also for much of the Oriental collection at Harvard. He brought the Harvard librarian, Ch'iu K'ai-ming, back with him to Yenching to reorganize the Yenching Library, and set down the policy that for every Chinese, Japanese, or Korean book bought for

Yenching University, a copy should also be bought for Harvard. If it was a rare book or a manuscript, he usually had it sent to Harvard on the grounds that Harvard could better afford it, but not before he had had a facsimile made for Yenching. He contrived to borrow from other libraries books that were not on the market to have facsimiles made for Yenching and Harvard. Nevertheless, he did not see himself as a "bibliophile," a lover of rare or beautiful books; for if cheap reprints of a rare book were available, he favored them over the original, the better to stretch the library dollar.

JUST WHEN many of Hung's earlier friends were becoming powerful members of the Nationalist government, he moved away from them. On one of his trips to Nanking to visit his brother David, he was told by a common friend that H. H. Kung, then Minister of Finance, wished Hung would come see him sometime. Hung said, "He should be thankful that I don't go to see him. There must be a roomful of people in his outer office waiting to see him every day. If I went to see him, he would feel obliged as an old friend to see me first. Now, this would inevitably give rise to many disagreeable situations, both for him and for me. People, thinking that I have great influence with a man of his position, would ask me to convey messages for them, to help them to secure employment, to do this and to do that. I would be pressured to comply with their requests, though I know full well that requests of this sort are the last thing in the world he needs."

Instead, Hung became deeply attached to a man who in mentality was closer to his father, a man who kept a concubine and was wrongly reputed to smoke opium, a man who obstinately refused to take root in the twentieth century. He was Teng Chih-ch'eng (Wen-ju), a historian of astounding erudition and phenomenal memory. It was said that he could name the day, month, and year of any major political event, and could recall the page number of any quotation from almost any standard classical text. He taught for many years at Peking University before he, like several other profesors, moved on to Yenching in the late 1920s when, owing to financial difficulties, Peking University dragged on for months without paying salaries to its faculty. He looked down his nose at anyone who went abroad to study, saving his strongest invectives for Hu Shih. "Hey, now there is back from America this fellow called Hu Shih, do you know him?" he would ask his students at class. Then shaking his head, he would sigh, "He is hopeless, hopeless!" His hostility may, however, have been merely part of an eccentric pose; for he made an exception readily enough for Hung.

Every Friday morning, Teng would arrive in a rickshaw at the Hungs in his long gown, with his cane. Being a gentleman of the old school, he never deigned to walk on the street even though he lived only five minutes away. He stayed for lunch and the rest of the afternoon, leaving behind him an ashtray heaped with smelly French cigarette stubs. Hung's eldest daughter Ruth disliked him so much that she hid a broom with the handle down behind the door whenever he came, a superstitious trick that she learned from the servants, which was supposed to get the guest out of the house. It never worked. Hung imbibed a tremendous amount of history and art from conversing with this dour man. Teng, in turn, obviously delighted in Hung's company.

The Hungs' house on the Yenching Campus at 54 South Compound was designed by Hung himself. It had a direct entrance to his study so that students who came to see him did not have to go through the living room. The living room and the dining room were separated by movable partitions so that the two rooms could be connected for sit-down banquets of twenty to thirty people. Outside in the garden was a pavilion at the entrance of which Hung had planted two wisteria trees. Every year in May, when the wisterias were in full bloom, Hung and Teng Chih-ch'eng invited some of the elderly men of Peking, well-versed in the art of making poetry, to celebrate the coming of spring properly with games, wine, and rhymed couplets, the way their fathers had done before them.

FOR MANY MONTHS IN 1931, Hung received in the mail formidable-looking publications in Russian, with no return address. Then one evening in the fall, when he was working late in his study, someone rapped on the window pane outside and Hung looked out to see a face pressed against the glass. After getting over his fright, he recognized Chang Wen-li, his former student, and quickly let him in.

Hung, true to his word, had taken Chang to Harvard so that he could realize his dream of studying with Thomas Carver. Carver told Hung that Chang was the brightest student he had ever had in all his years of teaching at Harvard. When Chang's year at Harvard was over, Carver recommended him to the U.S. Department of Agriculture as a consultant-specialist. The work enabled Chang to travel all over America collecting agricultural specimens and comparing farming methods. He went to say farewell to the Hungs early in the summer of 1930 before he left for Europe, where he planned to spend several weeks reading Karl Marx's manuscript of *Das Kapital* at the British Museum and then go on to Denmark to study the farm cooperatives there. Hung had not heard from him since.

Now Hung found out that Chang had been in the Soviet Union. He had been contacted by a Russian agent in Denmark. The Russians knew that he was familiar with the cultivation of cotton in the southern part of the United States, and they wanted him to help Russia grow its own cotton. Chang accepted the invitation and spent several months travelling in Russia, testing soil. He was provided with an interpreter and was paid handsomely by the government. Since he had difficulty spending his salary, he bought books and government documents with the rubles and sent them to Hung's address in Peking. When conditions appropriate for cotton were found in the Ukraine, he was put in charge of organizing the cotton plantations there. As soon as it appeared that the plantations would be successful, a beautiful woman was sent to teach him Russian. Chang realized that the Soviet government wanted to keep him there. On a trip to Siberia, therefore, he quietly slipped away from the party. Hiding during the daytime and walking at night, he made his way to Manchuria. By the time he reached Peking, he had exhausted his money and sold all his possessions.

Hung gave Chang a hearty meal. After he had bathed and changed into clean clothes, Hung asked him what his plan was now. Chang said that his conviction that China needed a rural revolution remained unshaken. He intended eventually to go back to his native Fukien, but he would like to stay a while in Peking so that he could clarify his own thoughts of what the basis of such a revolution should be.

Chang stayed with the Hungs for four months, during which he worked out a paper entitled "Productionism" ("Sheng-ch'an chu-i"), summing up a set of political, economic, and educational principles that he felt would turn a chaotic China into a powerful state. He drew from such diverse sources as Mencius, Jesus, Lincoln, Lenin, and the Bulgarian agrarian revolutionary, Aleksandr Stambolisky (1879–1923). His prescription for China was an authoritarian, socialist government based not on the maxims of Marx but on humanitarianism. With some revisions by Hung, the paper was printed in the form of an anonymous pamphlet for private circulation. Some of those who read the pamphlet suggested that the presentation was too dry and that in order to be accessible to more people, it should be worked into a utopian novel.

Hung jokingly answered that if he were ever stranded in a desert, away from people and books, he might just attempt such a work to kill time. It was not Hung's fate to be stranded in a desert; but he was imprisoned by the Japanese for five months, where composing just such a novel in his mind helped keep Hung sane. In the meantime, Chang Wen-li went south to pit his ideas against a harsh political environment.

CHINA'S largely self-sufficient economy was barely affected by the Great Depression. For Hung, however, it had two consequences. First of all, the Harvard-Yenching Institute underwent some belt-tightening and the budget for the Sinological Index Series project was cut. Secondly, it brought his friend Pinkie Thornburg to China.

Hung received a long telegram from Pinkie in 1933 saying that he was planning to visit China that summer and asking could Hung arrange a program for him. Just as Hung was wondering how Pinkie could have time to travel with all his business ventures, he showed up in Peking in April, unannounced. He said that all his businesses had come to a standstill, most of the stocks he owned were now worthless, and he was being sued by different associates for twenty million dollars. His lawyer had advised him to take a trip somewhere, so he planned to stay in China for six months. This put Hung in a quandary. There was nothing he would enjoy more than acting as a travel guide to his dear friend Pinkie; but with two more months of school to go, what could he do with this restless, vigorous man? He had the brilliant idea that during these two months, Pinkie should make himself an expert on Chinese porcelain and start a collection of his own. This drew an enthusiastic response from Pinkie. So Pinkie pored over English, French, and German books on porcelain that Hung brought home from the library and made a decision to specialize in crackleware — pottery with fine cracks produced by premature cooling — the aesthetic value of which was then not fully appreciated.

Rhoda took upon herself the responsibility of taking Pinkie around to the antique dealers, but she soon found out he did not need her at all. He knew all the tricks of getting a good deal. His corpulent, genial person, the very image of a Buddha, made him a favorite among the Chinese merchants. He also had a repertoire of amusing antics. Rhoda related to Hung how one day, a beggar woman thrust her basket in the face of this amiable-looking foreigner, only to be repelled by these indignant words: "No, no, I don't need it. Thank you very much."

When the woman persisted, Pinkie acted as if he could no longer decline and took a copper coin out of the basket as he thanked the woman profusely, to the general hilarity of the crowd that had gathered around him. Transferring his negotiating skills from American corporate boardrooms to the marketplaces of Peking, Pinkie was able to assemble a fine collection of Chinese crackleware for less than two thousand dollars—little more than it took to ship the pieces back to the United States.

When summer arrived, Hung and Pinkie, along with seven students, embarked on a memorable trip that took them to Shansi, Shensi, Honan, and Shantung. Carrying their bedding with them and staying in old-style Chinese inns and in barns, they found an inland China virtually unchanged from what it might have been a hundred years earlier. There were a few hints of change: While brides were still carried to their future homes in covered red sedan chairs, the placard that used to proclaim the groom to be an imperial degree-holder now announced that he had graduated from the county primary school. And the villagers were very curious about the world outside. Still, both their questions and their sources of information reflected their isolation. One of them asked Hung whether it was true that Americans were so much fairer in complexion than Chinese because they drank milk while Chinese drank tea. Another time, a member of the party asked whether he could get a newspaper anywhere. Newspapers were produced for his benefit—some in English, others in French, all several years old.

One evening in Shansi, they arrived at around eight o'clock in the evening in a village. The whole village had gone to bed, even though the summer sky was still light. But when the word got around that the party was from Peking and included a distinguished professor and an American, everybody got up and surrounded them with their torches. They asked for some food but were informed that nothing was to be had.

"Do you have eggs?" Hung asked.

"Eggs? Of course, we have eggs. Do you people eat eggs?"

Hung gave them a one-yuan bill, which in Peking would have fetched them 120 eggs. In a few minutes, two men returned carrying between them a basket of eggs and placed it politely in front of Hung.

"How many eggs are in there?" Hung asked, astounded.

There were four hundred! And the villagers gathered around to watch them be eaten.

In Shansi, before coming to their first major destination, the city of T'ai-ku, they passed through the Millionaire Village (Pai-wan ts'un), an impressive collection of high-walled residences. Having belonged to the old-style Shansi bankers who had dominated private banking in China from the Ming dynasty until Western-style banks drove them out of business, the buildings were now in sad disrepair. At a street vendor's stall, Hung picked up a Yuan edition of a book on chess for next to nothing. In T'ai-ku itself, he came across an even more intriguing find in the City Temple. A plaque predating the Opium War (1839–1842) commemorated an oath against opium taken by all the heads of households in the Millionaire Village. What specially interested Hung was that the oath had been led by the magistrate of T'ai-ku, one Ch'en Li-ho. Hung recognized Ch'en as the publisher of scholarly works by the historian Ts'ui Shu (1740–1816). Other writings by Ts'ui Shu had come into Hung's possession by accident, and he was just in the process of publishing them. When he saw Ch'en's name, he felt as if he had run into a colleague.

When they reached the Shansi capital of T'ai-yuan, the party paid a call on Governor Yen Hsi-shan to see whether he could help them with transportation. They walked through half a dozen courtyards, each heavily guarded by soldiers with machine guns, before reaching the gubernatorial residence. Governor Yen gave them a lavish banquet. He took an immediate liking to Pinkie and had his secretary draw up a document proclaiming him his "honorary consultant," before sending them on their way in a small bus.

ALL THIS TOOK PLACE against a background of war. In the south, the Nationalist government had hardly subdued the warlords when it found itself engaged in a life-and-death struggle with the Communists. In the north, the Japanese were busy grabbing as much as they could of China before a powerful central government could emerge. The Japanese gained control over Manchuria in 1931 and were inexorably inching their way towards Peking. In 1935, the Nationalist government, to buy time for itself, concluded a secret agreement with the Japanese to withdraw its army from North China and allow the area to be governed by a newly created autonomous body, the Hopei-Chahar Political Affairs Council. When the secret agreement became known, the students of Peking, especially those from Tsinghua and Yenching, were stirred into action. The idea that the Nationalist government should continue to fight the Communists but not the Japanese was anathema to them. Big demonstrations were organized. At this point in his life, Hung was simply glad he had nothing to do with university administration and felt sorry for his friend, Lu Chih-wei, who did.

Lu Chih-wei was the Acting Chancellor of Yenching from 1934 to 1937. A brilliant man with a Ph.D. in psychology from the University of Chicago, he was much respected for his fearless outspokenness. Looking back in 1978, Hung said of Lu Chih-wei, "He was a man who, to use an old Chinese phrase, 'detested evil as if it were his personal enemy.' Whenever he encountered something he thought was wrong, he wanted to root it out right away. There was no room for compromise. A man like that takes an awful lot on himself. It explains why he was so attracted to Communist ideology; it also explains why he suffered so much under the Communists."

During the December Ninth Movement in 1935, when the students organized to protest the Nationalist government's policy towards Japan, the mastermind at Yenching was Ch'en Chieh. He was the grandson of the emperor's tutor, Ch'en Pao-ch'en, and was known among the students as Ch'en the Fat or Ch'en the Dilettante. He wore only silk and rode a private rickshaw around the campus. But he was also a known Communist. On December 8, when they were organizing the demonstration, Ch'en went to see Lu Chih-wei to request the use of university busses the following day. Lu told him that the busses were university property and he could not authorize their use for political purposes. Later that day, at a general meeting of the students, Wang Ju-mei (who later changed his name to Huang Hua and, after a distinguished diplomatic career, became Foreign Minister of the People's Republic of China in 1976) declared that Lu was a traitor and suggested that the students punish him. When the news of this reached Lu, he said, "Let them kill me, this will be an honorable way to die." But his wife Mary was in tears and called Hung on the telephone for advice. Hung sent for Ch'en Chieh, who assured him Lu was in no danger: "We just wanted to scare him a bit."

"That evening, the students went around the campus and the neighborhood asking for donation of towels. They expected blood to be shed. The following day, they marched twenty miles in the ten-degree weather; but when they reached the city wall, they were intercepted by the police and prevented from joining the students in the city. A strike ensued at Yenching and Tsinghua that lasted for two months. Sung Che-yuan, the Chairman of the Hopei-Chahar Political Affairs Council, felt he had to do something about the situation. As he did not want to take on the

Americans, he did not touch Yenching; but he sent three thousand soldiers to surround Tsinghua in order to arrest the Communists. No Communists were found; but on that occasion the young, handsome Dean of the College of Engineering, Ku Yü-hsiu, an M.I.T. Ph.D. who wrote poetry, came out, dressed in an immaculate white flannel suit, to reason with the soldiers. They thought he was a student and slapped him in the face. That caused further uproar.

"It turned out that Sung Che-yuan, an old-style military man, was vain of his good name. He respected learning and was stung by the disapproval of the academic community. One afternoon, when I was taking a nap upstairs, my daughter Gertrude burst into the bedroom, carrying a large calling card. On it was inscribed, 'Sung Che-yuan.' I hurried downstairs and found him waiting for me, in a blue cotton gown. He evidently had come incognito. The first thing he said was, 'Mr. Hung, you are wise in these matters. Look at me, do I look like a traitor?'"

"'Well,' I said, 'How could you be a traitor? You should not bother yourself with the idle talk of young people. What your soldiers did at Tsinghua was not right; but no one knows their names, so they denounce you instead. I know that you are a patriotic man.'

"'How do you know?'

"'It is plain for all to see. You have no alternative to your present course of action. If you don't do it, they can easily find some traitors to do it.'

"'I never thought I would find such an understanding friend in you.' He sighed appreciatively.

"He stayed and talked for a while. As he walked out of our door, I saw that the street was heavily lined with policemen. That was the first and only time I ever saw him."

Hung was reluctant to endorse the confrontational tactics of the students. His ideal of a patriot was embodied in Thomas Masaryk (1850–1937), founder of the Czechoslovakian Republic, whose son Hung had met through the Crawfords. Hung admired Masaryk's uncompromising adherence to the truth even as he worked passionately for his country's liberation. He attributed Masaryk's success to strategies grounded in a thorough understanding of the political situation and urged his students to follow Masaryk's example.

ABOUT THIS TIME, Hung's brother Arnold, who had been teaching high school in Foochow, died suddenly of food poisoning. Rhoda went south to help with the funeral. Arnold had left his wife, a daughter, and a baby yet to be born. Rhoda helped her sister-in-law get into a normal school so that she would have a means of livelihood in the future. When a boy was born, the mother wrote Hung with the request that as the oldest uncle, he give the baby a name. Hung named him Wei, for "comfort" in Chinese, in the hope that he would bring some comfort to his widowed mother.

With the death of Arnold, Hung felt even more keenly the need to be closer to his two surviving brothers. Fred had been teaching nearby at Tsinghua ever since he returned from France, but David had been serving as an engineer with the government in Nanking. His life, on government salary, had been quite harsh. Hung persuaded him to take a leave of absence from his job to teach at Tsinghua for half a year. Those few months in which the three brothers were together again were some of the happiest of Hung's life.

On December 12, 1936, Chang Hsueh-liang, son of the warlord whom the Japanese assassinated in 1928 before they invaded Manchuria, took Chiang Kai-shek hostage and demanded that he unite with the Communists to fight Japanese aggression. Hung and his brother David had spent the day leisurely hunting for rare inkslabs at Liu-li-ch'ang. Hung had a collection of inkslabs which he planned to distribute among his students when he retired, in the tradition of mendicant monks who pass on their begging bowls to their disciples. After dinner, David was holding a newly acquired inkslab against the light to examine it when the phone rang. Hung answered the phone, "What, Chiang Kai-shek taken hostage? How could Chang Hsueh-liang do such a thing?" David, catching half of the disturbing conversation, let the inkslab drop from his hand. It broke into two on the floor. The following day, they had the pieces glued back together by an artisan; but a fissure remained, irreparable. David wanted to throw the inkslab away; but Hung stopped him, saying they should keep it as a memento of the occasion. So they went to an engraver and had him etch three characters on the back of the inkslab, *Ching-tuo-yen,* ("The Shock-fallen Inkslab"), along with the date, and an explanation of the event that led to the name.

CHAPTER FIFTEEN

Work and Students During the Thirties

RELIEVED OF ADMINISTRATIVE DUTIES, Hung embarked on a decade of prodigious scholarly activities following his return to China in 1930. A partial list of his publications in the 1963 issue of the *Harvard Journal of Asiatic Studies* lists forty-one publications during this period, most in Chinese, a few in English. The Harvard-Yenching Institute Sinological Index Series (HYISIS), which he conceived, developed, and supervised, is regarded by many as the most important reference series produced in the first half of the twentieth century for the study of traditional Chinese civilization. In this series, Hung and his small staff set themselves to evaluate systematically the most important books ever written in China, establish any textual variants of these books, and provide them with indices or concordances. It perhaps is no exaggeration to say that the appearance of the Sinological Index Series revolutionized scholarship in China. Henceforth, vague references to Chinese historical figures, institutions, documents, and so forth, would no longer be acceptable; for the means to be specific were there. With cross referencing made convenient, meanings of words, as well as dates and places of events, could be easily established, making it possible to clear the air of much pedantic obfuscation. Many a cherished misconception—in history, philosophy, religion, literature, and science—tumbled down; and new criteria were set for "historical truths."

The history of the development of the Sinological Index Series and the problems encountered by the staff with regard to such matters as methodology, format, and the choice of books, editions, and variant readings are recounted by Hung in his paper on "Indexing Chinese Books" (8) and in a volume incorporated into the Series, *On Indexing* (21). Prior to the Sinological Index Series, a few ancient Chinese texts had been indexed by European, Japanese, and Chinese scholars, but not on a systematic basis. In its first two years, the Series staff experimented with lesser works, such as an index of a chronological chart of Chinese history from 106 B.C. to A.D. 1911 produced by Hung's History 161 class at Yenching (9) and an index to documents concerning the seventeenth-century Mi Garden on which Yenching University was built.

The Series eventually encompassed sixty-four titles. In twenty-three cases, not only the index but also an authoritative text of the actual work was published; these twenty-three were numbered separately and called "Supplements." Only one title is strictly concerned with belles lettres, namely the *Concordance to the Poems of Tu Fu* with a preface by Hung (38). Indices or concordances were completed for all but one of the traditional "Thirteen Classics." Hung himself wrote the prefaces to the indices for the *Yi Li* (18) and *Li Chi* (33) and for the *Combined Concordances to the Ch'un-ch'iu, Kung-yang, Ku-liang, and Tso-chuan* (34). His protégé Nieh Ch'ung-ch'i wrote the preface to the *Concordance to the Analects of Confucius* (HYISIS Supplement 16) and the *Concordance to Meng-tzu* (HYISIS Supplement 17).

The first four of the "Twenty-four Standard Histories" were each indexed. Over the centuries, each new Chinese regime has felt obliged to write for posterity an official history of the previous dynasty. (A draft of the Twenty-fifth Standard History, that of the Ch'ing dynasty has been completed; and the Peking government is at present assembling a team to write the history of the Republican Era.) These undertakings have frequently employed hundreds of historians, with the finished product often running into dozens of volumes. The four Series indices give easy access to the official histories of the remote past through the year A.D. 250. Separately, and covering a much longer time span, the Series brought out the *Combined Indices to the Economic Treatises of Fifteen Standard Histories* (HYISIS 32).

Partly at the suggestion of the historian Ku Chieh-kang, an index was prepared for the sixth-century *Water Classics and Commentary* (HYISIS 17), one of the oldest Chinese books on geography, which traces the courses of 137 rivers and their tributaries as well as locating lakes, ponds, and canals. It was so accurate that it was still heavily relied on in the eighteenth century, when a geography of the empire was compiled.

Concordances were published for the important pre-Han philosophers, Chuang-tze (HYISIS Supplement 20), Mo-tzu (HYISIS Supplement 21), and Hsun-tzu (HYISIS Supplement 22). The entire first press run of the *Concordance to Chuang-tzu* was destroyed after the Japanese army occupied the Yenching campus; but luckily, one copy had been taken out of the office and could be the basis for a second printing in 1947.

Fifteen titles are indices of personal names in works on Chinese history, arts, and literature. Turning to these indices, the scholar could find in a moment the most important, if not the complete, biographical records concerning anyone above a certain rank from the late tenth through the late nineteenth centuries. Specialized name indices also enabled the historian to distinguish among the many persons with the same name in a given era or through history and to identify correctly the many appelations a single individual might acquire during a lifetime.

A project particularly close to William Hung's heart was the compilation of indices to pre-modern bibliographies, intended to facilitate access to information on the existence and condition of China's rich legacy of written works. The most famous of pre-modern book catalogues was that compiled by order of the Ch'ien-lung Emperor late in the eighteenth century, the critical and descriptive *Catalogue of the Complete Library of the Four Treasuries* (*Ssu-k'u ch'uan-shu tsung-mu*). "Four Treasuries" refers to the four traditional categories of Chinese bibliography, the classics, histories, philosophical works, and belles lettres. Between 1773 and 1782, the Ch'ien-lung emperor had employed more than three hundred fifty scholars to review and evaluate what he hoped were all the books in the empire. Some thirty-four hundred books were then selected into a new imperial library. The catalogue consisted of bibliographical and critical notes on these works, as well as on sixty-eight hundred others. The notices are masterpieces of Ch'ing scholarship and are useful to this day in resolving questions of the authorship, dating, and authenticity of the texts. In 1932, the Sinological Index Series staff published an index to these ten thousand titles (HYISIS 7), with a preface by Hung which gives a critical account of the imperial collection (20). A smaller companion index, published in the same year, covered a study of works compiled under imperial auspices during the Ming dynasty (HYISIS Supplement 3).

More significant than either of these was the *Combined Indices to Twenty Historical Bibliographies* (HYISIS 10) that appeared in the following year. Beginning with the Han dynasty (206 B.C.–A.D. 220), the imperial houses had regularly collected and kept bibliographies of extant books. These lists were later usually incorporated in a bibliographical section of the official history of each dynasty. For those dynasties that lacked such lists, later scholars had reconstructed them. The *Combined Indices* was a guide to the contents of fourteen official and supplemental dynastic bibliographies, as well as to six other bibliographies of books written during the Ming and Ch'ing periods. For the first time, the availability of books through successive dynasties could be traced readily. Although the scholar must still consult more specialized, private bibliographies, the *Combined Indices* gives, at a glance, a good indication of when a title first appeared and when it disappeared, or whether it was still extant in recent times. It is thus also a valuable scholarly tool in the detection of forgeries.

The Series also published indices to Buddhist and Taoist texts and two bibliographies of twentieth-century Japanese Sinological studies. Several volumes in the Series are useful primarily for determining the dating and integrity of texts because the books they cover either quote at length from other works no longer extant or are themselves concerned with textual criticism.

The Sinological Index Series is important, first, because it achieves its primary objective of providing scholars with easy access to the texts and, second, because in cases of the more important works, it also provides authoritative texts, meticulously edited and punctuated, with all variant readings listed. Many of the prefaces are major pieces of research that give a modern evaluation of the nature of the work and discuss the history of its transmission and the merits of the various editions. To modern Chinese scholars, who no longer learn the classics by heart, the indices and the concordances are now extremely helpful in understanding the literary and historical allusions of the post-classical period.

All told, the Sinological Index Series had only ten years of production under favorable circumstances and three years under unfavorable. The budget was six thousand dollars a year in the first two years, four thousand dollars a year thereafter. There were only ten persons on the staff at any one time. Given more time and more resources, what else could the Sinological Index Series have accomplished? On being asked this question in 1979, Hung simply said that he regretted not having done a combined index to the functionaries, which would help scholars negotiate the maze of titles and functions of government offices through the centuries; and a combined index to geographical entities, giving their names, sizes, and changes through time. If Hung had had more time and more resources, we can speculate that the rest of the Standard Histories might also have been indexed.

HUNG ATTRIBUTED MUCH OF THE SUCCESS of the Sinological Index Series to the help of two former students. On the research and editorial side was Nieh Ch'ung-ch'i, a fastidious scholar and a strict Confucian with a magisterial bearing. His views were universally respected on the rare occasions when he expressed them. On the production side was Li Shu-ch'un. He apprenticed himself in the printing trade for a full year to become acquainted with all facets of book production so as to ensure that the press for the Series was organized in the best, most efficient way possible. A system was worked out whereby information on index cards could be transferred directly to print, without going through a manuscript stage, thus saving time and eliminating many chances for errors. The small additional staff was occasionally supplemented by voluntary labor supplied by Hung's students, for doing work on the Series was considered very good training.

In his teaching, Hung was constantly on the lookout for students whom he might train for historical research. He looked for students who were capable of clear, logical thinking and possessed the independence of spirit necessary for original intellectual exploration. To these special individuals he gave attention and praise. They learned from him how to grasp the essence of a historical problem; how not to be confused by details; how to make hypotheses, test, and discard them; and how to present their findings in an intelligent, persuasive way. Above all, they learned to document their sources meticulously and exhaustively. He encouraged his protégés to become fluent in foreign languages and assisted them in getting further training abroad. His intention was no less than to raise a new breed of Chinese historians whose purview encompassed the whole world, and who could be relied upon to rediscover and conserve those permanent values in China's cultural heritage not incompatible with modern requirements. A list of some of the more important students he trained and their subsequent affiliations is found in Appendix I. They are some of the foremost Chinese historians of our time.

The manner by which he was able to get one of them, Weng Tu-chien, to Harvard gave Hung special satisfaction. Weng Tu-chien was a Fukienese who had graduated form the Foochow Anglo-Chinese High School, the successor of Hung's alma mater, the Foochow Anglo-Chinese College. Slightly crippled from polio contracted as a child, he learned to speak Japanese and English, read Mongolian, French, German, Russian, and Manchu. In sedulous emulation of Hung, he had taken up pipe smoking and earned the sobriquet of "William Hung Number Two." While Weng was still an undergraduate, Hung asked him to look over a manuscript of his former Harvard student, James Ware, and was impressed with Weng's comments. Hung then put him to work on the index of the Taoist Canon. In the meantime, without Weng's knowledge, Hung wrote to the Harvard-Yenching Institute, recommending him for a fellowship to do graduate work at Harvard, and urged James Ware, who was already teaching at Harvard, to put in a few words for him. When the telegram of acceptance came, Hung handed it to Weng, chuckling. Weng was thoroughly stunned. "Why didn't you tell me you were working on this?" he asked.

"I was afraid I might not be able to swing it," Hung laughed, as he savored again, in the surprised joy of his student, his own youthful happiness when he learned that he was going to study in America.

HUNG'S MAIN VEHICLE FOR TRAINING future historians was his "Seminar on Historical Methods," more popularly known on campus as the "Seminar on Rubbish." Hung paid a library clerk to go out on Sundays and buy scrap paper for him. The scrap paper, mainly drug prescriptions, calendars, pornographic literature, magic charms, and so forth, came from all sources and was sold in bagfuls by illiterate vendors to other merchants as wrappings for merchandise. Hung stored these bags of miscellaneous inscriptions in the crawl space between the ceiling and the roof of the library. Later, the rubbish overflowed into the crawl space in the adjacent chemistry building and the biology-geology buildings as well. On Wednesday afternoons, the students enrolled in the course, numbering not more than ten, would come equipped with wash basins for scrubbing their hands once they had finished digging through the piles of rubbish. They attempted to identify the nature of each inscription and to establish its time and place of origin. When anyone discovered something of historical significance, Hung encouraged the finder to write it up and publish the article in the "History and Geology Supplement" of the newspaper, *Ta-kung-pao (The Fair Press)*. They worked from three to six in the afternoon, after which either Hung took them home for dinner or they all went to eat at a small restaurant called Ch'ang San immediately outside the campus. Often, when the findings were intriguing, they went back to the library and worked late into the night.

There were some valuable finds in the rubbish pile. Once, the students discovered some documents that belonged to the Imperial Archives and returned them to the government. Another time, they found a long letter written in small Chinese characters. It was from the famed classical scholar Liu Shih-p'ei (1884–1919) to the Manchu Governor-General Tuan-fang, offering to spy on the revolutionaries! Hung published it in the *Ta-kung-pao* with some editorial comments (29). This provoked a letter of reprimand from the ruling Kuomintang Party, which for some reason found the document offensive.

Also discovered in the rubbish was a collection of poems in the handwriting of the Ch'ing iconoclast, Ts'ui Shu (1740–1816). Ts'ui Shu was a brilliant scholar who, by relying only on historical information that was verifiable, cast doubt on the veracity of many historical accounts and exposed as forgeries many supposedly historical documents. He was clearly a man ahead of his time. Unfortunately, he was isolated from other scholars who might have recognized his worth; and he lived a life of grinding poverty, his studies constantly interrupted by illness and the necessity of making ends meet. Only Ch'en Li-ho, the magistrate of Taiku, realized the value of Ts'ui's work. Having met Ts'ui at a chance encounter and read his work, Ch'en spent the remainder of his life printing Ts'ui's manuscripts and exhausted his fortune in the process. The labor of printing was made specially difficult by Ts'ui, who made frequent revisions; and the manuscripts had to be transmitted by friends over long distances. By the time Ch'en died penniless, a decade after Ts'ui's own death, fewer than half of Ts'ui's manuscripts were printed, the rest were scattered. Ts'ui's writings were neglected in China until Hu Shih called attention to them.

In 1931, after Hung discovered the collection of poems in the rubbish at Yenching University Library, he published them with notes explaining their attribution and the reasons for deducing that the handwriting was that of Ts'ui himself (12). He also constructed a table of the various editions of Ts'ui's works (11). Later that year, Hung took a trip to Ts'ui's hometown in Ta-ming, Hopei, with other historians including Ku Chieh-kang, Jung Keng, and Cheng Te-k'un. There, Hung's judgment that the handwriting belonged to Ts'ui Shu was confirmed by a comparison with the style of the inscription that Ts'ui wrote on his brother's tombstone. They found Ts'ui's own tomb, discovered his grandson (who was an illiterate laborer), and acquired some manuscripts. They wrote a joint report on their week-long visit (13). As a result of their visit, a resident of Ta-ming subsequently mailed to Ku a fragment of another manuscript by Ts'ui, which Hung also published with notes with Ku's permission (28). All four pieces were later re-printed in 1936 by Ku Chieh-kang in a volume on Ts'ui that included all surviving writings by Ts'ui.

The kind of historical detective work that Hung was teaching his students and practicing with his colleagues underlies much of his scholarly publication in the 1930s. For instance, he edited a text from a scroll found at Tun-huang and argued that it was from an encyclopedia compiled in the Southern Liang dynasty (A.D. 502–557) (22). He used internal evidence to date another Tun-huang manuscript (24). Both of these manuscripts were among the scrolls brought out by Paul Pelliot, the Frenchman whose work had first convinced Hung in 1928 that he could not ignore the Sinological research being done in the West.

Establishing dates, provenance, and historical significance of several hitherto unpublished documents from the Ch'ing dynasty also occupied his attention. In addition to the letter from Liu Shih-p'ei found by his students, Hung published two articles based on diaries by Manchu noblemen (15, 16). He also published five manuscripts by a writer early in the dynasty that give a close look at northern China under the Manchu conquest (35). A major publication was the eight fascicles of a manuscript found in the Yenching library that contain biographies of about eleven hundred Ch'ing painters with a preface by Hung describing the uniqueness of the compiler's contribution (26). His review of Carrol Brown Malone's *History of the Peking Summer Palaces under the Ch'ing Dynasty* allowed him to draw on his own research about the vicinity of the Yenching campus and publish information on the correct location of one of the famous gardens (30). It was, in fact, during the 1930s that Hung published many of his findings on the historical geography of Yenching.

A pamphlet published by the Yenching University Graduate School, called *Suggestions Concerning Research Papers* (*Yen-chiu lun-wen ko-shih chü-yao*) summed up Hung's advice to students on what should go into a research paper and set down standard practices for technical matters such as punctuation, transcription, and bibliographical notation (36). It has been reprinted many times on the mainland, on Taiwan, and in Hong Kong. It reveals Hung the meticulous scholar; but he was also a man who thought about the practice of history in the context of large issues. In 1936, he wrote a long paper in Chinese on the various world maps of Matteo Ricci (1552–1610), citing extensively from Latin, Italian, French, German, English, Japanese, and Korean sources (32). The paper itself is a testimonial to how historical research might be conducted with international cooperation. His hypothesis that Paoli Li, whom Matteo Ricci mentioned as one of the publishers of his maps, was the same person known as Li Ying-shih in Chinese documents was later confirmed by a Japanese scholar who discovered Li Ying-shih's map in Korea. In this paper, Hung also explored the extent to which familiarity with Matteo Ricci's world map changed the insular view of the world common among Chinese. Hung's conclusion was that, sadly enough, it changed very little.

Of course, his major scholarly efforts at this time were devoted to the Sinological Index Series. Hung himself wrote the monographic introductions to seven volumes in the Series. These introductions are book-length works, the culmination of years of study and research. Hung's preface to the *Li-chi* index (33) won him the Prix Stanislas Julien. But his preface to the concordance of the text and commentaries of the *Spring and Autumn Annals* (34) was perhaps his greatest scholarly triumph. On the day in July, 1937, that he was writing the last words of this work, Japanese planes were bombing the Nationalist West Barracks only a few hundred yards from the Yenching campus. All day the house shook and windows cracked, but Hung was determined to shut out the chaos and concentrate on his task at hand. In the preface he proved that the *Spring and Autumn Annals,* traditionally attributed to Confucius himself, is a true record of its time. The proof lies in the fact that thirty of the thirty-seven recorded eclipses between the eighth and fifth centuries B.C. in China can be verified in the eclipses calculated in Oppelzer's *Canon der Finsternisse* and that the seven eclipses which cannot be verified can be credibly explained. Hung then went on to unravel the complicated relationship between the text of the *Spring and Autumn Annals* and its various commentaries, showing that the most widely read commentary, the *Tso-chuan,* was not a late-Western-Han (206 B.C.–A.D. 8) forgery as many nineteenth- and twentieth-century scholars had argued. Hung Hsi, had he been living, would have been very pleased with his son's vindication of these Chinese classics.

IN LARGE PART, Hung's dedication to scholarship during the 1930s was a response to the rallying cry of Liang Ch'i-ch'ao and Hu Shih to "Set in order our national legacy." He joined the ranks of Ku Chieh-kang, Ch'ien Mu, and Fu Ssu-nien in a massive "housecleaning" task to chip away the scholarly accretion of the centuries and expose China's intellectual legacy to the harsh light of twentieth-century rationalism. The expenditure of such prodigious energy on the past was dismissed by some as futile and viewed by others as escapism. Whether or not the endeavor was justifiable in the eyes of contemporaries, it was timely. For the relative calm in China lasted less than two decades. The country was soon engulfed in a war against the invading Japanese and a rapid succession of debilitating internal conflicts. When the dust settled, a whole generation of intellectuals had been swept away or had left their most productive years behind them. Nevertheless an astonishing amount of work was completed in that short period of relative calm; and much of it could have been done only by scholars like Hung, whose generation was one of the last in China to have been brought up on the Confucian classics. Not the least of their contribution was the punctuation of many of the old texts. It is almost impossible for present-day students, untrained in the traditional manner, to read solid pages of words, to know where one clause ends and another begins. Without reference works, such as the *Sinological Index Series,* developed by Hung and others of his generation, much of China's historical and literary past would be totally inaccessible to us today. Their views on all that had gone before them, including texts and artifacts, will be heavily relied upon by future generations, even as the world they knew so intimately recedes in time.

CHAPTER SIXTEEN

In and Out
of Enemy Territory

ON JULY 28, 1937, the Japanese took Peking. They soon controlled most of China and set up two puppet governments, one in north China, the other in central China. Outside the Japanese-controlled areas in northern China, the Communists organized the population into anti-Japanese units and provided order and discipline. In the south, the Nationalist government continued its resistance against the invading force. This was essentially the situation that lasted for eight years, from 1937 to 1945.

FOR FOUR YEARS, until the outbreak of American-Japanese hostilities, Yenching University occupied an enviable, anomalous position in this scheme of things. While the other northern universities followed the Nationalist government in its evacuation to the hinterland in the southwest—tens of thousands of students and professors carrying books and laboratory equipment with them, trudging *en masse* on foot over the mountains in whatever vehicles they could command—Yenching raised an American flag on its high campus pole and dared the Japanese to touch the property of a non-belligerent nation. Stuart now dropped all pretense that Yenching had ever been administered by a Chinese chancellor and resumed public command of the university. He dealt with the Japanese in a way calculated to keep them at a respectful distance. The Japanese were treated with unfailing courtesy but were not permitted to enter the campus except by special arrangement. When asked to admit Japanese students, Stuart's response was to show that no Japanese applicant did well enough on the entrance examination. About the only concession Stuart made was adding a Japanese professor to the faculty, Dr. Ryuzo Torii, a seventy-year-old archeologist highly esteemed by the Chinese. But the task of keeping Yenching above political and military entanglements was not easy, because most of the students and some of the professors were engaged in one activity or another against the Japanese. Stuart's policy was to discourage such activities on campus and encourage individuals who were indiscreet to join the government in the south. In his negotiations with the Japanese authorities, he was greatly assisted by Hsiao Cheng-i, a native of Taiwan and a Yenching graduate whom Hung had recommended. He spoke elegant Japanese and understood all the fine points of Japanese protocol. Stuart made him initially, in 1937, a lecturer in Japanese and Secretary of the President's Office and then, in 1940, Secretary-General of the University.

We have several letters Rhoda wrote to Ruth Crawford Mitchell that give us some glimpses of what it was like at Yenching during those four years:

Written several letters but they may not have reached you as most letters are destroyed by the Japs after censoring them. I am now writing hastily as a friend is going in half an hour to America and am sending this by her. We have gone through a lot of bombing across from us which shook our houses and campus, street fighting near our campus . . . Our campus was a refugee camp for nearly two weeks in the early stage of the war. Our home had three families all so frightened. We ourseles had to be calm and tried to help others . . . The University has started its work with about 500 students. Outwardly calm, but faculty and students are in a nervous state. We are not allowed to have meetings or to express any views or even look displeased. Going in and out of the city we, as well as common folks, are subject to very thorough examinations at the city gates. Peiping [i.e., Peking] is full of Japanese soldiers and trucks, and tanks, at the city gates—really thousands of them everywhere—beautiful public buildings, schools, universities are used as barracks. The whole atmosphere is most unbearable at times. The whole of China is bombed . . . It is hard for China to go to war but the only thing to do when the country is invaded is to defend. The problem here is the refugees and the sickness, thousands out of work, no income. We get half pay but we are fortunate at that . . . (October 15, 1937)

The roaring of heavy bombers and searching planes, explosion of bombs and artillery fire . . . This is occupied area but there is no lack of warfare . . . Most of the movements are during the night, still there is enough that can be seen . . . [B]oth in Tientsin and Peking every one was forced to exchange their national currency for the Federal Reserves notes which are worthless. The Japanese also investigated all banks, not only seized the national notes but all deposits with large accounts must be furnished . . . Several of the wealthy persons have been kidnapped and heavy ransom demanded for their release. Poverty is the best protection these days . . . New dangers appear in the city which alarm me greatly because I am a mother of three girls . . . the kidnapping of young girls for illegal purposes . . . (June 22, 1939)

Life is difficult for many people this winter . . . Increasing number of death[s] from starvation and cold, suicide, murder, etc. Even among students there is great depression and several attempted suicide. Ruth and Gertrude spent the whole of New Year Day trying to cheer a friend and took from her the drug. Later she went home and made the attempt there. We understand she is critically ill . . . We do all that is possible to encourage wholesome activities and sports and live a normal life . . . (January 8, 1941)

By 1941, the Hungs had decided that Peking had become too unhealthy and too dangerous a place for their daughters. With the help of some friends, they sent the two older ones to continue their education in the United States, though they kept Agnes with them.

HUNG'S OWN LIFE became busier than it had ever been. A constant stream of visitors came to his home and his office. In addition to the usual friends and students, jobseekers and fundraisers, there was an increasing number of foreigners. Foreigners of all races and ideological stripes were pouring into Peking now, encouraged by the incredibly favorable rates of exchange their foreign currency would bring. Some were attracted by the luxurious mode of life available to those with even modest wealth; others came in pursuit of romance in a war-torn country; still others—White Russians and European Jews—were seeking a home. He tried to accommodate them all in his schedule, give them fatherly advice, and bring them to a better understanding of China's position.

With Hsiao Cheng-i acting as a bridge between them, Hung became a very close friend of the Toriis. Dr. Torii was almost fanatical in his love of everything Chinese, tracing even such common a Japanese word as *kawa* (river) to a Chinese origin. In his scholarly pursuits, he had three able assistants in his wife, who spoke Mongolian; his eldest daughter, who had studied in Paris and spoke French; and his younger daughter who had studied in Boston and spoke English. Like most Japanese intellectuals, Dr. Torii could read, but could not speak, Chinese.

"Among the Toriis, I spoke least with Mrs. Torii and most often with Midori, the younger daughter. She often served as interpreter between her father and me. But I admired very much her older sister, whose name I cannot now recall. She was so refined, so beautiful, and such a splendid French cook. She was once married to a Japanese but the marriage did not work out; that was why she and her little girl were living with her parents. One morning, my wife Rhoda was upset with me for no apparent reason. At my insistence she explained she saw in her dream the older Torii daughter sitting on my lap. It was only when I started to laugh that she realized the absurdity of the whole thing and laughed along with me.

"Later on, Midori fell in love with one of my students, Chang Yen-shen, and I found myself father-confessor to both parties. When they got married, they asked me to be sponsor of the wedding."

HUNG was turning prematurely gray. In a letter to Ruth Crawford Mitchell, he described himself as "a weary man in his forty-eighth year." Therefore, when in 1940, he learned that he had an opportunity to travel to Cambridge, Massachusetts, he heartily welcomed the chance to get out of the country for a while. Yenching University had acquired a new piece of land adjacent to its campus. Hung suggested that it be used to build ten bungalows for the use of Western scholars in residence at Yenching. The idea meshed well with Stuart's overall plan to develop Yenching as an international institution. By then, Yenching had already established relationships with not only such American and British universities as Harvard, Princeton, and Oxford, but also with French, German, and Italian institutions. Hung was to lay the plan for the bungalows before the trustees of the Harvard-Yenching Institute in Cambridge (who readily approved it when he arrived).

When Dr. Torii learned that Hung was going to the United States by way of Korea and Japan, he insisted on accompanying him as far as Japan to ensure that Hung did not have any trouble from the military authorities. The next day, Midori came and asked whether she could come along to take care of her father. So Hung and his two "body-guards" took the train from Peking to Pusan, Korea, and from Pusan a boat to Yokohama.

IN TOKYO, Hung wanted to visit the Iwasaki Memorial Library of the Seidako Bunko, built on the tomb of the financier, Baron Iwasaki Yano-suke (1851–1908) to house his rare book collection. Supposedly in the collection was a facsimile of an edition printed in the Sung dynasty of the earliest known Chinese work on the art of writing history, the eighth-century *Shih-t'ung* (*Study of Historiography*). Hung had been studying the *Shih-t'ung* since 1923 and had amassed a library of his own on the subject, but the earliest edition he had yet seen was one from the thirteenth century. Dr. Torii wrote a letter of introduction for Hung to the librarian, Morohashi Tetsuji, later known for his immense *Kanwa Daijiten,* a Chinese-Japanese dictionary that is the world's finest dictionary of classical Chinese. Morohashi received Hung in formal Japanese attire and had tea brought in ceremoniously, but they were soon speaking Chinese. After the preliminary pleasantries, Morohashi disappeared into the bookstacks and came out with only two volumes of the book, Volumes One and Four, taking the librarian's customary precaution of not making a whole set of books available to a guest, lest he abscond with it. Hung was annoyed at this sign of distrust on the part of Morohashi. As soon as he opened one of the volumes, he knew it was not a copy of any Sung text. He clapped the book shut and returned it to Morohashi. At that point, as Hung fondly recalled, the following exchanges took place:

"You seem to have solved your problem." Morohashi said, surprised.
"I have."

"Would you be so good as to tell me what was the problem?"

Hung said that before the book came into the possession of Baron Iwasaki, it had belonged to the nineteenth-century Chinese scholar Lu Hsin-yuan, who claimed that it was the facsimile copy of a Sung printed text of *Shih-t'ung*. Hung was interested in seeing whether it was or not, and he had decided that it was not.

Morohashi was rather put off. "Professor Hung, you must be an erudite scholar, but you have made your decision with barely a glance. Many Chinese and Japanese scholars have examined this—do you mean that they were all mistaken?"

Hung replied that the proof was not in these two volumes, but in the other two. Morohashi, by now visibly angry, clogged back noisily into the bookstacks and brought out the rest of the book, along with the box and its shimmering, silk wrapping. Hung opened up the second volume and pointed out to him the last line of Chapter Seven. There was a note made there by a sixteenth-century scholar named Lu Shen, which established beyond the shadow of a doubt that the edition was not a Sung facsimile. Morohashi was as impressed as he was embarrassed.

THE PRESIDENTIAL LINER crossing the Pacific Ocean was bustling with discussions of the wars in Europe and China and the upcoming American election. Hung travelled second-class. When he wandered among the third-class passengers, he heard a single, unanimous opinion, that Roosevelt should be reelected for a third term. In the first-class compartments, however, Roosevelt was bitterly attacked and the talk was all for Wendell Willkie. Hung's sympathies were for the Roosevelt side; but he resolved not to make any comments on the subject, knowing his opinions would displease his Republican friends in the United States.

Arriving in September of 1940, Hung made his first stop in Pittsburgh, where he visited his American sister, Ruth Crawford Mitchell. From Pittsburgh, he took a night train to Pennsylvania Station in New York, where he intended to have a leisurely breakfast and make a telephone call to Pinkie. He waited until the rest of the passengers had disembarked before he stepped off the train. As he did, he saw coming towards him a small group of people bearing flowers, followed by a band playing loud music in the otherwise empty station. They waved to him; and he, though surprised, waved back. When they came closer, however, he discovered their eyes converged on a point behind him, so he quickly turned around. It was Wendell Willkie, the presidential candidate, right behind him.

Pinkie—his legal and financial problems long over—was married and had moved to Quaker Hill outside Pawling, New York, to be near the Pawling Rubber Company he founded. His wife Pherbia was the sister of the broadcaster Lowell Thomas. They were both active in the American Committee for Non-Participation in Japanese Aggression, which advocated a U. S. embargo on the sale of scrap iron to Japan and a boycott on the purchase of silk stockings. It also held essay contests for high school students to encourage them to discuss the war in China. Pinkie was proud to have Hung meet his wife, and to show him his beautiful estate. He was especially pleased to show him a room lined with glass cabinets in which were displayed the crackleware he bought in China in 1933. They had dinner the next day at Lowell Thomas's house down the street. After dinner, Pinkie took Hung to see New York Governor Thomas Dewey. Pinkie wanted the governor to hear what Hung had to say about Japan.

Hung found Dewey a gracious host. The first thing he said to Hung was, "Before you begin, I want to confess how ignorant I am about

China. Everybody nowadays keeps referring to the government in Chungking. I can't even find it on the map."

They sat down and Hung gave them his views of the war in Asia. He stressed that the Japanese were decent people, but that they were bitten by a "Prussian militarism" which compelled them to feel that unless they conquered China, they would not be able to meet their God-given destiny. Hung predicted that Japan would eventually fall. Like a snake trying to consume a cow, it would suffer severe indigestion. Dewey interrupted Hung to go upstairs and pull his two young sons out of bed. He brought them down in their pajamas, for he wanted the boys to remember what the Chinese gentleman had to say.

Before Hung left for Cambridge, Pinkie also introduced him to Dorothy "Missy" Thompson (Mrs. Sinclair Lewis) of the New York *Herald Tribune.*

Several weeks later, Hung received a call from Pinkie at the Harvard Faculty Club, where he was staying. "William, here is your chance to shine. Missy was so taken with you, she wants you to be one of two speakers on the last evening of the New York Tribune Forum she is organizing. The other speaker is President Roosevelt."

Hung was greatly flattered by the invitation but had to decline it. Since he was in the United States on university business and had to go back to live in a Peking under Japanese occupation, he dared not speak in public on the situation in China. He suggested that they ask the Chinese Ambassador to the United States, Hu Shih, instead and took the opportunity to go see his old friend to tell him what he would like to have said. Hu welcomed Hung, who was greatly relieved to find him unchanged—their common friend George Birkhoff, the Harvard professor of mathematics, had warned Hung that Hu Shih had adopted a permanent smile since becoming ambassador. In Washington, Hung declined Hu's invitation to stay at the embassy, but he did take his dinners there and had many opportunities to observe the disagreeable side of a diplomat's life. Dinner was often interrupted by long-distance calls from T. V. Soong, the brother-in-law of Chiang Kai-shek and Chiang's personal representative. He would look annoyed and excuse himself to take the call in another room. Despite such interruptions, Hu and Hung worked out a ten-minute speech for the Tribune Forum, which Hu practiced in front of a mirror. Hung, the more experienced speaker, then suggested he cut two minutes off to allow for applause, which Hu did.

Hung spent Thanksgiving with Ruth Crawford Mitchell in Pittsburgh.

Ruth had conceived and brought to reality the successful Nationality Room cultural project at the Cathedral of Learning of the University of Pittsburgh. Hung was gratified to see the completed Chinese Room, which he had helped plan when he was in the United States in 1930, and whose designer, T'eng Kuei, was recommended by him. He was glad to see the University Chancellor, John G. Bowman, again. Chancellor Bowman had prized Hung's friendship so much he had framed and hung in his office a Confucian passage in Hung's calligraphy. Later, Hung was to advise Bowman in the establishment of a Chinese studies program at the University of Pittsburgh.

Ruth and Hung attended Thanksgiving service at the Heinz Chapel, across a lawn from the Cathedral of Learning: "The preacher that Thanksgiving Day was a Pastor Kerr. He preached a sermon on 'Failure,' on how Jesus, Confucius, and Socrates were all regarded as failures by their contemporaries and yet their lives have changed the direction of history. Ruth kept pinching me during the entire sermon. Finally, towards the end, Pastor Kerr said, 'We are thankful for the successes; but we are also thankful for some of the failures, depending on the kind of failures they are. Let me tell you, the idea for this sermon is not mine. It is from a Chinese thinker whose name I have forgotten. A week ago, I happened to be at the University of Pittsburgh Chancellor's office. While he stepped out for a few minutes, I found a pamphlet on failures, and I read it through.' After the service was over, Ruth introduced me to the pastor and said, 'I want you to meet my Chinese brother, William Hung—he is the one who wrote that pamphlet.'"

On New Year's Eve, Hung was with Ruth in Times Square, New York. The mood was euphoric. Roosevelt had won a landslide victory. America had climbed out of the Depression and was not yet embroiled in the war. For many blocks, the two of them were carried along by the pushing, shoving, merry-making crowd, their feet hardly touching the ground. This sensation of having no control at all over the direction one was going made a deep impression on Hung. It seemed so true of so much in life in general.

Since his trip over had worked out so smoothly, Hung was emboldened to take a Japanese steamer back to China in January of 1941. The voyage was free of incident.

CHAPTER SEVENTEEN

Incarcerated by the Japanese

PEARL HARBOR DAY was December 7, 1941, in the United States; but in China, across the International Date Line, it was already December 8. Early that morning, the phone rang at the Hung residence. It was Chang Tung-sun, Professor of Philosophy at Yenching University and a political activist of liberal sympathies, telling Hung that the war between Japan and the United States had started. Hung roused Rhoda and Agnes out of bed. The servants said that Japanese soldiers were already posted at the university gates.

The Japanese had not decided what they wanted to do with Yenching. One thing they were certain of, however, was that they wanted to capture the Lindsays. The Hon. Michael Lindsay, later to succeed his father as Baron Lindsay of Birker, had been teaching at Yenching since 1937. He and Hung used to spend long, quiet evenings together in front of the fireplace, each smoking a pipe, reading and talking, until one decided it was time for bed. Without his colleagues' knowledge, Lindsay had been smuggling explosives, medical supplies, and radio parts to the Communist guerrillas over the Western Hills. In the summer of 1941, he had married his young accomplice, Li Hsiao-li, a Yenching coed and daughter of a Nationalist general. As soon as the university ceased to be neutral ground, the Japanese headed straight for their home; but a few hours earlier, the Lindays had fled in Stuart's car to the Hills. The Lindsays were to spend four years with the Communists, building for them a sophisticated radio communication system.

Stuart himself happened to be in Tientsin. The Japanese gendarmes entered his office and rifled his files. It was learned afterwards that he was arrested and jailed by the Japanese.

That evening, the Japanese rounded up twelve faculty members and eleven students, kept them overnight in the rooms of the Administrative Building, then took them away in a truck the following afternoon. As they passed through the main gate of the university, the prisoners were deeply moved to see Professor Torii standing there alone by the gate, in formal Japanese attire, bowing to the truck in quiet defiance of the military.

There were no Christmas celebrations on the Yenching campus that year. A certain Major General Arisue, who was high in the Japanese Command, tried but failed to persuade the senior faculty members and administrative staff to reorganize the university under Japanese auspices. Several weeks later, having decided to convert the campus into a military hospital, the Japanese disbanded the student body. Some students went home; others sneaked over the Western Hills and either joined the Communist guerrillas or made their way to Nationalist territory in the southwest. Many continued their education at the makeshift Yenching University in Exile, which was formed by a faculty committee in Chengtu, in the province of Szechwan.

THREE DAYS AFTER CHRISTMAS, Teng Chih-ch'eng was having lunch at the Hungs' when Japanese gendarmes came into the house and took Hung and Teng to Stuart's office. While they were waiting, Teng wrote the Chinese character *ch'iu* ("prisoner") tentatively with his finger on his pants. Hung nodded in silence. The Japanese came back with another person, Stephen Ts'ai, the university's provost and business manager, and took all three of them to the Administrative Building of the Third College of Peking University, which they had made headquarters of the Japanese Gendarmerie. There, the three men were fingerprinted, their pockets emptied of all contents, and the items carefully noted and put into separate envelopes. Then they were shoved into separate detention cells in the basement, where they were to remain for a month and a half.

After Hung's eyes became adjusted to the dark, he saw that there were little mats on the wooden floor, and in one corner, a wooden commode. Another man was in the cell; he was big and had a long beard. As soon as the guards tramped away in their heavy boots, the hulking figure crawled over to Hung's side and whispered, "You are Professor William Hung of Yenching University, aren't you?" He was Tu Ch'ao-chieh, an alleged Soviet spy. A few days later, when Tu discovered that Teng Chih-ch'eng was also in the building, he laughed, "I have no doubt that the Japanese will lose this war. They are a bunch of stupid soldiers. What good does it do them to arrest the students? Now, they have even moved you and Mr. Teng, two useless antiques, here into jail. What a joke!"

Each prisoner was given a blanket and a mat and allocated a piece of paper a day to wipe themselves with, but they all saved the bigger part of the paper to write on. Generally, the gendarmes would come in the morning to search their clothing for instruments, pencils, matches, and other contraband material. In fact, there was always a supply of such contraband among the prisoners, hidden in nooks and crannies of the cells. For one thing, the families were allowed to send them food and a change of clothes every day; and small items like scissors, pencils, and cigarettes, could be easily sneaked in. For another, the prisoners were allowed to come out into the open air once a day to dump the contents of the commodes. Although they were tied bodily to each other when they came out, a great many maneuvers could be made so that articles could be exchanged. The most coveted item was fruit, because it helped bowel movements; and the most coveted information concerned the kinds of questions the Japanese were asking during interrogation. Some people were released after the interrogation; others were brought back to the cells moaning, their bodies and faces disfigured from torture.

ABOUT A WEEK after Hung was jailed, a Korean man came into Hung's cell and took him upstairs. He was ushered into what used to be a seminar room, about seven by nine feet, with a small window and a blackboard at one end. In the center of the room was an oblong table, on which was placed a stack of documents. A Japanese officer with a military cap was reading at the table; he sat straight up in his chair as soon as Hung entered. The Korean went over to sit on a stool at his right.

"Please bow to His Honor," the Korean said to Hung in Chinese.

Hung felt humiliated that he, a man almost fifty years old, was ordered to bow to a soldier in his twenties. He followed the order and bowed; but as he did, he said, "I am bowing to military might."

The officer told the Korean to get a chair for Hung, and Hung was placed directly across the table from the officer. The officer asked Hung his name, his age, his birthplace, his education, why he had studied in the United States, how many times he had been in Japan, whether he had friends in Japan, and so forth. Occasionally, he would ask Hung to write down the names of people and places. This went on for about half an hour. Then the nature of the questions changed suddenly.

"Are you against the Japanese cause?"

"I am," Hung answered simply.

"What is your reason for resisting Japan?"

Hung replied, "There are two ways I can answer that question. To answer it in a general way, I can tell you that I have no choice but to resist Japanese aggression. But to answer in specifics, I shall need twenty minutes in which I am not interrupted."

The officer said Hung would be given twenty minutes.

This was the opportunity Hung had been waiting for. He made a speech, a portion of which he had already prepared in his mind and a portion of which had just occurred to him in a flash of inspiration.

"I am a historian. When I was young, I studied the history of China; then I went abroad and studied world history, which includes the histories of Japan and Korea. I have come to an important conclusion, which is that the use of military force to conquer other countries, to enslave other people, to make other people submit against their will, can only succeed temporarily. There is bound to be a reaction, and in the end, retribution. When the end finally comes, the oppressors suffer as much as the victims, sometimes worse than the victims."

Hung then drew examples from the history of the West, beginning with Alexander the Great and coming down to Kaiser Wilhelm II in World War I. Then he pointed out that the Chinese had overthrown the Mongolians and the Manchus who had conquered China. "Look at the Manchus, they have now all become beggars and the Han Chinese have to take care of them.

"I am not against the Japanese people. I admire the Japanese people, but not the Japanese military machinery of which Your Honor is a part. Your propaganda says that you have come to conquer China because the Chinese government is corrupt. That was certainly true of the warlords but not true of the Nationalist government. I am not a member of the Kuomintang, and there are a lot of things about the Kuomintang that I don't approve of; but the Kuomintang had started to industrialize China before you came.

"The Japanese military first conquered Manchuria. Then you occupied north China. Now you are fighting the whole world. I don't know when the end will come, but I know it will. When it does, the Japanese people will suffer.

"I am sorry for the Japanese people. They are lied to by the military. The minute they realize they are lied to, they will find out that all the propaganda is empty. You claim that you are establishing a co-prosperity sphere for the Asians. How do we know it is a lie? Just look at the history of Korea, starting in 1885 when Japan first became interested in that country. China went to war with Japan because the Koreans were not able to defend themselves. After you won the war, you annexed Korea. Now whether the Koreans like it or not, they are drafted into the Japanese army and put into subordinate positions. You want to do to China what you did with Korea."

When Hung reached the part about Korea, tears streamed down the face of the Korean interpreter. The Japanese officer turned pale. He did not wait for the interpretation, but interrupted Hung, "It's lunch time. Take him down."

As the Korean took Hung down into his cell, he said, "What you said was true. Keep it up. I think His Honor was also moved."

Hung was so euphoric he could not eat lunch. When he told Tu in whispers about his questioning, Tu commented, "Wonderful! The Japanese bully whom they can, but they respect people with pluck."

Hung was all ready to launch into another speech that afternoon when about two o'clock, the Korean returned to fetch him. As in the morning, the Korean said, "Please bow to His Honor, the officer." And again Hung bowed, saying as he did, "I am bowing to military might." But to his great astonishment, the officer looked at him in silence for a moment; then he put his hat on the table, retreated to the end of the room where the backboard was, and bowed back to Hung, saying in perfect Chinese, "I am bowing to a man who is fearless in speaking his mind!"

"I have forgotten exactly what I said to him. I must have said something to the effect that I did not know His Honor spoke Chinese. He explained to me that he had learned Chinese in college and that he was only doing his duty, and that he wanted to speak to me in private later on."

That evening, the officer called Hung into his room and plied him with tea and pipe tobacco. They had a long conversation as they smoked. He told Hung that his name was Kurozawa and that he was a second lieutenant. He asked Hung what he thought of Chiang Kai-shek. Hung said that he was no admirer of Chiang Kai-shek but that one had to admit Chiang was a moral man and a hero. Hung said that Chiang was a dissipated gangster before he married Sung Mei-ling, but after he was converted to Christianity, he stopped smoking, drinking, gambling, and whoring. Then the Japanese made him a hero. The very fact that the Japanese tried so hard but failed to catch him made him a hero. Kurozawa nodded in agreement.

HUNG'S EXPERIENCE during the interrogation was singular. Most of the other Yenching faculty members arrested were not so lucky. Lu Chih-wei had almost all his teeth knocked out. Others were given the "hose": a water hose was aimed at the face of the prisoner tied on the floor so that the water poured incessantly over him until painfully struggling for breath and choking, he would gradually lose consciousness.

The rest of Hung's stay in the detention cell was relatively uneventful. Once, a number of Japanese were brought in. Along with other prisoners, they were fed three times a day; but the food was terrible. The Chinese shared with them what they had from their families. A student of Hung, James Tzu-chien Liu, was put into the same cell with Hung and Bearded Tu for a brief period. While he was there, he did Hung's washing for him. Later, Hung became seriously ill. He was so weak one day that when the gendarmes came in for the morning search, he could not stand up. A physician was sent in to see him and gave him some aspirin. Hung lay down in his fur coat and did not eat until he recovered.

Some days before the Chinese New Year, a jailer came and told Hung to follow him. He was led to a room where he found ten other Yenching members. They thought they were about to be released; but a man came with handcuffs and locked them all together by pairs, the last prisoner being handcuffed to one of the jailers. Aside from the ones whom Hung had known were imprisoned (Teng Chih-ch'eng, Stephen Ts'ai, Chang Tung-sun, and Lu Chih-wei), there were Chao Tzu-ch'en, the Dean of the School of Religion; Liu Huo-hsien, professor of journalism and a prominent Catholic layman; Ch'en Ch'i-t'ien, Dean of the College of Public Affairs; and three younger members of the faculty, Lin Chia-t'ung, Hou Jen-chih, and Chao Ch'eng-hsin.

Up to this moment, Hung had had no sense of fear at all; but at the sight of the handcuffs, he felt his heart sink. He prayed, "Oh God, I am so ashamed of myself. I have made up my mind not to be afraid. Give me courage so that I can live up to it."

Hung was handcuffed to Chang Tung-sun.

"What does this all mean? Are you scared?" he asked Hung.

"I was, but I am not now."

"If you aren't, then I am not either."

Hung quoted a passage from the Confucian *Analects* to him, "The virtuous man is not alone; he always finds a neighbor."

Chang grinned at that.

They were put in a truck and driven past the Russian Orthodox Church into a Japanese military prison. They did not know where they were; but since they could hear the bells of the church ringing every four hours, they figured that they must be somewhere in the northeastern corner of the city of Peking. They were fingerprinted again, stripped naked for a search before they were allowed to put their clothes back on. They were each assigned a number and were called thereafter only by their number. Hung's number was 506.

For the first eight days, all eleven of them were put into one huge cell and ordered to sit on mats all day facing the wall, which was about two feet away. Guards paced back and forth along the wooden cell gate, crudely latticed. There was no commode, only a foul-smelling hole at one corner of the cell. They were fed twice a day, once at ten in the morning and once around two in the afternoon. The meals consisted of a shallow bowl of steamed millet mixed heavily with sand and ashes (the sand was thought to help their bowel movements), a cup of soup made by boiling scraps from the Japanese table in salty water, and a cup of hot water. These were passed through the holes in the latticed gate, sometimes with chopsticks, sometimes without so that they were forced to eat with their fingers. The two cups of hot water were all they got, for drinking and for washing. Hung therefore often did without the soup, which tended to make him thirstier, and used part of the liquid to wash his face and hands. Fleas and lice soon thrived on their bodies, making them itch all over.

Though they were forbidden to communicate with each other, they whispered every chance they had; and before long, they had developed two sets of code for spelling out messages in English. The first code consisted of a series of scratching movements. The Adam's apple stood for A, the brow for B, the cheek for C, and so on. Out of the corner of their eyes, they could observe these signals; and they were amused when their guards, being suggestible, were soon scratching themselves wildly, too. The second code was transmitted by sounds. Dividing the first twenty-five letters of the alphabet into a matrix of five across and five down, and placing A on the first line, first column, B on first line, second column, and so forth, they could transmit messages by having a rap followed by a second rap standing for A, a rap followed by two raps standing for B, while two raps followed by a single rap stood for F and so on. The sound code proved to be extremely useful later when they were put into solitary confinement. In all their communication then and later, they elicited no response from Ch'en Ch'i-t'ien, the Dean of the College of Public Affairs; and they began to suspect him of intending to cooperate with the Japanese.

Across the corridor, some Japanese soldiers were imprisoned. They were beaten regularly by the guards, but they were fed very well. When the aromatic smell of good food wafted in at mealtimes, the starving Yenching members were driven to distraction. Every week, the soldiers were weighed, which led the Chinese to conclude that the soldiers were there for disciplinary reasons and would be sent back to the battlefields as soon as their sentences were up. The Chinese watched with amazement Japanese military discipline in action. The lowest Japanese officer could slap the face of anyone inferior to him in rank; and the subordinate, having been slapped, was obliged to bow deeply and thank his superior for the honor.

The Chinese were not allowed to lie down until after eight o'clock at night. Then they had to sleep with the naked light bulb shining in their eyes. One of the eleven was sick during this period when they were all together in the big cell. The guard was informed, and the sick man was given permission to lie down. A few days afterwards, another guard, passing the cell, saw the man on the floor and came in to kick him. The first guard told the second that the man was sick and was therefore allowed to lie down. The second guard saw Chang Tung-sun also on the floor, so he kicked him. Hung could hardly keep from laughing when Chang told the guard sulkily, "I am sick too." The guard told Chang he was not sick, kicked him some more, and ordered him to sit up.

Afterwards, when they were separated in a row of small cells for twenty-four days, they came to realize that loneliness was worse than hunger, thirst, cold, and vermin. Again, Chang was the first one to break down. Coming from a wealthy and cultured family near Hangchow in Chekiang, Chang had never slept alone in a room before in his life. The unremitting loneliness, night after day, day after night, became intolerable to him. He had studied in Japan in his younger days but had refused to read, write, or speak any Japanese after he returned to China. In his solitary cell, he could be heard calling out in Japanese to the guard, "Your Honor, Your Honor!"

And the guard would yell at him, "What do you think this is, a hotel? This is a prison! Shut up!"

Then Chang would start cursing him in Japanese. Ignored, he would curse the whole Japanese military establishment, the Japanese nation, the Japanese emperor. "*Baka!*" he would scream. "*Baka!* Donkey! Ass!" The guard would eventually feel compelled to go into his cell and beat him up, while he screeched shrilly. After the guard left, he would dash his head against the cement wall trying to kill himself.

Hung, some eight or nine cells away from Chang, was deeply disturbed. He felt that he, too, was losing his mind. He told himself that no help was forthcoming, except from God. Therefore he pressed his hands over his ears to prevent himself from hearing, leaned his head against the wall and prayed.

"William Hung," he said to himself, "for years you have been complaining that you do not have any time to yourself. Do you realize you now have nothing but time. For once in your life, you've got all the time you want. With your education, you should be able to decide what to do with it!"

He called to mind the examples of Jesus, who spent forty days in the wildneress; Mohammed, who withdrew to spend time alone; and Martin Luther who hid himself in the small town of Wittenberg to meditate. As he prayed and scratched the number of days on the wall with a long fingernail to keep track of the days, he resolved to shut out everything else and formulate a Utopian novel based on his student Chang Wen-li's productionism. He placed the story in 1965 and tried to imagine what China would be like after Japan had been defeated and the Kuomintang and the Communists were cooperating to build a new nation based on productionism. He worked out an elaborate code system and mechanisms whereby crucial data on population, employment, and production for the whole of China could be effectively collected and measured, making possible a planned economy. He conceived an intricate network of political and social control. Around the dry explication of how such a country might work, he built a plot of romance and mystery.

By March 14, 1942, Hung had practically completed a detailed outline of the story in his mind. Suddenly, the cell door flew open and a man was pushed in. It was none other than the Dean of Religion, Chao Tzu-ch'en. They figured the prison must be getting crowded for them to be doubling up. Hung discussed his novel with Chao, and Chao provided Hung with theological support for his vision of a New China. They also spent hours together surreptitiously composing poetry, for

Chao was a poet of no small distinction. There were poems on such subjects as eating on the floor, on dreams, on scratching fleas, on longing for their wives and children, on a sunbeam finding its way to their cell, on the willow tree outside the small window, on hearing the sounds of church bell. (After his release, Chao wrote down his own poems. There were 170 in all, published under the title *Collected Poems of a Prisoner (Nan-kuan-chi)*. Sixty-seven of these, including several addressed to Hung or written in the same rhyme scheme that Hung used, later appeared in the 1971 issue of the *Yenching University Alumni Bulletin.*) Their discussion and poetry-making caused them almost to forget their physical discomfort.

In contrast to Hung, Chao did not eat much of the millet but drank the soup. One day, he knocked on the floor to call Hung's attention. Hung glanced up to see a big grin on his face. Chao had found a piece of pork in his soup, which he held up by a piece of hair still attached to it. Hung felt a surge of pity. Chao's wife was a marvelous cook with a reputation for making delicate Soochow pastries, and here the husband was gloating over a hairy piece of pork.

After seventeen days of sharing a cell with Chao Tzu-ch'en, Hung was taken out of Cell 29 and led to Cell 34 where he found Liu Huo-hsien and the young Yenching professor, Lin Chia-t'ung. As the weather now grew warmer, Hung became perpetually thirsty, so he traded his food for part of the others' water. In their hunger, their minds kept reverting to food. Lin fantasized about a nicely roasted suckling pig; Liu about a *i-p'in kuo,* a hot pot of mixed delicacies; and Hung about platefuls of raw oysters served with tomato sauce, lemon, and horse-radish, to be followed by a honeydew melon.

"What we are eating now is pigfeed, really," one of them sighed.

"We are no common pigs, we are His Majesty, the Emperor's pigs," Hung quipped.

They all burst out laughing. Two guards rushed in immediately, shouting, "Who was talking?"

Hung said that he was, whereupon the older guard said, "The penalty for talking is beating."

Hung was moved to see the younger guard say, "He is too old to be beaten. Let me take the beating in his place." So he bent down on the floor while the older guard gave him two perfunctory raps.

An epidemic of typhus broke out in prison. Chao Ch'eng-hsin almost died of the disease. Men came in to spray green powder in the cells; and Hung could hardly breathe owing to his allergy. But as a result of the epidemic, they were given baths at two different times, their fingernails were clipped and their heads shorn.

On April 14, handcuffed and bound with a cord, Hung was led out of the prison walls about a mile away to the headquarters of the Japanese military court. He was asked whether he regarded Japan as an aggressor and if so, why. Hung gave the same arguments he had given Kurozawa at the Gendarmerie. He was then asked why he did not go over to Chungking and participate in the war of resistance. Hung answered he was too old to bear arms, and besides, he believed in passive, rather than active, resistance. Did he love America? Hung responded that he loved both China and America. Did he believe Japan would lose the war? Hung said he hoped peace would come soon because he did not believe the average Japanese wanted war. Then Hung was asked to explain his social and political ideals.

The following day, he was taken out again. Not knowing that it would be warm, Hung again had his fur overcoat on. There was a blazing fire in the room in which he was interrogated, and Hung asked if he might be unbound so that he could take off his coat. The interrogator interposed, saying that the procedures would be over in a few minutes; but the young stenographer, whose eyes Hung had avoided all this while because he was convinced they were shot through with hatred, extended his hand across the table and offered Hung a box of Japanese cooling pills. Hung looked up in gratitude and found in the stenographer's eyes nothing but sympathy. At that instant, Hung felt that his prayers would be answered and that he would soon be released.

DURING THE DAY, they were still forced to sit on the mats and face the wall. One of their favorite pastimes was to turn their heads to look at the opposite wall when the guards were not looking, and see whether the cobwebs had made any new pattern. One morning, Hung turned his head and noticed that the cobwebs had formed some intriguing patterns on the rough, dirty cement wall.

"There was a jungle; in front of the jungle was the upper part of a man with a little moustache. He was bald and had very sharp, penetrating eyes like an Arab. His arms were stretched out on either side of him, with the back of his hands to the front. Then I saw there were wild beasts behind the man, which the man seemed to have waved back with his hands. I averted my eyes for a moment and looked again. This time, I discovered that above the man's head and beyond the outstretched hands were pieces of wood. It was a picture of the crucifixion! Seeing this, I trembled in fear. When I looked again, I saw to my even greater surprise red blood trickling down from the spot where the man's heart should be! I almost fainted away. Surely, I must be hallucinating and finally losing my mind! So I decided to investigate. I stood up to use the latrine at the corner of the cell and passed directly in front of the wall on my way there. The picture was not visible at close range, but the blood was definitely there. On my way back to my seat, I found out where the blood came from. Someone had killed a bedbug on the wall, and the blood was smeared down the wall! When I sat down and turned my head to look again, the picture was still there. I coughed and caught the attention of Liu Huo-hsien, who was sitting a couple of feet from me. I asked Liu to look and see if he found anything on the opposite wall. Liu shook his head: He couldn't see anything. At 10:00 A.M., when the guards were being changed, I suggested that he change places with me. When he turned his head around, I saw him shudder.

"'What did you see?' I asked him.

"Instead of answering, he asked me if I knew what day it was. I said it was Friday.

"'It's Good Friday,' he said.

"I USUALLY HAD DIFFICULTY falling asleep at night because of the light-bulb shining in my eyes, and I am used to sleeping in the dark. On the evening of May 15, I stayed awake and tried to recall as many happy words as possible beginning with C, because the tungsten in the light-bulb formed the letter C. I had played this game before; but only words such as *calumny, complaint, cough, callous,* came to mind. This evening, what came to me was a chain of eleven words: *Court calls completed. Charge cancelled. Case concluded. Cannot continue. Confinement cut.*"

The next morning, three of them, Hung, Teng Chih-ch'eng, and Liu Huo-hsien, were called to appear before the military court. The major general told them that although the authorities were not happy with their attitudes towards the Japanese army, there was not enough evidence to sustain the charge that they had violated Japanese military law. He apologized for the long detention and wished them a speedy recovery of health. He said that he hoped they would soon join the new government and share the glory of the victory of Japan and her allies.

They were given back the personal belongings taken from them when they were first arrested, and were asked to sign a statement on the envelopes saying that nothing was missing. Then their Japanese jailer shook hands with them and asked whether there was anything he could do. Teng asked for rickshaws to take them home. It was then that new addresses were given to them and they learned for the first time that their homes on the Yenching campus were no longer theirs.

The Japanese had evidently concluded that it would do them no good to have the academics die on their hands. In about a month, the rest of the Yenching eleven were also released. Hung had lost twenty-five pounds during his incarceration. All of them had to recuperate in the hospital for various lengths of time. Lu Chih-wei was carried out on a stretcher. Chao Ch'eng-hsin reached the door of his home in a rickshaw, but his family found him collapsed in a heap on the ground when they answered the doorbell. Ironically, Chang Tung-sun, who among all of them had clearly suffered the most, was completely cured of his ulcer while in prison.

CHAPTER EIGHTEEN

Victory

AFTER HUNG WAS MOVED from the Gendarmerie, his wife Rhoda could not find out where he was. The packages she sent to him were returned with no explanation. She and the other ten wives met to exchange news. It became Rhoda's task to carry on the search among the foreigners. All the British and Americans were either repatriated or put into concentration camps; but German citizens, their country allied at war with Japan, were left free. She appealed to Helmut Wilhelm, Walter Fuches, Wolfgang Franke, and other German Sinologists in Peking. They tried to help but to no avail. For a time, she was told that all the Yenching prisoners had been shot. It was not until the last few weeks of their imprisonment that the wives learned of their whereabouts and were allowed to send them clean clothing and halibut oil pills for vitamins A and D.

Upon his release, Hung took the rickshaw to Hsin-k'ai Road, where Rhoda had many years earlier bought him a house as a refuge from his callers, to provide him with a place where he could do his work uninterrupted. He found on his arrival that a physician, Dr. Feng Ying-k'un and his wife were occupying the premises. They told him that Rhoda and Agnes had been staying with Dr. S. T. Wang of the Peking Union Medical College. A phone call was put through to the Wang residence; and when Hung got there, he was greeted with chicken soup and tears.

Many friends came to congratulate him on his release. An unusual package came from Dr. John C. Ferguson, an American who served as adviser to successive Chinese governments. Ferguson had not been interned by the Japanese on account of his advanced age and great prestige. He had valued Hung's opinions on the authenticity of Chinese scrolls, which he acquired in large number. In the 1930s, a book trader had shown a rare 1577 edition of *Shih-t'ung* to Hung. This was known as the Chang Chih-hsiang edition, by far the best of the extant texts. The asking price was 300 yuans, almost Hung's entire monthly salary. While Hung was agonizing over whether to buy it, the book was sold to Ferguson. Now he had sent Hung the book as a present along with his note of felicitation.

As the euphoria of having been released subsided, Hung came to realize how harsh life had been for Rhoda while he was away. Lacking any income, she had been forced to sell their possessions piece by piece. For the same reason, the Hsin-k'ai Road house had been rented out. Even though Dr. and Mrs. Wang had been most gracious, the Hungs felt they could not remain with them indefinitely. Arrangements were made for them to move back to the Hsin-k'ai Road house, sharing it with the Fengs. More things were sold just to pay for food. Off went more rugs, Hung's English typewriters, Hung's Chinese typewriters. Also sold was a beautiful set of prints over which Rhoda cried because it had originally been a birthday present to her from her husband. Finally they had to sell a set of the *Twenty-Four Histories* on the margins of which Hung had made valuable comments over the years. Fortunately, before they were totally destitute, Dr. S. T. Wang came up with timely financial advice: They should mortgage their house for cash, which could be deposited in Chinese-style banks in return for interest. Over moral scruples — for they knew that the bank lent the cash again at usurious rates — they decided on that course.

Some financial assistance came to the erstwhile Yenching prisoners from a remarkable businessman, Sung Fei-ch'ing, the owner of the Tientsin East Asia Textile Company. The company was widely known for the good wages and fringe benefits it provided its employees. It ran a school for the children of employees, and scholarships were available for those dependents who wanted to go on to higher education. There were also profit-sharing and pension plans, all of which were virtually unheard of at that time in China or in the West. One night at around midnight, this Mr. Sung came in a rickshaw to see Hung, bringing with him rolls of banknotes which he asked Hung to distribute among his colleagues. To keep the Japanese from being suspicious, he wanted Hung to say that he, Sung, had offered to buy old Chinese scrolls from these professors; and if they wanted to, they could send him some fake ones. Hung divided the money evenly among ten of the eleven prisoners. None went to Ch'en Ch'i-t'ien; for by that time, his cooperation with the Japanese was common knowledge. He had moved back to the

Yenching campus and was seen walking around behind Japanese officers with a briefcase in hand.

The Nationalist government in Chungking had also appropriated funds to aid the ex-prisoners from Yenching. The exact amount was not known, but it was thought to have been substantial. By the time the money reached the professors, however, having passed through many hands, there was barely enough to buy a pound of meat.

Being unemployed, Hung concentrated on setting down on paper the novel he conceived in jail. He wrote it in English so that Rhoda could enjoy it. He gave it the title *The Harvest is Plenteous*. He also worked on an annotated bibliography of Chinese bibliographies, as well as a reference work on Chinese phonology. The novel was never published, and the other two works were not completed.

To STAVE OFF mental depression and to escape the marital tension that so often preys on poverty, many of the Yenching staff took to playing mahjong. One evening, after a late game, Hung talked on late into the night with Lu Chih-wei, who had a Ph.D. in psychology but who had turned to traditional phonetics when he realized how difficult it was to conduct psychological research in China. Lu asked Hung what his greatest ambition in life was. Hung said he hoped to make contributions in the fields of religion, education, and government. Lu remarked that Hung's goals were too diffuse and confided that, as for himself, he wanted to be China's Minister of Education for a year so that he would have a chance to try out some of his long-standing ideas on education. He had been Yenching's Acting Chancellor from 1934 to 1937 and worked to raise academic standards throughout the university.

"When Yenching University is restored, I hope to become the Chancellor. I don't think I did a bad job as Acting Chancellor before the Japanese came."

"I guess the two most likely candidates for the chancellorship are you and I," Hung said. "You have my full support. From the chancellorship of Yenching to the Ministry of Education, that is but a short distance."

"And yet," Lu mused, "I don't think I want to be a minister of education under the Kuomintang. I'd much rather work under the Communists."

Hung and Lu diverged sharply over their opinions on the Communist Party. Hung liked the socialist ideas of the Communists, but their materialistic view of history clashed with his Confucian and Christian outlook on life. He also objected to their program of destroying everything traditional in order to build an entirely new society. Hung believed that the progress of mankind is cumulative and to destroy something simply because it is old would be too wasteful. Yet it was precisely the forceful and incisive way with which the Communists carried out their plans that appealed most to Lu. To Lu, as to many intellectuals at the time, Chinese society was a hopeless accretion of disparate and mostly useless traditions. It would be an impossible task to sort things out. It was much simpler to start anew. Between 1946 and 1952, Lu did become the head of Yenching, but he suffered mass criticism and died in humiliation under the Communists.

DURING THIS PERIOD, Hung counted among his closest friends several persons outside academia. Sung Fei-ch'ing was one. There was also Liu Shih-sun, a former banker and the father of Hung's student, James Tzu-chien Liu. Both Mr. and Mrs. Liu attributed their excellent health to Taoist meditation performed several times daily in which the meditator sits upright with legs crossed and focusses the mind first on emptiness and then on a shifting point in imagination that follows a circuit around the body. They convinced Hung to try the regimen, but he ran out of patience. Another non-academic friend was Sun Ping-ju, owner of a big flour company in Tientsin. When he came into Peking, he would spend the night in Hung's study. Together they would go out drinking and hold long discourses on books and business conditions. There were Wang Cheng-fu and his wife, Liao Feng-hsien, whom Hung knew from his students days in the United States. The Wangs ran what amounted to an open house for their unemployed friends.

TOWARDS THE LAST MONTHS of the long war, when it became increasingly likely that Japan would lose, the Chinese who had collaborated with the Japanese started to be very nervous and began to lavish presents on those members of the community who were thought to have the stature to plead their cause should the defeat come. Individuals like Hung, Lu Chih-wei, and Stephen Ts'ai were above suspicion of having compromised themselves by accepting gifts. But Chang Tung-sun, who continued to live rather well, was rumoured to have succumbed; and Teng Chih-ch'eng, who was impoverished, was also held suspect.

Hung decided to pay a visit to his old friend Teng, whom he had not seen for some time, to find out for himself. As Hung made the hour-long hike across the city to Teng's house, he ruminated over the reasons why Teng was such an easy victim for malicious rumors. Surely, it was partly due to the fact that Teng himself did not restrain his caustic tongue when it came to criticizing his colleagues. The story about his keeping a concubine was true. She was a woman who had fled from a family that treated her cruelly. But the rumour about Teng's being an opium addict was disposed of conclusively when they were all in jail together. Teng displayed no withdrawal symptoms whatsoever.

It was not quite dark, but Hung found Teng eating dinner alone. A look at the food was enough to reassure Hung that his friend had not sold out. The dinner consisted of a big piece of *wo-wo-t'ou* (a coarse bread made of kaoliang), a small plate of salted vegetable, and a small plate of fried peanuts. Hung sat down at the table and questioned Teng in a mock-formal manner.

Had such and such a person come to see Mr. Teng?

Yes, Mr. Teng said, he had.

Had Mr. Teng kept the offered present?

Teng laughed and asked Hung would he be eating the food on the table if he had.

Hung wondered aloud how did Mr. Teng decline the present.

Teng said, "You, my dear Mr. William Hung, might have had difficulty declining the present with due decency. But it was very easy for me. I just asked him whether he had offered the present to Mr. William Hung. As he answered in the affirmative, I asked if Mr. William Hung had kept the present; and he said no. Thereupon I said, 'If Mr. William Hung did not keep the present, I don't think I am going to keep it either.'"

The two friends had a hearty laugh together.

HUNG received his first news that the war was definitely ending from Rudolf Loewenthal, a Jewish refugee whom he had taken under his wing in the 1930s. When Loewenthal's teaching at Yenching did not work out, Hung gave him a job at the library. Later, Hung sponsored him for Chinese citizenship, and Loewenthal became a loyal friend of the family. While Hung was in jail, he was constantly turning up and asking Rhoda in his lilting English, "Mrs. Hung, do you need some money?" Because he was a person of anomalous status, a German Jew with Chinese citizenship, the Japanese did not quite know what to do with him. He had access to a great deal of news. It was he who first told Hung of the Potsdam Conference in July, 1945. A few days later, Stephen Ts'ai came to bid Hung farewell. He was tired of sitting in Peking doing nothing and had decided to make the six-week trip to join Yenching University in Exile in the south. Hung was able to dissuade him from leaving on the strength of what he had heard from Loewenthal.

Soon news of the atomic bombs dropped on Hiroshima and Nagasaki was all over Peking. On the evening of August 14, Loewenthal came to see the Hungs again and relayed to them the yet unconfirmed report that Japan had surrendered. They looked around the neighborhood and saw that all the lights in Japanese residences were extinguished. They were all sitting quietly expectant in the courtyard when, suddenly, someone banged on the gate. In burst a man with a bicycle, yelling at the top of his voice *"Dou-hang le! Dou-hang le!"* It took them a few seconds to realize that it was James Liu's eldest brother, and he was yelling "Surrendered! Surrendered!" in Shanghainese. The news certainly called for celebration. Dr. Feng went in the house and brought out all the soft drinks and wine he could find. He also brought out his patients' book; for ever since Hung had been released from prison, Dr. Feng had maintained the fiction that Hung was under his care for a nervous disorder. It had been his way of keeping Japanese officials at bay when they came around asking questions. Now, under Hung's name, he wrote in a great big character, "DISCHARGED." They laughed and talked and ate and drank to a near stupor that night.

Early the following morning, Stephen Ts'ai showed up, embraced Hung, and gave him a kiss on either cheek. "Thanks to you," he said, "I am here today. Otherwise I'd be on the road somewhere between Peking and Chungking. Let's find out where Stuart is and reopen Yenching at once." Everywhere on the street, they saw Japanese soldiers and civilians kneeling on the ground, weeping.

Chang Tung-sun, who could always be counted on to sum up a situation vividly, made the memorable remark that, "The Japanese have been shitting on our heads for fifty years. We finally got their asses off!"

BANKERS came in droves to offer unlimited credit to Yenching. For the first few days, Stephen Ts'ai, as the university business manager, deputized Hung to be in charge of financial matters. Hung made the first check to Dr. and Mrs. Torii and personally took it to their residence.

He found Mrs. Torii drawing water from the well in the yard, bare-footed. The past few years must have been miserable and lonely for them. They had neither Chinese nor Japanese friends.

Stuart was released in a few days. The Japanese had held him under guard in a private house for nearly four years, as a possible emissary between the Japanese government and Chiang Kai-shek. The Yenching faculty met at a temple near the American consulate to discuss plans for reopening the university. They set a reopening ceremony for 10:00 A.M. on the Double Tenth Day (October 10, the Chinese Republic Day). Hung was elected to make the opening speech. Rhoda had a hood and gown of black satin specially made for him to wear on this solemn occasion.

Much had to be done to restore the Yenching campus before it could function as a university again. The buildings were filthy, and the Japanese had ripped out all the bathroom fixtures and replaced them with Japanese equipment. Yet more than the physical facilities, reopening the university meant reassembling the faculty, which was scattered far and wide. They were also faced with the delicate question of whom to invite back. Those who had clearly collaborated with the Japanese, such as Ch'en Ch'i-t'ien, would not be tolerated, even though, like him, most of them had acted out of desperation. But what about those who were under a cloud of suspicion, such as Chang Tung-sun? Could decisions be made in an equitable way without setting up formal investigations?

Hung advocated inviting Chang back; for he felt that whether Chang had secretly received money from the Chinese politicians in the puppet government or not, he did suffer grievously in prison, and the Japanese would not let him commit suicide for fear of creating a martyr. After one discussion, Hung thought that the matter was settled; but on the next day, Stuart again proposed that they not invite Chang back. Upon being pressed to explain, he disclosed that Chiang Kai-shek had asked him not to re-employ Chang Tung-sun because Chang had always been a political gadfly and a thorn on the side of the Kuomintang. Hung hit the ceiling. If Chang were not allowed to come back, Hung said, he, William Hung, was not going to stay. As a result, Chang was invited back.

Hung was not so successful, however, with two other individuals in whose behalf he exerted himself. T'ien Hung-tu, the university librarian whom Hung had arranged to receive training at Harvard in 1930, had continued to run the library under the Japanese. Hung argued that his motive was to keep the Yenching collection intact, but the other members of the faculty were not convinced. The other was Jung Keng, who had accepted a teaching post at Peking University under the puppet government. Hung pointed out that Jung had been a very active member of the resistance movement; in fact, he had founded the anti-Japanese magazine *Torch* in which many faculty members had contributed patriotic articles and had accepted the post at Peking University only because he had to eat. But that motion, too, was rejected in the general wave of revulsion against anybody "tainted" by dealings with the occupational forces.

As soon as Hung had the chance, he went to inspect the condition of the Harvard-Yenching Sinological Index Series office. The printing presses were all gone. Inquiries revealed that they had been sold to a private company backed by a collaborator with the Japanese. Hung immediately laid claim to them as American property, but the government officials sent up from Chungking to take over Japanese properties insisted that these now should belong to the Nationalist government. Hung's assistant, Li Shu-ch'un, was still in the process of negotiating for the presses' return to Yenching when Hung left China in 1946.

BEFORE THE HUNGS moved back to the Yenching campus, while they were still cramped in their house on Hsin-k'ai Road, they received a call from a distinguished visitor, Li Tsung-jen, one of the most widely respected military and political figures in China during the first half of the twentieth century. He was enlightened in outlook and had built a firm power base in China's southwest before the rise of Chiang Kai-shek. He cooperated with Chiang not from any great love of the man but in the interest of national unity. After the war with Japan ended, he was appointed by Chiang to be director of the presidential headquarters in Peking. Li came to see Hung to offer him a position on his staff as secretary-general, with a military ranking of major-general.

"Li Tsung-jen came with a number of attendants in military uniform. He had a rustic cast of face, and his complexion was yellowish; but his bearing was dignified, and his speech and manners showed him to be a man of good character. I suspect he had presidential ambitions and saw in me someone who might be of use to him in dealing with the Americans."

Hung declined the offer but assured Li Tsung-jen that he would be glad to give him his opinion on issues about which he felt knowledgeable. Consequently, Hung was invited to have dinner a couple of times with Li. Li consulted Hung mainly on his estimation of prospective appointees. Hung also became one of the only two civilians, along with Lu Chih-wei, to be present at a banquet given by Li for General Albert C. Wedemeyer at Huai-jen-t'ang, the audience hall of the late Empress Dowager in the Forbidden City. The banquet provided Hung with the occasion to make one of those extemporaneous speeches of which he was proud and the opportunity to conduct the kind of personal diplomacy at which he excelled.

"At the end of the dinner, Li Tsung-jen got up, as the representative of the Generalissimo to welcome the Americans. All the while, a Chinese general interpreted for him. Then Wedemeyer made a speech, an excellent speech. His main point was that China had not been able to become a great power contributing to world peace and prosperity because of two main enemies. The first enemy, an external one, was Japan. For half a century, Japan had been manipulating Chinese politics, causing so many problems and so much suffering that China was hardly able to survive. Now the Americans, as friends of China, had helped China defeat Japan. It would be a long time before Japan would be able to bother China again.

"'And yet,' he continued, 'I would not be doing my duty as a friend to China without mentioning another enemy of China, against whom unfortunately we Americans can do very little to help, because it is your internal enemy. The name of this enemy is greed. Before you can enjoy real freedom and contribute your full share to the world's welfare, you have to eliminate this enemy, greed.'

"His interpreter, General Bliss, who spoke perfect Chinese, translated the whole speech; but he omitted the part on greed because the Chinese generals were all there, and they were mostly corrupt! I could not stand it. So I rose from my seat and said, 'General Li and friends, I beg your permission as a civilian guest to say something.' Everybody was astounded.

"I said, 'First of all, as a civilian and a student of history, I want to express my appreciation for the wonderful speech of our friend and great soldier, General Wedemyer, and I am grateful to General Bliss for his accurate but very diplomatic translation. To save the face of the Chinese, he omitted to translate the second part of the speech. Now I will give the translation in Chinese.' After I finished, the whole hall was completely silent.

"When the banquet was over, I took Wedemeyer aside and put him in the Empress's throne chair. I told him he deserved the highest honor because he was a real friend of China. Then I said, 'General, I have a request to make of you. You have thousands of American boys all concentrated in the southwest of China. It is the backyard of China—while the scenery is beautiful there, the culture is backward. Many of these boys are now ready to sail home, and they have not seen the real China. I wonder if you would allow those who so desire to spend a few days in Peking at U.S. Government expense?'

"Wedemeyer said he would see to it. So I organized a committee among university faculties and students to welcome the American soldiers, and I made a speech at Yenching to prepare the students for their arrival. That became the article on Chinese-American relations which was published in the magazine, *Ta-Chung* [51]."

HUNG had had no news of either his brothers or sister since 1941. After his family moved back to the campus, he received a telegram from David sent from New York saying that he hoped to see Hung very soon. One evening when Hung was having dinner at a friend's house in the city, he was called to the telephone. His brother David had already arrived at the Hung's residence at Yenching and wanted to see him immediately because he could not stay long. Hung decided this was the time when he could use his influence with Li Ts'ung-jen. He called Li to borrow a car and asked to have the West City Gate opened so that he could get out of the city. The two brothers were reunited after nine years of separation.

David disclosed that during the war years he was responsible for demolishing roads, railways, and bridges as the Nationalist army retreated to the south. He thus supervised the destruction of many bridges he himself had designed, including the famous Hsiang-chiang Bridge he had thought would ensure him a place in the history of Chinese engineering. Towards the end of the war, he was exhausted to the point of paralysis and was sent by his superiors on a study tour to the United States as an excuse to give him some much needed rest. In New York, many of his old classmates from Rensselaer Polytechnic Institute came to see him and offered him high-paying positions working for them in railroad and steel companies in the United States; but David was resolved to go back to China, for his one dream in life was to see China crisscrossed by railroads. When the war was over, the Ministry of Transportation cabled him to return immediately.

A government airplane met him in Tsingtao to take him back to

Chungking. While it stopped over in Shanghai to pick up another passenger, he saw an American military airplane a few yards away. He went over to strike up a conversation with the pilot and found that the plane was *en route* to Peking, whereupon he asked for and received a free ride to Peking to see Hung.

After a few days' visit with Hung, David was whisked off again. He found that he was to be assigned the impossible task of scheduling an orderly transport of government employees and their dependents back to Nanking. This job had very little to do with civil engineering; rather, it had to do with David's reputation of being a selfless and impartial administrator.

HUNG was called upon for advice by a great variety of people in the hectic days right after the war. Hsiang Che-chün, a long-time fraternity brother, dropped by on his way to Tokyo, where he was to lead the Chinese judicial delegation to prosecute Tojo and other Japanese war criminals in the International Tribunal for the Far East — the Asian counterpart of the Nuremberg Trials. He asked Hung to find him an assistant with adminstrative ability, who spoke both Japanese and English. Hung said that he had just the right person, James Tzu-chien Liu, who, in addition to Japanese and English, knew French and some Russian. He had, moreover, the distinction of having emerged from two stays in Japanese prisons bruised but free from any bitterness against the Japanese. On the latter score especially, Hung received nothing but praises about him. Hung was also approached by a group of paper merchants who were planning to make a proposal to the government to let them take over the paper factories left behind by the Japanese. They wanted to operate these factories on a fifty-one, forty-nine partnership with the government. The merchants asked Hung whether he knew of any Chinese with Western training in papermaking who could help them run the factories. Hung immediately thought of Dick Uong. He promised the merchants that he would get in touch with Uong as soon as he reached the United States.

His help was also sought by those in personal predicaments, and his contacts across the political spectrum proved useful. A former Yenching student who found herself alone, homeless, and pregnant after time spent with guerrillas "over the hills" appeared in his study one day, baffled by where else to turn. Hung's answer was to go himself to see another former Yenching student, Wang Ju-mei — now Huang Hua of the Communist Party. Hung had recently seen him at a cocktail party inaugurating the "Three Parties Team," the team of representatives from the Kuomintang, the Communist Party, and the U. S. government that sought to develop a *modus vivendi* for the three powers active in China after the war. Huang Hua agreed to see that she was taken care of; and after a few days, she was gone from the Hungs' house.

ON NOVEMBER 6, 1945, Hung wrote a long letter to Eric North and, because the postal system was not yet normalized again, sent it care of Leighton Stuart, who was departing for a trip to the United States.

We moved back to our University residence on October 8th. It was exactly three years and ten months and eleven days since I was taken and imprisoned by the Japanese gendarmerie. Though an extended repair was given to our residence just a few days before our removal, the house was still in a really bad condition. All ceilings were black with smoke and the floors dirty and smelly. All the window screens were off and shades missing. Most of the door locks were torn and keys missing. Several of the radiators were broken and the plumbing system was severely damaged. The garden was in a fearful mess, the lawn was replaced by several patches of cabbage cultivation, the flower plants were gone and the bamboos were dead. The trees have grown considerably. Even up to now we are still living in a semi-camping style and the task of tidying up here and there is still going on . .

I feel that I was practically cut off from the outside world for a period of four years. I know practically nothing of what happened during these four years in the academic world. I am eager to get in touch again with the Sinological activities of the Harvard Yenching Institute in America and in free China. Here at Yenching we are planning to restore the Index Press to a degree of usability. If we can locate the whereabouts of the good paper which we bought from America four years ago and if we could regain it in part or in whole, we shall begin to publish some of our indices and the *Journal of Chinese Studies* . . .

Perhaps our University Trustees and the United Board may start some financial campaign for the University after consultation with President Stuart. I proposed to President Stuart that I shall be willing to come to America later this winter or early next spring if our University Trustees wish to make use of me in connection with any such campaign. President Stuart is very agreeable to this idea, and he informed me that he has already written to the Trustees about it.

I would like to spend only a few months in America, to return to Peiping in time for teaching and research and any administrative work no later than the autumn of 1946. I wish to take Rhoda with me to America this time. Perhaps it may be fair for the University Trustees and the Harvard Yenching Institute to bear our travelling expenses half and half. The University Trustees may be willing to defray the half since my time in America will be used mostly on the campaign; the Institute may be willing to defray the other half since during a period of fifteen years I have not had a furlough . . .

During the period of the 'Babylonian exile' we wrote no letters and received none. Only a few days ago we received a cable from our second daughter Gertrude informing us that she is already married and is working for Station W.P.A. at P[u]rdue University where her husband Sheldon Chang is pursuing graduate work in physics. She informs us also that her elder sister Ruth is married also and is living with her son, Billy, in Alhambra, California, and that Ruth's husband, S[e]rgeant Young Chin, is on the service somewhere in the Pacific theater. I am hoping that I can bring Rhoda to America so that she may have the joy of seeing our children and the grandchild.

The bitter war years have exhausted all of our savings. I have sold part of my own library, more than half of the house furnishings and all of Rhoda's jewelry except the wedding and engagement rings. The debts at the present conversion rates will be about several million local dollars. Fortunately they are mostly from friends who will not press for the return. I am not at all unhappy. The joy of being alive and at work without the Japanese oppression will more than compensate the economic losses. But our financial status is such that I need to request aid from our University and the Harvard Yenching Institute Trustees to pay also for Rhoda's travelling expenses.

I am enclosing a copy of another letter to Dr. Elisseeff. I am not at all certain of my present status with the Harvard Yenching Institute, but I presume Dr. Elisseeff and the Trustees of the Institute will, perhaps, welcome my findings that may have a bearing on the future work of the Institute in China . . .

There was a note of desperation in the letter, and a certain amount of self-pity and self-doubt very uncharacteristic of Hung. Between Eric North, who was a trustee of the Harvard-Yenching Institute, and Serge Elisséeff, its director, arrangements were made for Hung to lecture at Harvard for a semester. With plans for Rhoda to follow in the summer, he left Peking in April, 1946. It became a long journey, for Hung was never to make his way back to China again.

Part Five

William and Rhoda Hung
Cambridge, Massachusetts, ca. 1970

CHAPTER NINETEEN

A Very Long Journey:
1946–1949

THE JOURNEY began inauspiciously with a prolonged airplane ride from Peking to Shanghai. It was Hung's first experience with the flying machine. The trip was supposed to take two hours; but when they were in the air, the pilot was instructed to search for another plane, which had crashed in the vicinity. Airplane crashes were daily occurrences; the carriers were generally none too airworthy to begin with, and they were invariably overloaded. After five hours of fruitless search, Hung's flight landed in the Shanghai airport late in the night.

Hung's brother Fred was in Shanghai, but Hung had only his office telephone number and not his home address. He asked where his fellow passenger, an American army officer, was going to spend the night. The officer said the the U.S. Army was billeted at the Park Hotel and if Hung liked, he could go with him and see whether he could be accommodated there. Feeling half like an impostor, Hung explained his plight to the Americans at the desk of the Park Hotel. The fact that he was on his way to teach at Harvard seemed to carry a lot of weight, and he was put up in a vacant room. But he was kept awake all night by prostitutes soliciting business. Every time the phone rang, there would be a different voice at the other end cooing, "Dearie, aren't you lonesome? Why don't you come down and buy me a drink?"

The next day, Hung called the office of the United Nations Relief and Rehabilitation Administration (UNRRA) to try to find Fred. Taking his family with him, Fred had retreated to Chungking with the Nationalist Government during the war and was now working for UNRRA in China. Since he was not in the office, Hung got in touch with an old student, Chang T'ien-tse, an editor at the Shanghai Commercial Press. Chang immediately came to see him. He told Hung that living space was virtually impossible to find in Shanghai and that it would be out of the question for him to stay with Fred, because Fred, his wife, three children, his mother-in-law, his wife's niece, and a maid were all eight crammed into one rented room. Chang urged Hung to take advantage of the offer of another Yenching alumnus, a businessman by the name of T'an, to stay in his apartment while he was away. Hung did stay there for almost a month while he waited for his travel papers to be processed and for a plane seat to the United States.

While he was in Shanghai, a painful carbuncle grew on Hung's neck. The sister of Chang Wen-li, Chang Ch'ün-hsia, happened to hear about it and came to nurse him. The protuberant growth was eventually cured by the new wonder drug penicillin, obtained in the black market. From her, Hung also learned what had happened to Chang Wen-li, whom he had last seen in 1933. It appeared that in fomenting a peasant revolution based on his concept of productionism in Fukien, Chang was implicated in the 1933–1934 Fukien Rebellion against Chiang Kai-shek. The rebellion was crushed, and Chang went into hiding. With the eruption of the Sino-Japanese War, however, men like Chang Wen-li were welcomed back to the fold of the Nationalist government; and Chang took advantage of the general amnesty. He changed his name to Chang Yen-che and for a couple of years served with distinction as city treasurer for Chungking. When Ch'en Yi was sent to take over Taiwan from the Japanese, Chang was assigned to accompany him as treasurer for the province of Taiwan. According to his sister, Chang had sent Hung a letter with some money after the war; but it evidently had not reached Hung.

In a bank one day, Hung happened to be talking to a Taiwanese. He queried him on the conditions in Taiwan, and the man launched into an emotional attack on Nationalist brutality on the island. He predicted that Taiwanese resentment against the Nationalist government would erupt into violence. Hung wrote a long letter to Chang expressing his concern but received no reply.

Hung found the disorganized and overloaded government bureaucracy, part of which was still in transit from Chungking, incapable of performing the most routine procedure in an orderly manner. Anything that got done at all was done through personal connections. After repeated difficulty in securing a passport, Hung paid a call on his friend H. H. Kung. It was often the case with the two rival brothers-in-law of Chiang Kai-shek that when T. V. Soong was in power, H. H. Kung was out, and vice versa. At this time, H. H. Kung was more out than in.

During the course of the dinner, Kung indicated that Yenching people had put out a feeler to him, asking him whether he would assume the chancellorship of the University; and he asked for Hung's advice. Hung was torn between his eagerness to be gracious to his host and his desire to speak his mind. After much deliberation, he chose to be candid: Kung had been on the Yenching Board of Managers for years and had held the chancellorship in a purely nominal way briefly before the war, expediently answering the political need of the university. Hung did not think Kung would ever take the post earnestly, whereas Lu Chih-wei, who wanted the job very much, had great plans he wanted to carry out. Hung felt he should give Lu Chih-wei a hand.

"If I were in your place," he said to Kung, "I would not take it. You are busy with your political activities, and I don't imagine you would really have the time to attend to academic and administrative details. Yet once you occupy the position, you would be inundated with all kinds of trivial requests—to act as sponsor at weddings, to be the arbitrator at disputes, to help people like me get passports. You'd end up with a lot of trouble for a title you don't need. Moreover Lu Chih-wei is doing the job right now. He should be given a chance to really prove himself."

"You are right. You are right," Kung said. But that obviously was not the response he had been looking for.

WHEN HUNG finally arrived in the United States in May of 1946, his daughter Ruth found him old, tired, and low in spirit. He was the picture of a man who had lived through a long period of traumatic experiences, to find at its end, not a peaceful respite, but more painful conflicts, more uncertainties, more calls for sacrifice.

Though the crowding was less extreme than in Shanghai, housing was at a premium in postwar Cambridge. For a while, Hung slept in the living room of the Harvard-Yenching Institute librarian, Ch'iu K'ai-ming. After Rhoda and Agnes arrived in August, they stayed at the house of Charles Sidney Gardner, an assistant professor at Harvard whom Hung had first met in Peking. The Gardners were spending the summer in Maine and let them use their house. On their return, the Hungs moved in with the widow of Professor William Arnold on Francis Avenue, until a few months later, when the heirs of Reverend William Worcester, whom they had known in 1928, found out about their living situation and offered to have them stay in his house at Five Bryant Street, while they put the house on the market for sale. The Hungs opened the doors of the splendid fifteen-room dwelling for other transients like themselves. When Lord and Lady Michael Lindsay came to Cambridge with their two young children, both born in Communist guerilla territory in North China during the war, they found accommodation with the Hungs at Five Bryant Street.

At Harvard, Hung taught a course on Tu Fu, the poet to whom his father had introduced him in his youth. As his father had predicted, Tu Fu's poetry grew on him as he went through turbulent experiences similar to those of the poet. In 1940, he had the satisfaction of bringing out in the Harvard-Yenching Sinological Index Series, a *Concordance to the Poems of Tu Fu* (38). For it he wrote a long preface that deals with the textual history of the poems, evaluates the two dozen or so known editions, and explains why he chose to base the *Concordance* on an 1181 edition instead of a purportedly earlier one, which he thought to be a forgery. When he was incarcerated by the Japanese, fragments of Tu Fu's poems haunted him. The turmoil, upheaval, and dislocation in Tu Fu's time was analogous to what was happening in China during Hung's own lifetime. Tu Fu's famous lines, "The nation is shattered; / Only the landscape remains," had been too heartbreakingly applicable. Yet Tu Fu lived his life bravely and unselfishly. Between 1946 and 1949, Hung was to lecture on Tu Fu at Yale, the University of Pittsburgh (48), the University of Hawaii, as well as at Harvard.

Hung eventually organized his lectures on Tu Fu into a two-volume book, *Tu Fu: China's Greatest Poet* (42; 43), published by Harvard University Press in 1952. The first volume offered a reconstructed account of Tu Fu's life, interspersed with 374 of Tu Fu's fourteen-hundred-odd poems. The second volume was constituted entirely of notes to the first, with references to source materials and discussions of spurious poems, chronological clues, and the sequence of the poems. The accounts of Tu Fu's life had hitherto been sketchy and contradictory, partly because the poet was not "discovered" until some half a century after his death. Hung, basing his inferences on both historical sources and close readings of the poems and more than thirty pieces of Tu Fu's prose, was able to piece together a well-documented history of the poet's life, which eliminated many misconceptions.* Because Tu

---

*Even Hung's own work eventually needed some revision. In 1957, the Shanghai Commercial Press published the *Sung-pen Tu Kung-pu chi* (*Sung Editions of Collections of Tu Fu's Works*). It contains a facsimile of newly uncovered fragments of the 1133 edi-

Fu's poetry was so inextricably interwoven with the events of the period, Hung's book also gave a vivid portrayal of eighth-century China—a most brilliant and poignantly tragic epoch in Chinese history. Hung described in arresting detail the political institutions, economic conditions, social climate, and intellectual milieu of the T'ang dynasty under the Emperors Hsuan-tsung, Shu-tsung, and T'ai-tsung. He apologized for the inadequacy of his English in the translation of the poems; but they read easily and smoothly, and critics gave him high marks for conveying the true sentiments of Tu Fu.

While Hung's choice of Tu Fu as his subject of study is easily understandable, his intense identification with the man is at times baffling. He seemed to take an almost personal offense at any negative comment on Tu Fu's character. He reacted vehemently to the characterization of Tu Fu in the *New Standard History of the Tang,* (*Hsin Tang-shu* published in 1060) as an undisciplined person who liked to make idealistic but impractical suggestions on political matters; and Hung reacted much the same way to A. R. Davis's remark that Tu Fu was guilty of ethnic chauvinism.

Many years later, in 1979, in a lecture at Harvard, Hung had the pleasure of lashing out at the writer Kuo Mo-jo, who was then still alive in Mainland China, for chiding Tu Fu for his refusal to accept the post of commissioner of police. Kuo Mo-jo accused Tu Fu of shirking the job because it was in a remote province. Hung pointed out that Kuo Mo-jo's geography was wrong and composed a biting poem of four couplets to ridicule him. Hung cited numerous sources to show that Tu Fu declined the job offer, even though he was desperately poor, out of repugnance at its nature, which was to administer whippings to draft evaders and tax delinquents. (Professor Yang Lien-sheng pointed out to me also that according to poems written by Tu Fu's contemporaries, a commissioner of police at that time might himself be subject to beating.)

Hung depicted Tu Fu as a man of great compassion, who entered into the feelings of creatures big and small. Moved by the sufferings of the common people, he articulated their griefs. His own life was tragic, but

---

tion, which Hung had hitherto suspected to be a forgery by Ch'ien Ch'ien-i. Although the facsimile showed that Ch'ien did misuse the 1133 edition, its undeniable existence compelled Hung to modify his harsh view of Ch'ien Ch'ien-i; and he revised his earlier remarks on several minor points as well in his 1962 article "Wo Tsen-yang hsieh Tu Fu" ("How I Wrote About Tu Fu") (54), in his 1971 review of A. R. Davis's book on Tu Fu (56), and his 1974 article "Tsai shuo Tu Fu" ("Discussing Tu Fu Again") (57).

he faced it bravely and with unyielding grace. Yet, Tu Fu was also a man of immense psychological complexity, inconsistent at times and ineffectual as a public official.

Why did Hung feel compelled to insist that Tu Fu was a paragon of virtue as well as a great poet? Knowing what we do of Hung's childhood, we may speculate that in depicting Tu Fu's frustrations and sufferings as a minor government bureaucrat, Hung might have identified the poet in his mind too closely with his own father, who shared Tu Fu's values and outlook on life.

The volumes on Tu Fu were the only full-length books Hung published. He had planned to publish his work on *Shih-t'ung* in Chinese, but did not live to finish it.

DURING THE FALL OF 1946, Hung was asked to give the Merrick Lectures at his alma mater, Ohio Wesleyan. This he considered an honor above all honors, for he remembered vividly how thirty years earlier, he had sat in the audience, awestruck by the force and eloquence of Charles Jefferson of the New York Broadway Tabernacle giving the Merrick Lectures. We have the following account from the January 1947 issue of the *Ohio Wesleyan Magazine:*

Lecturing on the Merrick Foundation, Dr. William Hung, '17, of Yenching and Harvard universities, spoke on the great changes taking place in China today in his country's rapid transition from age-old tradition to modern life. He commented upon the breaking up of the family system and the movement toward individual expression; the struggle to overcome illiteracy, without which true democracy is impossible; the need for reforms which will improve the living conditions of the oppressed peasant class; the uncertain political development of the future . . .

Hung accepted a teaching appointment at the University of Hawaii for the spring of 1947. He had been in Hawaii several times, including once in 1927 when, as a participant at the Second Institute of Pacific Relations Conference, he had engaged the Japanese delegation in spirited debates. Consequently, he had a group of loyal local Chinese supporters who, over the years, had been sending their sons and daughters to Yenching. From Hawaii, Hung was planning to take his family back to China. But the news from China was not good. There had been intense fighting between the Nationalists and the Communists even before the war with Japan was over. In the fall of 1946, President Truman appointed Leighton Stuart to be the U. S. Ambassador to China in the vain hope that a man highly esteemed on both sides would be able to effect a peace treaty and forge a coalition government in China. By the spring of 1947, it became apparent that negotiations were hopeless, neither side being willing to make any concession; and the civil war dragged on. In the meanwhile, the economy continued to deteriorate. The Nationalist currency lost its value about ten percent every day. The exchange rate declined to 12,000 Chinese yuan to one U. S. dollar in April. Money became meaningless and people relied more and more on barter. Among the hardest hit were government employees and teachers, who received fixed salaries. Families pooled their resources and ate meals together; still that was not enough. The desperate plight of China stood in sharp contrast with Hung's surroundings in Hawaii, with its half-naked bathers lolling in the sun amid lush tropical flowers, where life seemed to be an unending garden party. Hung found himself so unsettled and distracted that he decided to move back to Cambridge that summer.

Since Number Five Bryant Street had been sold to an association of Jewish students and turned into the Hillel House, the Hungs moved into a series of apartments while Hung flung himself into feverish activities. In addition to teaching at Harvard and working on his book on Tu Fu, Hung hit the lecture circuit again. He maintained that the United States should throw its weight behind the Nationalists because although the Nationalists might be corrupt, the Communists were violently intolerant of any views of the world other than their own. He told his audience that under Communist rule, there would be a place for neither the Confucian values he himself treasured, nor the Christianity or democracy his audience believed in. At his own expense, he travelled between Cambridge, New York, and Washington, enlisting the support of men like Henry R. Luce of Time-Life to have the State Department release the aid funds appropriated by Congress for the Nationalist government. At one point, he was also deeply involved with the Church Peace Union, an organization promoting world peace through religion.

ON ONE OF HIS TRIPS to New York, Hung suddenly remembered that his old friend and colleague Timothy Lew had been living in New York. It had been a long time since they had seen each other. When he went to call, he found Lew in bad shape.

"He was not well at all, coughing all the time. I felt very sad for him. He called to his daughter Grace, of whom he was very fond, and said,

'Baby, come over and see your Uncle William.' His wife Catherine was busy with all kinds of medicine. Not long after that, he passed away; but I did not hear of his death until 1948. That is one of the regrets of my life. Timothy Lew and I had such a close, beautiful friendship. He was a few years older than I am. I always looked up to him because he was older. Yet I was not able to maintain that very close relationship. Even now, with Timothy Lew dead many years," said Hung in 1979, "every time I think of him there is a tug on my heart."

BY SEPTEMBER, 1947, the financial situation of Yenching University had become so alarming that Hung had to cancel a purchase for some microfilm equipment authorized earlier for the Yenching University Library. Hung had been away from Yenching for a year and a half. In view of the unsettled situation, he was inclined to wait before committing himself to return. In a letter dated October 11, 1947, to Carl A. Evans, associate treasurer of the United Board for Christian Higher Education in Asia, which oversaw the finances of Yenching and other Christian universities, Hung wrote concerning his annuity and summarized his contractual arrangements with Yenching University in the previous twenty-five year period:

I was away from the Yenching campus during the whole fiscal year of 1946–47. During the first half of the year I was still on Harvard-Yenching Institute duties, and I was paid out of the Cambridge budget of the Harvard-Yenching Institute. The second half of the year, I regarded as my furlough . . .

For the present academic year, 1947–48, I have from Yenching only a leave of absence, and you will note that for the year 1947–48 I am no longer on the Yenching end of the Harvard-Yenching Institute budget. If the annuity plan had better be continued, I believe I should personally pay for it out of my earnings during the present year. I shall appreciate your advice on this matter . . .

By way of explanation, I might summarize here a little history. When I joined Yenching University in 1922, the understanding I had with President Stuart and the Board of Trustees was that my salary and other treatments should be similar to those of a missionary. I was indeed so treated during the years, 1922–1929. After I had returned from Harvard in 1930, the salary schedule at Yenching was considerably changed. A sharp distinction was drawn between the Chinese and the foreign members of the staff. The latter alone were to be paid in part in U.S. currency. When the [exchange rates] climbed up, the disparity became more and more glaring. Not wanting to be the only Chinese teacher to receive an unusually big salary on account of the Exchange, I notified the Administration that until further notice from me, I should be willing to receive the treatment according to the schedule for Chinese, considering the balance as my contribution to the University. This explains my inability to take advantage of the annuity plan for many years, for out of the reduced income I had to continue my premium payments in America . . .

Hung was offered the presidency of the Fukien Christian University in 1948. As in many other schools, student disruptions there had gone totally out of control; and the administration had hoped that Hung, with his prestige and experience, might be able to grapple with the situation. Hung felt that in response to the clear call of duty, he had to return to China now. He had always felt guilty about not having done anything of worth for his native city of Foochow. Now was his chance. But missionary teachers from his Foochow Anglo-Chinese College days, the Gowdys as well as Ralph Ward, who were much closer to the scene, all advised him against going back. Communism was coming like a tide, they told him; no valiant effort on the part of any one person could turn it back.

In a letter to Dr. Robert J. McMullen, executive secretary of the United Board, he wrote explaining his decision:

About twenty-two years ago I was invited to the same position. I was then obliged to decline it because I felt it wiser to continue my tolerably acceptable work of teaching and research than to venture forth into the realm of academic administration in which my lack of preparation, patience, and tact might harm a university with all the chances of development. Now after all these years I have found I have not made up much of the deficiency so keenly felt then.

On top of this I have found myself unsuited to work in an area where a Communist political regime might impose some educational regimentation. I am not opposed to the economic policies advocated by the Communists. My difficulties with Communism are basically ideological. A few years ago I said that I could accept Communism if the Communists could modify their stand on three items. I have felt that the Communist hostility to religion is against the basically moral and spiritual nature of man. The thorough-going materialistic interpretation of history is lopsided and therefore inaccurate. The advocacy of violence as an instrument of progress is unnecessary and certainly contrary to the teachings of Chinese ethics. To my regret I have found that the Communists either in China or anywhere else are not at all inclined to modify their stand on these items.

Although Hung's unhappiness with the political situation was sufficient to play an important part in his refusal to return to Foochow, his decision not to go back to China at all did not become final until the outbreak of the Korean War. His internal struggles were violent, for the decision meant the abandonment of his life's work in China and smacked of evasion of duty. But the strength to live once more in material privation under a hostile political regime had been sapped from him; he no longer had the will.

When his brother David came to Washington on official business, Hung tried to persuade him to wait it out in the United States. David replied sternly, "My situation is different from yours. You have been a civilian all your life, while I have been living off a government salary. I have the duty to stand and fall with the government I serve." Having said what they each had to say, the two brothers fell silent and could only stare at each other sadly.

In the fall of 1948, Hung was able to get Nieh Ch'ung-ch'i to Cambridge on Harvard-Yenching Institute funds to teach a course on Chinese bibliographies. For years, Hung had tried to get Nieh to go abroad. He was one of Hung's brightest students; and after the Harvard-Yenching Sinological Index Series was firmly established, Hung had left administrative matters largely in his hands. During the Japanese occupation of the Yenching campus, Nieh had continued the index work under the auspices of the Centre Franco-chinois at the Sino-French University, according to a secret emergency plan formulated earlier by Hung. Several important books were indexed as a result, but Nieh suffered from not being totally familiar with Western Sinological works. In the past, Nieh had refused to leave Peking because he did not want to take long trips away from his mother. Now she was dead, and he came to Cambridge. But in December, when the Communists took Peking, Nieh hurried back, in true Confucian fashion, to make sure that his sick older brother was all right.

The Nationalists lost the capital city of Nanking to the Communists in August of 1949. Stuart, who had presided over the American presence in China as U. S. Ambassador during the preceding three years, watched helplessly as the Republic by which he had set so much store disintegrated chaotically. He stayed on in Nanking waiting for the new government to get in touch with him to discuss the establishment of diplomatic relations with the United States. But all foreign diplomats were told that they would henceforth be treated as private citizens, and a virulent anti-foreign campaign was launched against them. Finally, it was with the help of Huang Hua that Stuart was able to leave China with dignity. He came to see Hung in Cambridge, a defeated man angry over U. S. State Department releases justifying America in freezing funds for the Nationalists in China. He felt they were unconscionably critical of the Nationalist government, with whom the United States supposedly still maintained friendly relations; and he was distressed that they quoted freely from many documents he had prepared in strict confidence. Stuart had a severe stroke in November from which he never fully recovered. He died in 1962.

The People's Republic of China was formally inaugurated in Peking on October 1, 1949. For Hung, it marked the end of half a lifetime of speaking out publicly on behalf of his country. He could neither support the government in Peking, which was bent on the destruction of some of the values he held most dearly, nor the government in Taipei with its fatuous claims.

CHAPTER TWENTY

In Exile

HUNG, at fifty-seven, counted himself lucky to be able to stay in Cambridge, loosely affiliated with Harvard as a research associate. Many other Chinese in his situation simply drifted from place to place, disoriented and suffering a perpetual sense of bereavement. They took up menial jobs in schools, hospitals, offices, moving among people who had no conception of the grand positions they had once occupied, of the important things they had accomplished. As the world they carried about with them faded even in their own memory, they gradually lost any sense of self-identity on which they could rely.

Typical of what happened to Hung's generation of Chinese liberals was the case of Wei T'ing-sheng. He was one of the promising Chinese young men on the make at Harvard whom Hung came to see in the summer of 1916. He returned to China in the 1920s to serve the government in Nanking where he helped lay the foundations of Nationalist financial institutions. Totally disgusted with the way fiscal matters were handled in the late 1940s, he did not move with the government-in-exile to Taiwan; instead, he and his wife went to Hong Kong, where they spent a few years, thence to Southeast Asia, and eventually took up residence in Cambridge, Massachusetts. When he was not offered a university teaching position as he had hoped, Wei landed a job preparing indices at Houghton Mifflin but soon quit it after being told his work was too slow. For a while, he gave Chinese lessons to the children of the Harvard-Yenching librarian Ch'iu K'ai-ming, but that did not last long either. Fortunately, his wife, a graduate of the Peking Union Medical College, was able to find employment at a pharmaceutical company in Boston, so that he did not have to work. She persuaded him to channel his energy into scholary pursuits. A parade of books and arti-

cles issued forth from his restless mind. These were published in Taiwan. Lacking historical training, he often arrived at startling conclusions. One of his pet theories, painfully documented with multilingual
sources, was that the Imperial House of Japan was descended from Hsu
Fu, a Chinese explorer of the third century B.C. He actually wrote the
Japanese Emperor telling him so. Another of his pastimes was writing
letters to American presidents. Every time he wrote Dwight Eisen-
hower at the White House, he would receive a polite reply. He pasted
all the White House letters in a big scrapbook and made careful annota-
tions on each of them. But the invitations to come to Washington that
he hoped for never came. His wife soon got tired of it all and ordered
him to stop writing letters.

"When John Kennedy became president, he also wrote to him, with
exactly the same result," Hung remembered. "Eventually his wife
stopped giving him money for stamps, and he came to borrow money
from me. So his wife seized his typewriter and locked it in a closet."

IN CHINA, the radicalized Yenching students and faculty greeted the
Communist takeover largely with jubilation. There were some two
years of honeymoon during which Chou En-lai personally reassured
Lu Chih-wei, now Chancellor, that New China would have a place for
a university like Yenching. While the faculty, students, and workers of
Yenching organized themselves into study groups to readjust to a new
political order, the trustees in New York continued to send money. But
when the United States entered into the Korean War and cold-war
hysteria on both sides of the Pacific Ocean mounted, posters began to
appear all over the campus attacking members of Yenching University
who had American connections. They were ordered to prepare statements of self-criticism. They had to confess as sins having gone to the
United States, even having desired to go to the United States, having
maintained American friendship, or having sent their scholarly articles
to the United States for publication. Faculty members whose self-
criticisms were found unacceptable were publicly castigated and removed from their positions. Lu Chih-wei, who had wholeheartedly en-
dorsed the Communist revolution as much needed by China and who
was convinced that it was not incompatible with his Christian faith, at
first insisted that he could not hate Americans because "I never hate
anybody or any class of people." Under great pressures, however, one
person after another stood up to accuse him of treasonous acts; even his

own daughter was under pressure to attack him for "poisoning the minds of the youth." His spirit crushed, Lu made a public confession that he had fallen into the imperialist trap of Stuart and had harmed a great number of students, that he had subconsciously hoped the Americans would return so that he could hand Yenching back to them. Finally in August of 1952, as part of a plan to reorganize higher education, Yenching University was officially dissolved by the new government and Peking (Beijing) University moved into its splendid, American-built campus.

News of these persecutions of his former colleagues, some of whom had suffered with him in prison under the Japanese for their patriotism, hardened Hung's anti-Communist stance. "For an intellectual to be forced to say something he does not believe in is like a woman being raped. Thank God for a country like the United States," Hung said, "Otherwise, where would people like me go?" He vowed never to return to China as long as the regime remained in power.

Yet Hung was not totally negative about the government in mainland China. He applauded their efforts to stem the flow of antiques outside the country, their decision to level all the graves accumulated through the ages to make way for more farmlands, their elimination of innumerable causeways in the fields that formerly marked the boundaries of tiny private plots, their penal system combining re-education and hard work. He was not fundamentally opposed to the idea of collectivism; he only decried the inefficiency resulting from the lack of competition. He believed in a system of free enterprise with mandatory profit-sharing and labor representation in management. He was, however, greatly enraged by the wholesale destruction of Confucian and Christian institutions and bitter about the nastiness of the political campaigns.

In 1950, Hung wrote Nieh Ch'ung-ch'i in Peking for his books, notes, and manuscripts on T'ang historiography. Nieh wrote back saying that he had mailed the books, except those more than fifty years old (the government had forbidden any "antique books" to leave the country), but that the handwritten materials would have to be submitted for government inspection before he could send them out. Mail service, however, between the People's Republic of China and the United States was cut off in 1952; and Hung never heard from Nieh again. Around 1961, when a Yenching alumnus working for the United Nations Secretariat in New York returned to China for a visit, Hung asked him to inquire once more into the possibility of bringing his notes and manuscripts on T'ang historiography out of the country. The government replied that Hung was welcome to come back and work on them in China, where it would provide him with a pension equal to his retirement income in the United States. Hung viewed the invitation as a kind of blackmail.

HUNG CAME TO RECONCILE himself to the harsh fact that in an America flooded with refugees, where prejudice against nonwhites still lingered, a person like him, additionally hobbled by the lack of a Ph.D., would not be offered a position commensurate with his ability. With money withdrawn from his pension fund, the Hungs made a down payment on a yellow, Queen-Anne–style house at 31 Gray Street in Cambridge, within walking distance of the Harvard-Yenching Library that he had helped to build. They took in boarders to help pay the mortgage. The house, with its quaint turret and stained glass windows, was furnished with heavy, turn-of-the-century furniture from the old Crawford summer house in Marblehead Neck. Old friends called and new friends dropped by. Emotions often ran high when discussion touched on the situations in mainland China or Taiwan. Otherwise, Hung settled down to an austere and quiet life of writing, occasional teaching, and counselling—for new generations of graduate students of Chinese at Harvard were quick to discover that here was a source of incomparable range and depth. Though he was barred from serving on any candidate's committee, many a Ph.D. thesis was written under his unofficial guidance.

Every weekday at three in the afternoon, for thirty years, he met with Francis W. Cleaves, professor of Far Eastern Languages at Harvard, whom he had first known in the 1930s when Cleaves was in Peking on a Harvard-Yenching fellowship. Their friendship had been renewed after the war when Cleaves, as a liaison officer in the U. S. Marines, had returned to Peking to participate in the transfer of Japanese properties back to the Chinese. Now these two men of very different temperament—one an old-fashioned gentleman perhaps more at home with his cows, horses, and fellow farmers in New Hampshire than with the academic intrigues of Cambridge; the other a pragmatic Confucianist adept at the art of living—daily discussed problems of mutual interest, read several pages of the Chinese classics or the dynastic histories together, or just sat sipping tea. In a way, the mutual respect and love of two such different men was surprising, especially since both were outspoken men who did not mince their words; but both were also erudite, fluent in many languages, recipients of the prestigious Prix Stanislas Julien. Cleaves's astonishing knowledge of the Western classics, of China's borderlands, and of the Mongolian period in China (A.D. 1260–1368) enriched Hung's sense of history. Partly inspired by their conversations, Hung wrote two articles, "The Transmission of the Book Known as *The Secret History of the Mongols*" (41), and "Three of Ch'ien Ta-hsin's Poems on Yuan History, Translated and Annotated" (46). Publication of the former was perhaps unfortunate; for Cleaves, who of the two was the real authority on Mongolian history, did not agree with Hung's conclusions and, out of a feeling approaching filial piety, withheld publication of his own research on *The Secret History of the Mongols* until 1985, after Hung's death.

In the 1950s, Far Eastern studies at Harvard was still dominated by the ebullient Russian, Serge Elisséeff, who ruled the department like a benign dictator. Steeped in old-world etiquette, he would send his secretary around in the summer to see that faculty members did not take their jackets off.

Elisséeff set Hung working on the Harvard-Yenching Dictionary project. The undertaking, as it was conceived in 1936, was to produce a dictionary organized on historical principles, with the meanings of each Chinese word traced through their evolution from antiquity to modern times. It was to be equal to the Oxford English Dictionary. Entries from sixteen dictionaries were cut out and pasted on three-by-five index cards and filed carefully in green steel cabinets. It was estimated that the project would take two hundred man-years, so with ten people, as the theory went, it should take just about twenty years. For a decade and a half, the project had involved such luminaries in the field of Chinese linguistics as Chao Yuan-jen, Li Fang-kuei, and Achilles Fang; but by 1950, the end was nowhere in sight. It became evident that even an institution as well-off as the Harvard-Yenching Institute was not in a position to see its completion. The entire undertaking would have to be abandoned unless other, massive fundings could be found. Hung was asked whether he could edit and organize the materials so that at least a few sample entries could be published, to show the academic world what the dictionary might have looked like. Hung spent a summer on what would have been the first word of the dictionary, *tzu*, and produced a twenty-seven page monograph published by the Harvard-Yenching Institute in 1953. The following year, a second monograph, on what were to be the second and third entries, the words *chieh* and *chüeh,* was published. The monographs (44) were greeted with enthusiasm by the Sinological community, but no financing was forthcoming. When the Harvard Far Eastern Department moved from Boylston Hall to its present site at Two Divinity Avenue, nobody knew what to do with the green filing cabinets full of index cards, so Francis Cleaves offered to take them; at this writing, they still line the basement walls of his farm in New Hampshire.

Many of Hung's publications from 1950 until his retirement from Harvard in 1963 were of a nostalgic nature, such as a touching poem in Chinese, "Mourning Teng Chih-ch'eng," in which he wrote about his old friend's death in Peking (52). The publication of which he was proudest from this period, aside from his works on Tu Fu, was his interpretation of a seventy-two word poem, "Broken Axe" ("P'o fu"), from the *Canon of Poetry* (47). He was very pleased when his student James Liu declared that Hung's use of historical materials and close reading of the poem set an example for how study of the *Canon of Poetry* should be conducted.

Having sworn off public discussion of politics subsequent to the collapse of the Nationalist government in China, in 1955 Hung nevertheless expressed his frustration and hope for better Chinese-American relations through his translation of a poem by Huang Tsun-hsien written in 1881 (45). The poem described the droll culture shocks experienced by the earliest Chinese students in the United States and bemoaned the shortsightedness of the Chinese government in sending the boys back to China for fear they were being contaminated by American values.

OUTSIDE HIS ACADEMIC WORK, Hung became deeply involved in the Fellowship in Prayer, which was founded by a former treasurer of the Yenching Board of Trustees, Carl Evans, and his secretary, Kathryn Brown. Their idea was that since all religions have the common element of prayer, one way to create peace in the world is for people of all religions to join in prayer. They convinced Hung to be its first president. Although Hung had strayed away from organized religion, he believed in the efficacy of prayer, of its ability to tap a person's inner resources. During one of the taping sessions on which this book is based, Hung summed up his view of religion this way: "We human beings are not very different from cats, dogs, and horses in our physical composition. What is different is that we have a set of values. We live on these values . . . A person tries to know himself, know his fellow men. But this is not enough. By training I know there are a lot of problems with Christiantiy. But the problems are only academic. In actual life, you feel there is a God. Voltaire the great Agnostic said that for the good of humanity, even if there were no God, it would be necessary to invent one. In many ways that is true. Then there is the brotherhood of man, which becomes a reality when they love the same God."

Clearly, Hung was more "of one piece" than most people. Even though he became a Christian, he never repudiated his Confucian upbringing. When he turned away from the ministry, he did not negate his religious experience. Although he was disillusioned with the Nationalists, he did not become radicalized. All this was not because William Hung did not hold strong views. He certainly did. It appears, rather, that Hung habitually sought a higher perspective whenever there was potential for his value systems to clash. In conversing with Hung, one had the impression that although his view of the world might have been influenced by the experience of a turbulent life, his basic values were never severely shaken. There was very little of the alienated intellectual in him.

In part, Hung had the good fortune to have been shielded from some of the most traumatic experiences of his generation. By the time he arrived in the United States, his parents had both died, hence he was spared much of the wrenching internal struggle of a Chinese adjusting to Western ways. He was away from China during the May Fourth Movement and the years immediately following it, when intellectuals felt that they faced a stark choice between the traditional and the new. He was again absent during the crucial years between 1928 and 1930, when the Nationalist government started a ruthless campaign to exterminate the Communists and many of his contemporaries were radicalized. Even though he suffered in a Japanese jail with his colleagues, he never had to endure the abject poverty many others were subject to during and after the Japanese occupation. In his later years, he did not, in his own words, have to "prostitute" himself in order to survive the Cultural Revolution.

To Hung, there were no deep chasms lying between the realm of the spiritual and the realm of the physical; no blank walls dividing the East and the West; no sharp ruptures severing the modern from the ancient. It was possible for him, therefore, to take up wholeheartedly the work of a non-sectarian organization dedicated to publicizing the efficacy of prayer.

"The Fellowship in Prayer operated out of a total budget of five thousand dollars, of which three thousand was contributed by Carl

Evans and the other two by Miss Brown. For some thirty dollars, we rented a small area in the lobby of the Hotel Seville in New York, where we placed two desks and one typewriter. The telephone could take only incoming calls. For outgoing calls, we had to go through the keyboard operator, for which we were charged ten cents. Every time Carl Evans wanted to make a call, he would take out a nickel and have Miss Brown make the call in a phone booth in order to save a nickel."

The organization advertised in the newspaper urging people to pray and published a newsletter which promoted the practice of prayer. Thanks partly to a speaking tour Hung and Kathryn Brown made to California, Indianapolis, and Chicago in 1964, the Fellowship in prayer was to be the beneficiary of a $2,000,000 bequest from Mrs. Eli Lilly. The effort to prevent parties interested in its wealth from seizing control of the organization was to take up much of Hung's energy in his latter years.

ONE OF HIS KEENEST PLEASURES was to meet Dick Uong, whom he saved from deportation in 1921, for lunch at the Old Mill Restaurant in Westminster, Massachusetts. As soon as he arrived in Cambridge in 1946, Hung had placed a call to the Fitchburg Paper Company to find Uong and discuss with him the Chinese paper merchants' proposal to have him help them manage the paper mills left behind by the Japanese in Manchuria and in Taiwan. Hung was told that Uong had risen to be the vice president and general manager of the company, and that he was in China at the invitation of Chiang Kai-shek. Dick Uong had made a name for himself during the war years by developing the paper with invisible fibers that was used by the U. S. government for ration coupons. He declined the Chinese government's offer to manage the paper mills in China, however, seeing that there was no way he could keep them from being political pawns.

Hung loved to tell about how one time, at the Old Mill Restaurant, the waitress came to the table when Uong stepped out. She asked Hung how long he had known Uong and then said, "I have to tell you that in this area, everybody knows him and loves him. He has been for many years the head of this big paper mill, and he is known to be always fair. I know because my husband works there."

To Hung, for a Chinese to be accepted and loved in a foreign country, especially to be so highly regarded by his subordinates, was one of the highest accomplishments possible.

HUNG rarely spoke in public now, except on scholarly topics and by invitation to some university or another from old friends who remembered him. He took pride in his students in the United States—Kenneth Kuan-sheng Chen, Fang Chao-ying, Tu Lien-chieh, James Liu, Teng Ssu-yü, and Y. T. Wang—all of whom held important positions in distinguished universities; and he enjoyed visiting with them.

In 1959, Hung was once again invited to assume the role of educator, as a member of a commission called by the governor of Singapore to determine whether official recognition should be conferred on Nanyang University. Nanyang University had been founded in 1954 by a group of wealthy Chinese in Singapore who felt strongly that the Malay Peninsula should have a university for Chinese speakers that could rival the University of Malaya, where English was the sole medium of instruction. The writer Lin Yu-t'ang was invited to be its first president. At that time, Lin had sent feelers to Hung to find out whether he would be interested in becoming Dean of the College of Arts. Hung had declined the invitation. His one piece of advice to Lin Yu-t'ang was to make sure that air-conditioners were put in the library. By 1959, Lin Yu-t'ang had long since left Singapore under a cloud of controversies and the first class of students was about to graduate, uncertain whether their degrees would be recognized as valid by the world. With the university presidency vacant for want of a taker, Hung's former student Chang T'ien-tse, as chairman of the Executive Council, was nominally head of the university. At his recommendation, the governor of Singapore wrote President Nathan Pusey of Harvard, requesting him to pick someone from the Harvard faculty to sit on the commission. Chang was hoping it would be Hung, and indeed Hung was appointed for the assignment. After about a month of investigation and confidential interviews, the findings of the five-member commission were, essentially, that Nanyang University was organized more like a business than an academic institution, and that, moreover, it was run as if it were a subsidiary of the Chinese Chamber of Commerce, which had complete control of its financial matters and the leading members of which decided virtually all university policies and faculty appointments. The commission reported adversely on the academic standards of Nanyang University, which gave rise to a great furor in the Chinese community and much ill-feeling against Chang for his presumed role in the investigation. As soon as the commission left Singapore, a certain member of the Chinese Chamber of Commerce expressed his anger against Chang by having his house smeared with buckets of manure. Chang had to leave Singapore shortly thereafter.

The work of the commission took Hung back to Asia after an absence of thirteen years. He welcomed the chance to see for himself what had become of the Singapore he had last seen when his steamer stopped there in 1928 and to visit with friends and acquaintances who had drifted there from China. He also took advantage of the opportunity to stop over in Hong Kong and Taiwan on his way back to Cambridge.

"In Singapore, we were put up in a very nice hotel. I stayed in a room on the third floor and Ch'ien Ssu-liang was on the second. Every day when we returned to the hotel, there would be a big bowl of assorted fruits waiting for us. I love the bittersweet flavor of pomelo, whereas Ch'en disliked it. So he would bring his pomelo and give it to me every day. When we were about to leave Singapore, he came up to ask me what my travel plans were. He insisted that I call him from Hong Kong so that he could meet me at the airport in Taiwan. He said his presence there might save me from some unnecessary aggravation with the customs officials. Thus when the plane arrived in Taiwan, I was expecting my brother David, my sister, and Ch'ien Ssu-liang all to be there. However, as I was halfway down the ladder off the plane, a band started to play and two little girls ran toward me with flowers. I had an eerie experience of *deja vu* and turned to look behind me; for the last time that a similar scene of band music and flowers greeted me was at the Pennsylvania Station at New York; and it was not me, waving back at the crowd, that they were greeting; it was Wendell Wilkie right behind me. But this time, the music and the flowers were indeed for me. Not only that, there was a general in the crowd, a certain General Hung who had claimed kinship with my brother David, and a movie star, too. It turned out that the granddaughter of my mother's sister, my Aunt Lin, had become quite famous as a movie actress. Her name is Wu Ching-hung. A man soon yelled out to me, 'William, William!' It was Hu Shih. He was there, too.

"They all wanted to set a date with me for dinner. So I told them I had only six days in Taiwan, just to consolidate their dinners into one big dinner."

Present at that dinner were Ch'ien Ssu-liang, the chancellor of National Taiwan University; Mei Yi-ch'i, former president of Tsinghua University, then the Minister of Education; Shen Ch'ang-huan, the

Minister of Foreign Affairs; and, of course, Hu Shih, his old friend the
former Chinese Ambassador to the United States, who, after several
years of self-imposed exile in New York, had accepted an invitation to
assume the presidency of the Academia Sinica in Taiwan. Also present
were many alumni of Yenching University in Taiwan, including Chang
Wen-li.

Chang—in whom Hung had seen so much promise that he took him
to Harvard at his own expense in 1928; who wanted to revolutionize
rural China starting with the peasants in his native Fukien; who had
proven his mettle in the Ukraine, in Chungking, as well as in Taiwan—
was now a broken man. According to Hung, he did an excellent job
handling the fiscal affairs of Taiwan when he was sent there in 1945 as
a deputy of Ch'en Yi. His wife, a devout Catholic, soon started a pro-
gressive kindergarten. Chang said he wept when he read Hung's letter
to him from Shanghai warning of the danger of civil unrest in Taiwan,
for he knew only too well the greed and the arrogance of the Nationlist
officials he had to deal with daily. When the Taiwanese actually rose in
revolt in February of 1947, he and his family were protected by Taiwanese grateful for what they had done for them. Subsequently, Ch'en Yi
was reassigned by Chiang Kai-shek to be the governor of Chekiang,
and he took Chang with him. In Chekiang, when Ch'en was arrested for
collaborating with the oncoming Communist forces and summarily executed, Chang was also arrested. At his release some two years later,
he became totally disenchanted with ideals of any kind and took to
heavy drinking. He drove Hung around in an old battered car while
Hung was in Taiwan those six days. Later, Hung heard he had died,
lonely and separated from his wife.

Hung was saddened to see how much his brother David had aged.
There was a wide range of subjects the brothers deliberately avoided in
their conversation lest they aggravate raw wounds. Hung went to look
at a steel bridge David had designed and built near Taichung, the Hsi-
luo Bridge. Neither the brochure describing the bridge nor the stone
tablet at the foot of the bridge mentioned David's name. It was so like
David, Hung mused, not to put his name on his work. He felt that
David was the only one among his brothers who lived up to the Confucian ethics of their father. Only a short poem in the brochure gave a
hint as to the creator of that engineering marvel:

> The river issues forth among the mountains in the cloud,
> Clear waters and muddy merge indiscriminately into the ocean;

> Down where the rice paddies and orchards form an expanse of green,
> A steel bridge is again erected across the blue ribbon.

The second line of the poem refers to the irony that some of the most conscientious as well as the most corrupt Nationalist officials were now congregated in Taiwan, and the last line refers to another bridge David had built earlier in China, the Hsiang-chiang Bridge, which he personally had to demolish to delay the Japanese advance during the war. When David died ten years later, in 1969, Hung wrote a touching account of him, which appeared in the August 1970 issue of the Taiwanese journal *Chuan-chi wen-hsueh* (*Biographical Literature*).

Hung's sister, when he visited her, took out from under her bed innumerable scroll-paintings for him to see. She had bought them as a hedge against inflation. Hung pleaded that he did not have time to examine them carefully, when, in fact, he did not have the heart to tell her they were all forgeries.

Between 1959 and 1962, starvation was rampant in mainland China owing to a combination of economic mismanagement and natural disasters. People were eating tree roots to stay alive. Hung, back in the United States, heard that Ch'i Ssu-ho, one of his prize students who was always teasingly called "the Fatty," had lost so much weight that he was now practically skin and bones. Coincidentally, Lien Shih-sheng, an alumnus of Yenching and a good friend of Ch'i Ssu-ho, had asked Hung to write some articles for the Nanyang Commercial Press in Singapore, of which he was the editor. Hung wrote a long article on "How I Wrote about Tu Fu" (54) and asked Lien to buy oil and dried meat with the money due him for the article and send them to Ch'i in Peking. The article, along with three of Hung's poems in Chinese, was later published in book form.

On Hung's seventieth birthday, the *Harvard Journal of Asiatic Studies* dedicated its 1963 volume to him, citing his "contribution to the study of Chinese history and letters, and the encouragement and guidance — characterized by both solicitude and the most exacting severity — which he has offered to three generations of scholars and students." Rhoda had planned a big birthday party for Hung on his seventieth birthday. On the day before the event, however, she collapsed of a heart attack.

CHAPTER TWENTY-ONE

The Survivor

DURING THE 1970S, a distinguished looking, silver-haired man was regularly seen striding briskly along the streets of Cambridge, his cane swinging vigorously at his side. He gave the impression of being much taller than his five-feet-eight inches, for he always carried himself straight as a rod and had not lost an inch in the aging process. There was something debonair about him. His face recalled a fine piece of wood in which the natural grain and structure becomes more evident with the passing years. William Hung was in his eighties and had outlived his wife, his sister, and all of his brothers except the youngest. He had endured the grief of his youngest daughter Agnes's untimely death and the even sadder suicide of his daughter Gertrude. His life had spanned the Empress Dowager of China and Jimmy Carter. Young acquaintances were conscious of being in the presence of one who contained within him a piece of the past that was now no more. Yet as soon as he began to talk, they found that he was a man who lived very much in the present. His mind was ever probing, querying, inquisitive of the latest fad in health food as well as recent developments in nuclear weaponry. He gave and attended parties where his reputation as a raconteur had not diminished; and in the absence of his wife, he had trained himself to be a superb cook, applying to the culinary art the same procedures of comparison and analysis that served him so well as a historian. There was something youthful in him that refused to change: His capacity for spontaneity, for play, and for the formation of new and long-lasting attachments remained very strong.

At gatherings, a group of people always collected around him to hear him talk. His manner was polished, his sentences peppered with striking phrases, memorable aphorisms, and literary allusions. He had an impish love of holding his audience in suspense, deferring and deferring the climax, which, when it came, was inevitably droll. Once in a while, he would startle his listeners by delivering a scathing remark on something or somebody. And he had a flattering way of taking even the youngest and humblest of his audience into his confidence and putting them at their ease.

If these new young acquaintances came to call on him at the turreted Queen-Anne-style house on Gray Street, they would climb the steps to a slightly dilapidated porch; once through the front door, they would find him moving among massive old furniture, lace-trimmed tablecloths, and well-worn rugs. There he was ready to listen to the problems of the young with generous empathy, equally eager to share an experience or a new recipe. Although not above indulging in a bit of faintly malicious gossip, he always returned in his conversation to ethical considerations: What would have been the right way to behave in the circumstances? He had a stubborn belief that life was ultimately just and that problems always had elegant solutions if only people took the right attitudes. Confrontational politics had no place in this ethical world. To him, the civil rights leaders and social activists of the 1960s were "pushy." Nevertheless, he took the issues of the day seriously and declared that his views on blacks and on women were "undergoing revisions."

He still agreed to read graduate students' dissertations and guide their work. He continued to meet with Francis Cleaves every weekday afternoon for scholarly discussion. He carried on a voluminous correspondence with friends and former students throughout North America and Asia, taking an active interest in their affairs. He exchanged clever Chinese poems regularly with several intimates, notably the writer Yeh Chia-ying, the botanist Hu Shiu-ying, and Sidney Dai of the Harvard-Yenching Library, often experimenting with new poetic forms and writing in the vernacular.

HIS OWN RESEARCH now centered on the *Shih-t'ung* (*Study of Historiography*) of the iconoclastic, T'ang-dynasty author Liu Chih-chi, about which he had begun collecting materials in 1923. The book, dated A.D. 710, dovetailed nicely with his research on the poet Tu Fu's period of history. In addition to a systematic and critical appraisal of the methods, formats, and contents of all major works of history prior to its time, *Shih-t'ung* offers intimate glimpses into the T'ang archival system and the inner workings of the Bureau of Historiography. Annotating *Shih-t'ung* would offer Hung an opportunity to tie together a lifetime of work on Chinese history and historical methods. Moreover, its refreshingly egotistical author, Liu Chih-chi, who did not hide his contempt for his contemporaries or his predecessors, appealed to Hung.

Hung's first publication on the subject had been an attempt to re-edit a chapter of *Shih-t'ung* (31). In this chapter of the book, Liu Chih-chi pointed out more than a dozen passages that were redundant within a single text or repeated in more than one, marking them in red and yellow ink; and he suggested some revisions of his own. Since none of the surviving editions of *Shih-t'ung* showed the color marks, Hung attempted to recreate them. The demands of the task led him to work eventually with some twenty editions in an effort to reconstruct every word of the original.

Unfortunately, because most of his work on *Shih-t'ung* had been left in China, Hung had to start again almost from scratch after he settled down in Cambridge. He intended to write a book that would be the crowning achievement of his career. In 1957, he published two articles relating to Liu Chih-chi. One, "A Bibliographical Controversy at the T'ang Court," (50), concerns Liu's part in a tumultuous dispute of the year 719 involving the Emperor, the Ministry of Proprietry, and the State Council, over which commentaries of certain classics should be adopted for the education of the young. As was often the case, Hung was accomplishing one thing in the text of his article and another in the footnotes. In the article, he presented the various documents related to the case and set Liu Chih-chi off against his contemporaries. In the voluminous notes, he made known his own views of the various commentaries on the *Canon of History,* the *Canon of Filiality,* the *Canon of Changes,* and *Lao-tzu.* In the second article (published in Chinese in Taiwan in an issue of *Academica Sinica* commemorating Hu Shih's sixty-fifth birthday), Hung showed that two of the three rhymed-prose pieces (*fu*) attributed to Liu Chih-chi in the *Complete Anthology of T'ang Prose* could not have been written by him (49).

In 1961, to strengthen his resolve to press on with his book, he gave up his pipe, vowing not to touch tobacco again until he had completed it. That year, he published an article describing how historical information was collected and compiled during the T'ang dynasty, as well as the development of the Bureau of Historiography, where Liu Chih-chi was employed (53). When his daughter Gertrude killed herself in 1967, he was heartbroken. He feared that he himself did not have long to live and would not finish his work. In an article entitled "A T'ang Historiographer's Letter of Resignation," he therefore included notes in which he clarified the provenance of each extant edition of *Shih-t'ung* in order to simplify the problems of textual variants for future scholars (55).

"After I am done with *Shih-t'ung,*" he said, "I shall write only poetry. Making a poem is like giving birth to a baby. It's pure agony until the child's born, and then what joy!"

FOR HIM, reducing a set of circumstances to a few rhymed lines was therapy, creativity, play. Having written a poem about a situation, re-ordered his thoughts, and captured his emotions in concise expressions, he could then move on to other things. Always a meticulous man, he became even more fastidious in his old age. All his cooking ingredients had to be categorized and put in their proper places. He insisted on settling all financial matters immediately. He wanted to keep his mind uncluttered.

He resisted temptations to accumulate things, quoting from Book XVI of the *Analects* of Confucius: "There are three things a superior man guards against. In his youth, when his physical powers are yet unsettled, he guards against lust. In his middle years, when he is full of vigor, he guards against contentiousness. When he is old, and his powers are deteriorating, he guards against greed."

On a trip to Francis Cleaves's farm in Alton, New Hampshire, in the summer of 1978, Hung was introduced to Cleaves's neighbors, Mr. and Mrs. Mel Drew. He was delighted with a pond he found on the Drews' property. It reminded him of one described in a poem by the Neo-Confucian, Chu Hsi, which Hung immediately recited and wrote down in Chinese for the Drews:

> Like a mirror, the square pond bursts upon my sight;
> In it, sunlight and shadowy clouds sway together.
> I queried the man as to its uncommon clarity,
> The living water is fed from a hidden spring.

The poem was one of Hung's favorites; and he often said that had Chu Hsi not been such a major philosopher, he would surely have been better known as a great poet. The pond symbolized to Hung the state of mind he wanted to attain. It was calm, reflecting everything around it; but it was not stagnant, for the water was kept fresh and clear by an inner source of renewal. Hung believed that by the "hidden spring," Chu Hsi was referring to *t'ien-liang,* the universal force of goodness immanent in man and nature. To Hung, *t'ien-liang* was no other than

God, the God to whom he believed Confucianism and Christianity
both ultimately led.

UNFORTUNATELY, the cool detachment to which he aspired eluded
Hung. Ambivalent, conflicting, and often painful feelings relating to
his friends, his relatives, the work he left behind in China were stirred
up again with the reopening of China. For about twenty-five years, with
the nearly complete cut-off of communications between the United
States and China, emotions had been in suspension; now they were revived. First, he was angered by the rosy picture American journalists
painted of life under the Communist government. He knew it to be un-
true. Then, although he applauded the United States's normalization of
relations with Peking, he was bitter about the unceremonious manner
in which Presdient Carter dropped the government in Taiwan. He felt
Americans were exchanging one set of myths, that the mainland should
be controlled by Taipei, for another, that Peking had rights over the
island of Taiwan. As the trickles of visitors to and from China became
veritable floods, hardly a week passed without some fresh news arriving that agitated him in new ways.

When his friend Stella Wong went to Peking to visit her mother,
Hung asked her to go over to Peking University, formerly the site of
Yenching, to find out whether the two wisteria plants in front of the
pavilion in his garden still existed. She came back with the news that
not only were the wisterias gone, the pavilion was no more; and his
house, quite run down, was divided up for occupancy by six families on
the crowded campus.

His student James Liu went back. His three brothers in China all
died during the Cultural Revolution. It is not clear whether they were
killed or forced to commit suicide. When he saw Chou En-lai, the
Premier said to him, "Excesses were committed by the overzealous; I
hope that you don't take it too hard."

As the true enormity of the Cutural Revolution became known, news
of other deaths reached Hung, among the most horrible of which was
that of Lu Chih-wei, the Chancellor of Yenching University when the
Communists took over. Lu was beaten senseless in 1968 at the height
of the hysteria. Confused and in a state of shock, he was locked up in
a room where he lived amid his own excrement for more than half a
year. After he was released, he became gravely ill and no attempt was
made to give him medical attention; death resulted.

Hung heard from his sister-in-law (Arnold's wife) and nephew, Hung Wei. During the Cultural Revolution Hung Wei was removed from his job as a chemical engineer and separated from his family. For months, they did not know where he was. Later, they found him working in a factory at a quarter of his former salary.

BUT there was also good news. Old friends sent regards. His student Chou Yi-liang, once head of the history department at Peking University was soon to be released from confinement and restored to his position. Chao Tzu-ch'en, with whom Hung had written poems in the wartime Japanese prison, was now in his mid-nineties, and, though an invalid, was being well taken care of by the government. The crippled Weng Tu-chien, for whom Hung had made arrangements for study at Harvard, was vice chairman of the Nationalities Research Institute of the Academy of Social Sciences.

By the fall of 1978, the government of the People's Republic of China had completely turned around in its policies towards the West. The slogan was now "Four Modernizations." It sought to heal the wounds of the past. One of its conciliatory gestures was to return all confiscated properties that could be identified. For the first time, Hung learned what had happened to his properties in China. The houses were, of course, occupied by other people. The government said he could have them back if he returned to China to claim them; otherwise they could pay him some compensation. The 30,000 some books in his personal collection and other personal effects had been moved to the former Imperial Academy. Hung entrusted the disposal of all his properties to his student, Wang Chung-han. Specifically, he instructed him to donate all items of historical significance to universities, libraries, and the Peking Historical Museum; to give his books to those among his friends who might make good use of them in their scholarly research, and to give to his nephew proceeds from the sale of personal effects. He also directed that an enlarged picture of his parents and a eulogy he wrote on the death of his father in 1912 be given to his nephew "so that he may have some idea what manner of man his grandfather was."

There was also his collection of rare inkslabs. Hung had written an article on inkslabs in Chinese history (37). When he first collected them in the 1930s, he had in mind giving them to his students some day before he died, as a symbolic gesture, to indicate that his work had passed into their hands. This wish could now be fullfilled: Hung requested Wang Chung-han to distribute these inkslabs to his students still living in China. When James Liu returned to lecture in China in the spring of 1980, he was able to bring back several rare inkslabs to the United States for Hung to distribute to his students here. Liu wanted none for himself. His family lost its fortune thrice during his lifetime and he had foresworn any attachment to possessions.

ALTHOUGH GREATLY GRATIFIED that his students in Peking were putting out a collection of his works, Hung repeatedly declined invitations to return to China for a visit. Nevertheless, the past that was connected with his life there laid its claims on him more and more. He became almost obsessed with reliving the past, re-evaluating all its events in the light of the subsequent developments so recently disclosed, explaining it. Whenever someone with whom he could share reminiscences came to visit, he would talk about the past all through the night, and sometimes for several sleepless days straight. His brother Fred, his sister-in-law Mabel, his niece Theresa and her husband Theodore, his students Lu Hui-ch'ing and Wang Tsun-t'ung, had all been subject to these marathons. In the spring of 1978, at my request, he began to dictate his memoirs. Meeting me almost every Sunday in his kitchen, with a kettle of hot water constantly simmering to refurbish the teapot, and the tape recorder running, Hung would talk from about two-thirty in the afternoon until seven or eight in the evening, as if unable to stop. The Sunday afternoon sessions lasted more than two years.

Gradually, the infirmities of old age overtook even William Hung. His hearing was the first to weaken; he started to have problems hearing the doorbell around 1977. Then he fell down several times, which caused him to curtail his long walks in the winter.

"My greatest fear is that I may go blind. I hope I die before I go blind," he said. Fortunately, his eyes were as sharp as they had always been up till the very end; and he never lost his physical grace.

He forced himself to learn the art of gracious receiving. His grandson Billy McLaughlin lived with him, and Hung let him do much of the heavy work. He relied more and more on friends, having Soonkih Min, Grace Mauran, Joe Fletcher, Anna Berry, Helena Shen, Ho Chien, Loh Wai-fong, and Tim Wixted do errands for him. Trying to treat old age with wry humor, he would say, "An old man is like a little child."

ON FEBRUARY 20, 1980, Ronald Egan, who taught a course in Chinese culture at Harvard, asked Hung to give a lecture on traditional Chinese education and the examination system. He had been a guest lecturer in similar courses at Harvard over the past years; he did not know this was to be his last. Hung was in form that day. Pacing back and forth on the platform and acting out his words, he told the class of some one hundred undergraduates the story of how his father extricated himself from being a stationer's apprentice by impressing the schoolmaster next door with a Confucian quotation: and he described what schooling was like when he himself was a child preparing for the civil service examination. Then he leaned far forward and thundered at his audience, "All the examination system did was to produce obedient, docile civil servants for the government and to preserve the monarchy. Although there were all these nice sayings in the *Analects* that the Heaven sees as the people sees, the Heaven hears as the people hears, and so forth, in the main, the government in China throughout history has not been one that was of the people, by the people, and for the people. That was why the monarchy needed to be overthrown and a republic established in its place."

He concluded his fifty-minute lecture by referring to the current situation in China, "They are returning to scholarship and discipline now that the so-called Gang of Four is vanquished and people realize that not everything wrong with China could be blamed on Confucius. It might be a step backward to the past, but sometimes, progress is made by stepping backward.

"Let me end my talk today by telling you a story. There was a little boy named Johnny and he was late to class one day.

"The teacher asked him, 'Johnny, why are you late?'

"Little Johnny answered, 'It is because the devil bedevilled my legs this morning so that for every step forward I took, I had to make two steps backward.

"The teacher said, 'In that case, I can understand why you are late, but I don't understand how you got here at all.'

"Little Johnny said, 'Well, I just turned around and walked here backwards.'"

The students had been completely spellbound by the eighty-six-year-old man. His timing was faultless. They were hanging on his every word. And now they roared with laughter, giving him rousing applause that lasted some five minutes.

ON MARCH 27, 1980, he fell again, during his daily fifteen-minute morning exercise. He used his arm to break the fall and fractured a bone in his elbow. The doctor made a cast for him, which was later changed into a sling. There was an annual meeting of the Fellowship in Prayer Board of Trustees the following week in Princeton, New Jersey. The doctor had advised Hung against going, but he went anyway. Mrs. Lilly's unexpected $2,000,000 bequest in 1973 had turned the Fellowship in Prayer from a sleepy little organization perpetually teetering on the brink of oblivion into an arena of power conflicts. Hung had spent much of his time and energy during the prior year building a case against someone who he felt was trying to seize control of the organization for selfish reasons. Armed with his files full of evidence, he had flown back and forth to Princeton; and by throwing his weight around behind the scene, he had succeeded in wrestling the organization back from his adversary. At this April 7 meeting, Hung had the satisfaction of seeing the persons he recommended securely installed as new officers of the Fellowship.

The summer came and went. Bonnie Oram, his granddaughter-in-law, came with Hung's great-granddaughter Toni to spend a part of the summer with him. Bonnie is one of those women who combine a warm, motherly instinct and shrewd, practical sense. She never left without completing some major household project for Hung. This time, she and Billy repainted the dining room. Hung also received visits from several guests from Peking, including Hou Jen-chih, who had been in prison with him during the Japanese occupation, and Ch'i Wen-ying, daughter of his old student Ch'i Ssu-ho, the "Fatty" to whom he had had food sent during the starvation years of the Great Leap Forward. They were both professors of history at Peking University, and both were kept up by Hung at night with his reminiscences of old times.

October 27 was his eighty-seventh birthday. As had happened for several years past, some fifty people gathered at his house to celebrate his birthday with him. There were his old Chinese friends, his more recent American friends, members of the faculty and graduate students from Harvard, his remaining daughter, grandchildren, and friends of friends. Hung was specially happy that evening because his niece Fanny was there from Szechwan. Fanny, David's daughter, disappeared from Shanghai one day in 1948 and was not heard of again until her sister Theresa somehow got in touch with her on a trip to China in 1979. Fanny had left secretly to join the Communists. She now came to visit her sisters in the United States.

In November, six weeks before Hung's death, Ruth Crawford Mitchell, whom he always referred to as "my American sister," herself a sprightly ninety who had just published a book on Alice Masaryk, flew to Boston to see Hung. They completed plans for the format and the inscription of the Hungs' gravestone. His and Rhoda's ashes were to be buried in the Smith-Crawford family plot in Pepperell, Massachusetts.

On December 16, Hung had turned weak almost overnight and reverted at times to speaking Chinese with those around him. Anna Berry, a nurse, was called; and she took Hung to the Mount Auburn Hospital in Cambridge, where it was determined that he had massive internal bleeding. For about ten hours, tubes ran in and out of him to drain the liquid from his lungs; he was in great pain. He was reduced to expressing himself in writing with a pen in a trembling hand. All his messages were the same: Take the tubes out! The doctor said Hung would stop breathing if he did. But Hung insisted. After a few hours of agonizing over the question, the doctor decided to take a chance. Hung lived six more days in relative comfort, during which he chatted charmingly with his family and visitors, who came from all over the country to say goodbye. His daughter Ruth Beasley, five grandchildren and their families, his brother Fred, and his niece Theresa, all came to see him. He died on December 22, 1980, lucid to the very last. That was the way he wanted it to be.

Epilogue

WILLIAM HUNG'S ASHES, along with those of his wife, were interred in the Smith-Crawford family plot at the Old Walton Cemetery, Pepperell, Massachusetts, on December 27, 1980, at a simple ceremony presided over by James Liu. Between January and February of 1981, the Harvard-Yenching Library had an exhibit of Hung's pictures and literary works. On April 14, a memorial service for him was held at the Central College of the Nationalities in Peking, drawing more than three hundred people. The invitations were sent out in the names of Wu Wen-tsao, Hsieh Ping-hsin, Lei Chieh-ch'iung, Lin Yao-hua, Hou Jen-chih, Weng Tu-chien, Chou I-liang, Chang Chih-lien, Ch'en Ting-wen, and Wang Chung-han, all of them prominent intellectuals who had survived the Cultural Revolution. The meeting was duly reported by the *People's Daily* on May 8. Hung's colleagues and friends in the United States held another memorial service for him on May 3 at the Harvard University Memorial Church. The speakers were Joe Fletcher, Francis Cleaves, and Glen Baxter; a message signed by 106 academics in China was read by Hou Jen-chih, who happened to be in North America. On June 1, 1982, the University of Pittsburgh honored him at a program at which, among others, Ruth Crawford Mitchell, Y. T. Wang. S. Y. Teng, and Chou I-liang spoke.

The China Book Bureau (Chung-hua shu-chu) in Peking brought out a selection of his works in Chinese, entitled *A Collection of Hung Yeh's Scholarly Discussion* (*Hung Yeh lun-hsueh-chi*) in March of 1981. The Fellowship in Prayer devoted the May 1982 issue of their monthly publication to him.

After claims against Hung's estate in China were settled, some 10,000 renminbi remained. Five scholarships were established in his name to be awarded annually to outstanding students of history at Peking University and the Central College of the Nationalities.

Appendices
Bibliography
Glossary of Verses
Glossarial Index

A Partial List of Scholars Trained at Yenching University by William Hung

Name	Subsequent Affiliation
Chang Chih-lien (Zhang Zhilian)	Peking University
Chang T'ien-tse	University of Hawaii
Ch'en Kuan-sheng (Kenneth Chen)	University of California at Los Angeles
Cheng Te-k'un	Chinese University of Hong Kong
Ch'i Ssu-ho (Qi Sihe)	Peking University
Chou Yi-liang (Zhou Yiliang)	Peking University
Chu Shih-chia (Zhu Shijia)	Peking Normal University
Ch'ü T'ung-tsu (Qu Tongzu)	Academy for Social Sciences, Peking
Fang Chao-ying	Columbia University
Feng Chia-sheng (Feng Jiasheng)	Academy for Social Sciences, Peking
Hou Jen-chih (Hou Renzhi)	Peking University
Liu Tzu-chien (James Liu)	Princeton University
Nieh Ch'ung-ch'i (Nie Chongqi)	Academy of Social Sciences, Peking
Teng Ssu-yü	Indiana University
Tu Lien-chieh	Columbia University
Wang Chung-han (Wang Zhonghan)	Central College of the Nationalities, Peking
Wang I-t'ung (Yi-t'ung Wang)	University of Pittsburgh
Weng Tu-chien (Weng Dujian)	Academy of Social Sciences, Peking
Yu Hsieh-chung	New Asia College, Chinese University of Hong Kong

A Summary of Hung's "Preface" to the *Combined Concordances to Ch'un-ch'iu, Kung-yang, Ku-liang, and Tso-chuan*

IT IS INSTRUCTIVE, and even inspiring, to observe how William Hung himself used the research tools that he created and others that were available to him. As an example, we may consider what many regard as Hung's most brilliant piece of scholarship, his "Preface" to the *Combined Concordances to Ch'un-ch'iu, Kung-yang, Ku-liang, and Tsochuan* (34). The *Ch'un-ch'iu* or *Spring and Autumn Annals* is a history of the state of Lu, supposedly written by Confucius himself. In traditional China, it was studied assiduously along with commentaries attributed to three masters called Kung-yang, Ku-liang, and Tso. Indeed, the four books held a place in Chinese culture roughly analogous to that of books of the Bible in the West.

In his "Preface," Hung set about to bring modern historical criticism to bear on questions concerning the reliability of the *Spring and Autumn Annals* as a historical record, its authorship, and the relationship of the commentaries to it and to each other. The *Annals* records in annalistic form the major events that occurred in the state of Lu from 772 to 481 B.C. and contains some reports of events from elsewhere as well. It was traditionally attributed to Confucius (551–481 B.C.), who was said to have written it to set the historical records straight and to pass judgment on the men and policies of his era.

In 221 B.C., when the king of Ch'in established himself as emperor of a unified China after a period of wars among rival states, he ordered the destruction of most of the Confucian classics, including the *Spring and Autumn Annals*. The Ch'in dynasty (221–207 B.C.), however, was soon succeeded by the Han dynasty (206 B.C.–A.D. 220), during which massive efforts were made to recover the writings of earlier times. Two versions of the *Annals* had survived, each in the form of text interspersed with added commentary. These are *Kung-yang* and *Ku-liang,* known by the names of the masters who were said to be the authors of the commentaries. In the middle of the Han dynasty, the scholar Liu Hsin brought forth a third manuscript on the Spring and Autumn period, which he announced he had discovered in the imperial vaults. In contrast to *Kung-yang* and *Kung-liang,* which gave elaborate comments on the moral implications of the terse chronological entries in the *Annals,* this manuscript provided long and vivacious narratives of the political and military life of the period. Liu Hsin identified it as the *Tso's Spring and Autumn Annals* (*Tso-shih ch'un-ch'iu*) mentioned by the great historian Ssu-ma Ch'ien (d. ca. 85 B.C.). Ssu-ma Ch'ien had said that *Tso's Annals* were written by Tso Ch'iu-ming, a contemporary of Confucius, to ensure that Confucius's views were correctly transmitted, and the same Tso Ch'iu-ming also wrote the *Kuo-yü,* another historical work of the Spring and Autumn period. Liu Hsin tried to persuade the emperor to give official recognition to his *Tso's Annals* by creating a chair in the Imperial Academy for its instruction; but the proposal was met by a storm of protest from the doctors of the Imperial Academy, who were not convinced that the manuscript was by Tso Ch'iu-ming and did not believe it was a commentary on Confucius's *Annals.* The emperor could bring a halt to the heated controversy only by sending Liu Hsin away from court. After Wang Mang usurped the Han throne, however, Liu Hsin was able to champion again the cause of his manuscript. Subsequently it became known as *Tso-chuan* (*Tso's Commentary*) and was actually read far more widely than the *Kung-yang* or *Ku-liang* commentaries because of its narrative interest. Nevertheless, doubts regarding the authenticity of the *Tso-chuan* persisted into the twentieth century. Among its detractors was K'ang Yu-wei (1848–1927), who argued that the book was a forgery by Liu Hsin.

The main issues surrounding the subject, then, are these: How reliable is the *Annals* as a record of the Spring and Autumn period? Was it written by Confucius? When were *Kung-yang* and *Ku-liang* written; by whom were they written; and how are they related to each other? Is the *Tso-chuan* a commentary on the *Annals,* or is it an independent chronicle? Hung systematically worked through these problems and issues related to them. A summary of his "Preface," therefore, can show how this master historian solved major scholarly problems.

ON THE GROUNDS that the *Annals* can be shown to report astronomical events accurately, Hung argued that the work as a whole is an authentic record of its time. He found in Oppolzer's *Canon der Finsternisse* more than sixty solar eclipses that could have been seen in the state of Lu in the 442 years covered by the *Annals*. Relying on a procedure worked out and published in 1928 by a Japanese scholar, Shinjō Shinzō, Hung converted the Chinese cyclical dates in the *Annals* to Julian dates. In a neat table, he demonstrated that out of the thirty-seven eclipses recorded in the *Annals,* thirty coincided with those listed in the *Canon der Finsternisse.* Of the remaining seven, three could be verified if the month in the *Annals* were changed. The other four were correct as to month but erroneous in either the day or the year given. In other words, the preponderance of the evidence from an unequivocally verifiable category of entry pointed to the conclusion that the *Annals* was a genuine but not flawless record.

The inconsistencies that did exist led Hung to his second point, which was that the *Annals* as we know it today must be marred by omissions and alterations from the original. Aside from occasional errors in dates, he showed that the *Annals* records only twenty-three battles, which does not agree with the statement, "The *Annals* has thirty-four battles," found in *Ku-liang.* Other books dating from the early Han say that the *Annals* records thirty-six instances of regicide and fifty-two instances of states being destroyed, but fewer of each appear in present-day editions of the *Annals.* Since the original copy of the *Annals* was written on bamboo strips, Hung hypothesized that some of the strips were lost or transposed. The loss of certain entries, however, would not challenge the accuracy of those that remained. Nevertheless, there is other evidence that the text has been tampered with. In the Sung dynasty, Wang Ying-lin (1223–1296) observed that the season of the year does not appear with the month in ancient texts. This could be accounted for by the fact that ancient Chinese astronomy was not sophisticated enough to relate the lunar calendar to the movement of the earth around the sun. Yet the season of the year is always mentioned before the month in the present version of the *Annals.* In another table, Hung demonstrated that conversion of some of the dates to Julian dates reveals that some of the season designations are obviously incorrect and must have been added by later scholars. The basic chronological integrity of the text, however, convinced Hung of its overall authenticity.

HAVING ARGUED FOR the reliability of the *Annals* as history, Hung moved on to confront the question of authorship. Citing examples from five pre-Ch'in works, including one no longer extant but quoted in another book, Hung reiterated that the term *ch'un-ch'iu* (*spring-autumn*) originally just meant historical records, for spring and autumn were the two seasons in which most acts of state were taken. He then showed that the only surviving pre-Ch'in works that had any bearing on the question of whether Confucius wrote the *ch'un-ch'iu* or historical records in question were *Mencius,* the two commentaries, and the *Tso-chuan.* The only one that lends any support to the theory that Confucius was the author is a passage cited by Hung in which Mencius appears to have said he had not seen the *Annals* compiled by Confucius, but such a statement is hardly the grounds for a positive identification. With the help of the *Concordances,* Hung listed all passages in the two commentaries and the *Tso-chuan* that relate to the writing of the *Annals.* Both *Kung-yang* and *Ku-liang* imply that Confucius improved upon the *Annals,* which suggests, of course, something other than original authorship. Likewise, nowhere in the *Tso-chuan* is there any claim that Confucius wrote the *Annals.* In fact, the *Tso-chuan* records that a certain Han Ch'i was said to have seen the annals of the state of Lu in a certain year, a year when Confucius was still a child. If the annals Han Ch'i saw were the *Annals* we now have, then Confucius cannot have been the author. Hung had no doubt that the annals (that is, the historical record) of the state of Lu, was used as a subject of instruction by Confucius; but Confucius's teachings might or might not have been transmitted as a book. He thought that the commentaries were almost certain to have reflected Confucius's views; but such conformity proved nothing about the authorship of the basic text. He concluded there was no basis for attributing authorship of the *Spring and Autumn Annals* as we now have it to Confucius.

THE AUTHORSHIP of the *Kung-yang* and *Ku-liang* commentaries was also a matter of some importance, for the traditional assumption that they had been written by different masters had influenced the way they were studied for century after century. Rival schools of thought had grown up in the belief that they offered differing interpretations. If in fact, however, they were based on a common source or were even written by the same person, then many of the controversies were pointless and much opinion could be jettisoned.

Hung traced the earliest mention of *Kung-yang* and *Ku-liang* to Ssu-ma Ch'ien but noted sacrastically that later scholars seemed to have fuller details about the commentators than the historian who lived closest to the time of the commentaries' composition. Making use again of the *Concordances,* he showed that the eponymous masters Kung-yang and Ku-liang are characterized in much the same way; each is treated in his own commentary as one among equals. Neither is quoted in the commentary bearing the other's name, but both quote a certain Master Shen. The two works contain many similar passages, and they cite many identical sources. Reasoning from the great similarities of the works and the lack of any early, authentic information about the identity of the authors, Hung concluded that the two commentaries must have emanated from the same source and must have been set down in writing within a short time of each other. He raised the possibility that Kung-yang and Ku-liang, both rare surnames, might have been corruptions of the name of the same person.

As for dating the commentaries, Hung noted that earlier scholars had pointed to passages in both commentaries that appear to have been lifted from *Mencius,* while the ideology reflected in the commentaries is that of Confucianism before the final demise of the Chou Kingdom in 256 B.C. Therefore, an anterior limit of late fourth century B.C. and a posterior limit of 256 B.C. can be set. Neither commentary, however, appears to have survived intact. Numerous passages in existing versions of both commentaries are unintelligible. Furthermore, annalistic entries lack an accompanying comment for thirty-seven years in *Kung-yang* and for fifteen in *Ku-liang.* Hung noted that such lacunae are the kind that occur in incomplete texts rather than as omissions in an oral tradition that was later written down. By comparing the present *Kung-yang* and *Ku-liang* to passages from them cited in other books, Hung suggested that of the two, the *Kung-yang* was the better preserved.

TRADITIONALLY, the *Tso-chuan* was treated as a third commentary on the *Annals,* and so Hung treated it next; but from the beginning, its differences from *Kung-yang* and *Ku-liang* have been self-evident. Again, questions of authorship are central to establishing a critical description of the text. Even though many scholars immediately after Liu Hsin accepted his assertion that the manuscript he discovered and identified as the *Tso-chuan* had indeed been written by Tso Ch'iu-ming, a contemporary of Confucius, questions about its author's identity were raised as early as the third century A.D. At that time, Fu Hsuan pointed out inconsistencies between the *Tso-chuan* and the *Kuo-yü,* which was also attributed to Tso Ch'iu-ming, inconsistencies that imply one author could not have written both works. In the Sung dynasty, Yeh Meng-te (1077–1148) pointed out other problems, including, for example, the fact that towards the end of the *Tso-chuan* the posthumous title of a man who died fifty-three years after the death of Confucius is given. Tso could not be a contemporary of Confucius and at the same time write a book some sixty years after the death of the Master. Yeh Meng-te was also suspicious of the fact that many of the predictions recorded in the *Tso-chuan,* supposedly made by diviners of the Spring and Autumn period, were so accurately fulfilled long after the book was purportedly written.

Hung patiently summarized the views of more than two dozen scholars on the date and authorship of the *Tso-chuan,* from Chu Hsi (1130–1200) to Chang Ping-lin (1868–1936), including the findings and views of the English Sinologist James Legge, the German Otto Franke, the French Henri Maspero, the Swedish Bernhard Karlgren, and the Japanese Shinjō Shinzō and Iijima Tadao. In his article "On the Nature and Authenticity of the *Tso-chuan,*" published in 1926, Karlgren had applied linguistic analysis to the *Tso-chuan* and concluded that the book was not written by a native of the state of Lu. He also suggested that since the *Tso-chuan* and the *Kuo-yü* are linguistically dissimilar to the corpus of other third century B.C. works, the *Tso-chuan* most likely dates from the fourth century B.C..

Shinjō and Iijima had brought modern astronomical data to the task of dating the *Tso-chuan* but reached different conclusions. Their shared premise was that since according to our present knowledge many of the dates given of astronomical events in the *Tso-chuan* are incorrect, what we have is a later account of the events. Furthermore, since the error in the *Tso-chuan* is not random (the earlier the year, the larger the error), an analysis of the progression in the margin of error should, they both argued, enable one to determine when the calculations were made. Iijima, whose articles began to appear in 1912, correlated the pattern of errors in the *Tso-chuan* with astronomical calculations based on movements of the planet Jupiter put forward by Liu Hsin. Iijima pointed out that Liu Hsin's calculations are now known to be inaccurate. A consistency between his miscalculations and the errors in the *Tso-chuan* would point, therefore, to a date of composition contemporaneous with his discovery of it. On the existence of such a consistency, however, the two Japanese scholars disagreed. From mathematical work recapitulated by Hung in the "Preface," Shinjō argued in 1928 for a date of composition some three hundred years earlier than Liu Hsin, between 365 B.C. and 329 B.C., to be exact.

In his 1931 article, "La composition et la date du *tso tschouan*," Maspero offered the novel idea that the *Tso-chuan* is a conflation of two originally distinct works, a chronicle and a commentary on the Spring and Autumn period. The chronicle, parts of whose surviving text is embedded in the present *Tso-chuan*, spans a period longer than that of the present *Annals*. Unlike the *Annals*, which is based on the calendar of the state of Lu, the chronicle in the *Tso-chuan* is based on the calendar of the state of Chin. Therefore, he argued, the *Tso-chuan* could not have been a Han forgery. If a Han scholar had wanted to forge a new commentary to the *Annals*, it would not have made sense for him to create a new chronicle on which to make the comments. Furthermore, the differences between the chronicle embedded in the *Tso-chuan* and that of the present *Annals* are mainly in such details as dates and names, not in any principles that would have made a forgery worthwhile. *Tso-chuan*, he concluded, must be an authentic pre-Ch'in-dynasty document. Maspero asserted that the astronomical events are mentioned only in the commentary and concluded, therefore, that errors concerning them do not invalidate the authenticity of the chronicle itself. He placed the date of the *Tso-chuan* between late fourth century B.C. and mid third century B.C..

Hung adopted many of Shinjō's and Maspero's views, and made use of Karlgren's linguistic analyses as well as traditional textual criticism, and added his own insights. He approached the dating of the *Tso-chuan* by first disentangling the relationship between the *Tso-chuan* and the *Kuo-yü*. The *Kuo-yü* covers more or less the same period as the *Tso-chuan;* but instead of dealing with the events on a strictly chronological basis, the stories in the *Kuo-yü* are divided into seven parts, each devoted to an important state of the Spring and Autumn period. Nearly half the book, however, is devoted to the state of Chin; other states are treated only briefly; and the *Kuo-yü* comes to only a third the length of the *Tso-chuan*. Many of the same stories appear in both works; and in many passages, wording is identical. Were the *Tso-chuan* and the *Kuo-yü* then written by the same author? Were they by different authors but based on the same sources? Was one based on the other? Hung favored the theory that the *Kuo-yü* was one of the sources on which the *Tso-chuan* was based. The *Tso-chuan*, like the *Kuo-yü*, is particularly detailed on the affairs of Chin, and both works lack information on Chin for the period between 607–592 B.C. But there are distinct differences in the use of language between the two works. Also, the *Tso-chuan* focusses on the narrative flow of events whereas the *Kuo-yü* uses events as occasions for recording speeches. When they recount the same events, the *Tso-chuan* shows evidence of condensing and combining the passages in the *Kuo-yü*. The *Tso-chuan* appears to have revised some passages in the *Kuo-yü* to make them more consistent with the ideology expressed elsewhere in the *Tso-chuan*. There is, Hung insisted, even an instance in which the author of the *Tso-chuan* appears to have misread the *Kuo-yü*. Since both the *Tso-chuan* and the *Kuo-yü* contain the posthumous title given to Chao Hsiang-tzu, who died in 425 B.C., neither could have been written before that date. There are no traces in the *Kuo-yü* of Ch'in and Han taboos, and the cosmology reflected in the *Kuo-yü* suggest it was written before the third century B.C. Therefore an anterior limit of 425 B.C. and a posterior limit of late fourth century B.C. for the authorship of the *Kuo-yü* could be set.

Hung postulated that not only was the *Tso-chuan* written after the *Kuo-yü*, it was also written after the *Kang-yang* and the *Ku-liang* commentaries; for there is an event recounted in the *Tso-chuan* about which both the *Kung-yang* and the *Ku-liang* profess ignorance, and there are other events of which the *Tso-chuan* gives full details but about which the *Kung-yang* and *Ku-liang* were unaccountably sketchy. All this suggests that the authors of the *Kung-yang* and the *Ku-liang* had not seen the *Tso-chuan*. On the other hand, the author of the *Tso-chuan* appears to have seen the *Kung-yang* and the *Ku-liang*.

Hung suspected that the *Tso-chuan* was based, as Maspero had proposed, on an incomplete chronicle of the state of Lu, one different from the present *Annals* as attached to the *Kung-yang* and the *Ku-liang*. Utilizing the *Concordances*, the differences can be verified by comparing passages on identical events in the *Tso-chuan*, the *Kung-yang*, and the *Ku-liang*. Where the chronicle he was using was incomplete, the author of the *Tso-chuan* appears to have drawn heavily from the *Kuo-yü*. Since the astrology found in the *Kuo-yü* appears to be that prevailing during the Ch'in dynasty, the *Tso-chuan* must have been written no earlier than the Ch'in dynasty. The version of the legend of the Nine Tripods found in the *Tso-chuan*, moreover, places its composition after the overthrow of the Ch'in empire. As collaborating evidence, Hung found in the avoidance of the Han emperors' names in the *Tso-chuan* traces of a taboo which suggested that the work was written in the early

Han, during the reign of Emperor Hui between the years 194 and 188 B.C..

Having narrowed his hypothesis about the date of composition, Hung conjectured that it was Chang Ts'ang (d. 152 B.C.), or someone close to him who wrote the *Tso-chuan*. Chang was an avid collector of books, who served briefly as *chu-hsia shih* ("historian below the column") under the First Emperor of Ch'in and had access to books and historical documents. Having displeased that despot, Chang fled from court and joined the rebel forces of the man who later became Emperor Kao of Han. He was subsequently enfeoffed as the Marquis of Pei-p'ing and served as Prime Minister under Emperor Wen of the Han for fifteen years. He is said in some sources to have presented the *Tso-chuan* to the imperial court. A great scholar as well as a great statesman, Chang Ts'ang was especially learned in astronomy. He was, Hung thought, a man who had the opportunity, the ability, and possibly the motive (i.e., an antipathy to the Ch'in empire and its destruction of historical records) to compile a book such as the *Tso-chuan*.

Hung concluded his monumental monograph with an authoritative discussion of the various recensions of the *Annals* and how they might have evolved over the centuries through the faulty transmission of the original chronicle of the state of Lu.

During the four decades after the appearance of the "Preface," many other studies on the subject appeared, some of them challenging specific points in Hung's monograph. Yet so masterfully had Hung built his case, plank by plank and brick by brick, that he said on several occasions that if he had it to do all over again, he would not change a single word.

Bibliography

Part I: A Partial List of the Publications of William Hung

An annotated list of forty-one of William Hung's writings can be found in the 1963 issue of the *Harvard Journal of Asiatic Studies* (vol. 24) dedicated to him. The list was updated and expanded to seventy-seven entries by his students Weng Tu-chien and Wang Chung-han in the collection of his works, *Hung Yeh lun-hsueh-chi,* 洪業論學集 published in Peking in 1981 by Chung-hua shu-chu. What follows is a list of the fifty-seven publications by Hung cited in this biography. They are arranged and numbered chronologically in the order of their publication rather than in the order of their appearance in the text; they thus provide a survey of his career. Each reference to a given work is followed in the text parenthetically by its assigned number.

1. *Failure.* New York, 1918. Peiping, 1939. Peiping, 1941.
2. *Get Acquainted.* New York, China Society, 1921.
3. "The Contribution of the Christian Church," in *China Her Own Interpreter.* Ed. Milton Stauffer. New York, 1927, pp. 68–93.
4. "Second Pacific Relations Conference," *China Weekly Review* 42:66–68 (17 September 1927).
5. "Ming Lü Ch'ien-chai Lü Yü-heng tsu sun erh mu-chih-ming k'ao" 明呂乾齋呂宇衡祖孫二墓誌銘考 , (The Funerary Tablets of Lü Chien-chai and His Grandson Lü Yü-heng of the Ming Dynasty), *Yen-ching hsueh-pao* 燕京學報 (Yenching Journal) 3:521–536 (June 1928).
6. *Nationalist China:* Discussed by William Hung, A. N. Holcombe,

and D. Z. T. Yui. New York, Foreign Policy Association Pamphlet 54, 1929.

7. Review of *A History of Christian Missions in China* by Kenneth Scott Latourette, in *International Review of Missions* 18.72:605–609 (October 1929).

8. "Indexing Chinese Books," *Chinese Social and Political Science Review* 15.1:48–61 (April 1931), and published by HYISIS as a pamphlet.

9. "Tu-shih nien-piao fu yin-te hsu" 讀史年表附引得序 ("Preface," *Chinese Chronological Charts with Index*), HYISIS Supplement 1, February 1931.

10. "Ch'ing tsung-shih Hsi-en shih-kao chiu ts'e pa" 清宗室禧恩詩稿九冊跋 (A Colophon to Nine Manuscript Volumes of the Poems of the Manchu Nobleman Hsi-en), *Yenching University Library Bulletin* 4:1–2 (28 February 1931).

11. "Ts'ui Tung-pi shu pan-pen piao" 崔東壁書版本表 (Tabular Presentations of the Varying Recensions of the Works of Ts'ui Shu), *Shih-hsueh nien-pao* 史學年報 3:1–6 (1931). Also in Vol. 1 of *Ts'ui Tung-pi i-shu* 崔東壁遺書. Ed. Ku Chieh-kang 顧頡剛. Shanghai, 1936.

12. Colophon to *Chih-fei chi* 知非集. Peiping, Yenching University Library, 1931.

13. "Ts'ui Tung-pi hsien-sheng ku-li fang-wen chi" 崔東壁先生故里訪問記 (A Joint Report on a Visit to the Hometown of Ts'ui Shu), with Ku Chieh-kang 顧頡剛, in *Yen-ching hsueh-pao* 9:1873–1897 (June 1931). Also in vol. 2 of *Ts'ui Tung-pi i-shu*. Ed. Ku Chieh-kang 顧頡剛. Shanghai, 1936.

14. "Chinese Picture of Life," *Asia* 31.9:586–592 (September 1931).

15. "Tu Ch'ing tsung-shih Ching-cheng jih-chi kao-pen" 讀清宗室敬徵日記稿本 (On the Manuscript Diary of Manchu Nobleman Ching-cheng), *Yenching University Library Bulletin* 19:1–2 (15 December 1931).

16. "Chi tu Tsai-ch'eng chi-shih-chu" 記讀載澂記事珠 (On the Manuscript Diary of the Manchu Prince Tsai-ch'eng), *Yenching University Library Bulletin* 20:1–2 (30 December 1931).

17. "Wei-hsiu-yuan hsiao-shih" 蔚秀園小史 (Brief History of the Garden of Elegant Refinement), *P'ing-hsi pao* 平西報 (1 January 1932).

18. "Yi-li yin-te hsu" 儀禮引得序 ("Preface," *Index to Yi Li*), HYISIS 6 (January 1932).

19. *As It Looks to Young China.* Ed. William Hung. New York, Friendship Press; London, Student Christian Movement Press, 1932.

20. "Ssu-k'u ch'üan-shu tsung-mu chi Wei-shou-shu mu yin-te hsu" 四庫全書總目及未收書目引得序 ("Preface," *Index to Ssu-k'u ch'üan-shu tsung-mu and Wei-shou-shu mu*), HYISIS 7 (February 1932).

21. *Yin-te shuo* 引得説 (*On Indexing*), HYISIS Supplement 4 (December 1932).

22. "So-wei *Hsiu-wen-tien yü-lan* che" 所謂修文殿御覽者 (The So-called *Hsiu-wen-tien yü-lan*), *Yen-ching hsueh-pao* 12: 2499–2558 (December 1932).

23. *Shao-yuan t'u lu k'ao* 勺園圖錄考 (An Investigation of the Paintings and Literature on the Ladle Garden), HYISIS Supplement 5 (February 1933).

24. "*Shang-shu shih-wen* Tun-huang ts'an chüan yü Kuo Chung-shu chih kuan-hsi" 尚書釋文敦煌殘卷與郭忠恕之關係 (The Incomplete Manuscript of *Shang-shu shih-wen* Found at Tun-huang and its Relationship with Kuo Chung-shu), *Yen-ching hsueh-pao* 14:185–191 (December 1933).

25. *Ho Shen and Shu-ch'un-yuan: An Episode in the Past of the Yenching Campus.* Peiping, Office of the President, Yenching University, January 1934; reprinted by the New York office of China Christian Universities, no date.

26. *Ch'ing hua-chuan chi-i san chung* 清畫傳輯佚三種 (Biographies of Ch'ing Dynasty Painters in Three Collections); HYISIS Supplement 8 (January 1934).

27. "Ho Shen chi Shu-ch'un-yuan shih-liao cha-chi" 和珅及淑春園史料劄記 (Notes on the Source Material for the Story of Ho Shen and the Garden of Modest Gaiety), *Yen-ta chou-k'an* 燕大週刊 6.22 (22 February 1934).

28. "Ts'ui Tung-pi *Ch'iao-t'ien sheng-pi* chih ts'an kao" 崔東壁莰田賸筆之殘稿 (The Incomplete Manuscript of *Ts'ui Tung-pi's Chiao-t'ien sheng-pi*), *Shih-hsueh nien-pao* 史學年報 2.1:1–20 (1934).

29. "Ch'ing-mo ko-ming shih-liao chih hsin fa-hsien—Liu Shih-p'ei yü Tuan-fang shu" 清末革命史料之新發現 — 劉師培與端方書 (A Newly Discovered Piece of Source Material for the History of the Revolution at the Close of the Ch'ing Dynasty—A letter from Liu Shih-p'ei to Tuan-fang), *Ta-kung Pao* 大公報 (2 November 1934).

30. Review of *History of the Peking Summer Palaces under the Ch'ing*

Dynasty by Carrol Brown Malone, in *Chinese Social and Political Science Review* 18.4:611–619 (January 1935).

31. *"Shih-t'ung* 'Tien-fan p'ien' i-pu" 史通點煩篇臆補 (An Attempt at Re-editing Chapter Forty-two, "Elimination of Tautology," of *Study of Historiography), Shih-hsueh nien-pao* 史學年報 2.2:149–160 (1935).

32. "K'ao Li Ma-tou ti shih-chieh ti-t'u" 考利瑪竇的世界地圖 (On the World Maps of Matteo Ricci), *The Chinese Historical Geography Semi-Monthly Magazine* 5.3–4:1–50 (11 April 1936).

33. *"Li-chi yin-te* hsu" 禮記引得序 ("Preface," *Index to Li Chi*), HYISIS 27 (January 1937).

34. "Ch'un-ch'iu ching chuan yin-te hsu" 春秋經傳引得序 ("Preface," *Combined Concordances to Ch'un-ch'iu, Kung-yang, Ku-liang, and Tso-chuan*), HYISIS Supplement 11 (December 1937).

35. "Yen Chen-hsien hsien-sheng i-kao wu chung" 閻貞憲先生遺稿五種 (Five Unpublished Manuscripts of Yen Chen-hsien), *Shih-hsueh nien-pao* 2.5:1–15 (1938).

36. *Yen-chiu lun-wen ko-shih chü-yao* 研究論文格式舉要 (Suggestions concerning Research Papers). Peiping, Yenching University Graduate School, 1939.

37. *The Inkslab in Chinese Literary Tradition*, Occasional Papers by the Scholars, Fellows, and Their Advisors in Chinese Studies at Yenching University, 3 (7 May 1940).

38. *"Tu shih yin-te* hsu" 杜詩引得序 ("Preface," *A Concordance to the Poems of Tu Fu*), HYISIS Supplement 14 (September 1940).

39. "Chung-Mei pang-chiao" 中美邦交 (Sino-American Relations), *Ta Chung* 大中 1.3:3–10 (March 1946).

40. "Education in Old and New China," in William Wyatt Davenport, ed., *The Pacific Era*. Honolulu, University of Hawaii Press, 1948.

41. "The Transmission of the Book Known as *The Secret History of the Mongols.*" *Harvard Journal of Asiatic Studies* 14:433–492 (1951).

42. *Tu Fu: China's Greatest Poet.* Cambridge, Harvard University Press, 1952.

43. *Notes for Tu Fu: China's Greatest Poet.* Cambridge, Harvard University Press, 1952.

44. *Harvard-Yenching Institute Chinese-English Dictionary Project:* Preliminary Print, Fascicle 39.0.1 and Fascicle 39.0.2–3. Cambridge, Harvard University Press, 1953, 1954.

45. "Huang Tsun-hsien's Poem 'The Closure of the Educational Mission in America.'" *Harvard Journal of Asiatic Studies* 18:50–73 (1955).

46. "Three of Ch'ien Ta-hsin's Poems on Yuan History, Translated and Annotated," *Harvard Journal of Asiatic Studies* 19.1–2:1–32 (June 1956).

47. "P'o fu" 破斧 (Broken Axe), *Ch'ing-hua hsueh-pao* 清華學報 New Series 1.1:21–62 (June 1956).

48. "China's Greatest Poet, Tu Fu," in *World Literatures.* Pittsburgh, University of Pittsburgh Press, 1956.

49. "'Wei-hsien' 'Shen so-hao' erh fu fei Liu Chih-chi so-tso pien" ‘韋弦’ ‘慎所好’ 二賦非劉知幾所作辨 (On Why the Two Pieces of Rhyme-prose "Wei-hsien" and "Shen so-hao" Were Not Written by Liu Chih-chi), *Bulletin of the Institute of History and Philology* (Academia Sinica) 28:583–592 (May 1957).

50. "A Bibliographical Controversy at the T'ang Court A.D. 719," *Harvard Journal of Asiatic Studies* 20:74–134 (1957).

51. "San-ti Shu-hsing hsing-shu" 三弟書行行述 (An Account of My Third Brother Shu-hsing), *Chuan-chi wen-hsueh* 傳記文學 17.2:59–62 (August 1959).

52. "K'u Teng Chih-ch'eng Wen-ju" 哭鄧至誠文如 (Mourning Teng Chih-ch'eng (Wen-ju)), *Yenching Alumni News*, 20 November 1960, p. 8.

53. "The T'ang Bureau of Historiography before 708," *Harvard Journal of Asiatic Studies* 23:93–107 (1961).

54. "Wo tsen-yang hsieh Tu Fu" 我怎樣寫杜甫 (How I Wrote About Tu Fu), *Nan-yang shang-pao i-chiu liu-erh nien yuan-tan t'e-k'an* 南洋商報一九六二年元旦特刊 , 1 January 1962, p. 6.

55. "A T'ang Historiographer's Letter of Resignation," *Harvard Journal of Asiatic Studies* 29:5–52 (1969).

56. Review of *Tu Fu* by A. R. Davis, in *Harvard Journal of Asiatic Studies* 32:265–284 (1972).

57. "Tsai-shuo Tu Fu" 再說杜甫 (Tu Fu Again), *Ch'ing-hua hsueh-pao* 清華學報 10.2:1–52 (July 1974).

Part II: Publications Consulted in Preparation of this Biography

Barbour, George B. *In China When.* . . . Cincinnati, University of Cincinnati, 1975.

Boorman, Howard L., ed. *Biographical Dictionary of Republican China.* New York, Columbia University Press, 1971.

Ch'en Wan-li 陳萬里 . *Hsi-hsing jih-chi* 西行日記 (Diary of a Western Trip). Peiping, P'u-she, 1926.

Ch'i Ssu-ho. "Professor Hung on the *Ch'un-ch'iu*," *The Yenching Journal of Social Studies* 1.1:49–71 (June 1938).

Chou Tse-tsung. *The May Fourth Movement: Intellectual Revolution in Modern China.* Cambridge, Harvard University Press, 1960.

Crawford, Frank L. *Morris D'Camp Crawford and His Wife Charlotte Holmes Crawford: Their Lives, Ancestries and Descendants.* Privately printed. Ithaca, 1939.

Edwards, Dwight. *Yenching University.* New York, United Board for Christian Higher Education in Asia, 1959.

Elman, Benjamin A. *From Philosophy to Philology: Intellectual and Social Aspects of Change in Late Imperial China.* Cambridge, Harvard University Council on East Asian Studies, 1984.

Fairbank, John King. *Chinabound: A Fifty-Year Memoir.* New York, Harper and Row, 1982.

Fairbank, John K., Edwin O. Reischauer, and Albert M. Craig. *East Asia: Tradition and Transformation.* Boston, Houghton Mifflin, 1973.

Fenn, William P. *Ever New Horizons: The Story of the United Board for Christian Higher Education in Asia 1922–1975.* New York, The United Board for Christian Higher Education in Asia, 1980.

Fenn, William P. *Christian Higher Education in Changing China 1880–1950.* Grand Rapids, Michigan, Wm. B. Eerdmans, 1976.

Garside, B. A. *One Increasing Purpose: The Life of Henry Winter Luce.* New York, Fleming H. Revell, 1948.

Grose, George Richmond. *James W. Bashford: Pastor, Educator, Bishop.* New York, The Methodist Book Concern, 1922.

Hsu, Immanuel C. Y. *The Rise of Modern China.* London, Oxford University Press, 1970.

Hummel, Arthur W. *The Autobiography of a Chinese Historian.* Leyden, E. J. Brill, 1931.

Lindsay, Michael. *The Unknown War: North China 1937–1945.* New York, The Two Continents Publishing Group, 1975.

Liu, James T. C., "William Hung: The Amazing Professor," *Fellowship in Prayer* 33.5:1–5 (May 1982).

Schneider, Laurence A. *Ku Chieh-kang and China's New History: Nationalism and the Quest for Alternative Traditions.* Berkeley, University of California Press, 1971.

Stuart, John Leighton. *Fifty Years in China: The Memoirs of John*

Leighton Stuart, Missionary and Ambassador. New York, Random House, 1954.

Tuan Ch'ang-t'ung 段昌同. "Shih-shui fei-ch'en erh-shih nien: Yi Nieh Ch'ung-ch'i hsien-sheng" 逝水飛塵二十年--憶聶崇岐先生 (Twenty Years – Rushing Water and Flying Dust: Remembering Mr. Nieh Ch'ung-ch'i), *Hsueh-lin man-lu* 8:69–76 (1983).

Wang Chung-han 王鍾翰 "Hung Wei-lien hsien-sheng he yin-te pien-chuan ch'u," 洪煨蓮先生和引得編纂處 (William Hung and the *Sinological Index Series*), *Hsueh-lin man-lu* 8:52–68 (1983).

Wang Chung-han 王鍾翰 "Li-shih hsueh-chia Hung Wei-lien" 歷史學家洪煨蓮(William Hung, the Historian) *Fu-chien hsueh-pao* 福建學報 1:9 (1982).

Wang Chung-han 王鍾翰 "T'eng-hua-hui i-shih" 藤花會逸事 (Reminiscences of the Wisteria Parties), *Hsueh-lin man-lu* 4:81–84 (1981).

Wang, Y. T. "Harvard Sinologist Nurtured Asian Studies at Pitt," *Pitt,* University of Pittsburgh (November, 1981) pp. 21–22.

Warner, Langdon. *The Long Old Road in China.* Garden City, N.Y., Doubleday, 1926.

Weng Tu-chien 翁獨健 and Wang Chung-han 王鍾翰 . "Hung Wei-lien hsien-sheng chuan lueh" 洪煨蓮先生傳略 (A Brief Biography of William Hung), *Wen-hsien* 文献, 10:154–164 (December 1981).

Weng Tu-chien 翁獨健, Liu Tzu-chien 劉子健, and Wang Chung-han 王鍾翰. "Hung Wei-lien" 洪煨蓮 (William Hung), in Chen Ch'ing-ch'uan *Chung-kuo shih-hsueh-chia p'ing-chuan* 中國史學家評傳, vol. 3. Honan, Chung-chou ku-chi ch'u-pan she, 1985.

West, Philip. *Yenching University and Sino-Western Relations, 1916–1952.* Cambridge, Harvard University Press, 1976.

Wixted, Timothy. "A Memoir of William Hung," *Fellowship in Prayer* 32.5:10–12 (August 1981).

Wu Hsiang-hsiang 吳相湘 . "Cheng-chih-hui ts'u-chin Chung-kuo hsien-tai-hua" 成志會促進中國現代化. (Ch'eng-chih-hui Promotes the Modernization of China), *Min-kuo tsung-heng-t'an* 民國縱橫談 Taipei, Shih-pao wen-hua ch'u-pan-she, 1980, pp. 143–159.

Yang Lien-sheng. "William Hung, *Tu Fu, China's Greatest Poet*," *Harvard Journal of Asiatic Studies.* 15:264–269 (1952).

Yu Ying-shih 余英時. "Ku chieh-kang, Hung Yeh yu Chung-kuo hsien-tai shih-hsueh" 顧頡剛，洪業與中國現代史學 (Ku Chieh-kang, Hung Yeh and Modern Historiography in China) *Ming Pao* 185:57–61 (May 1981).

Yenching News. (December 1943–November 1950)

Yenching University Alumni Bulletin. Hong Kong. 1971; Palo Alto, 1973; Taipei, 1974; Palo Alto, 1976.

Glossary of Chinese Verses

This glossary provides the original Chinese for verses that appear in translation in the text. Characters for words, phrases, sentences, and proper names that appear in the text but do not occur in the bibliography appear in the glossarial index.

from page 21

> 甘白俱能受
> 升沉兩不驚

from page 22

> 一片一片又一片
> 兩片三片四五片
> 六片七片八九片
> 飛入梅花都不見

> 白狗忽變大
> 黑狗忽變白
> 大明好江山
> 萬里清一色

from page 23

昔年麂焚東魯
大聖惟恐傷人
今日水淹南關
丈夫何心問馬

from page 24

花未開完香不減
春雖老去色猶艷,

from page 213

半畝方塘一鑑開
天光雲影共徘佪
問渠那得清如許
謂有源頭活水來

Glossarial Index

Chinese characters are provided for names of persons and places, titles of books, and terms when they are needed for precise identification. They are omitted for famous public figures like Chiang Kai-shek, scholars like James T. C. Liu who have established careers in the West, and well-known placenames like Peking.

Harvard East Asian Monographs

STUDIES IN THE MODERNIZATION OF THE REPUBLIC OF KOREA: 1945–1975